Emotions and Social Movements

Most research on social movements has ignored the significance of emotions. This edited volume seeks to redress this oversight and introduces new research themes and tools to the field of emotions and social movements.

This volume takes both the sociology of social movements and the sociology of emotions in an exciting new direction. Truly international in scope, the contributions to this volume cover diverse issues such as the Women in Black in Israel, the Chinese student movement, care and feminism, and the techniques of the Adbusters Media Foundation. The contributions show how emotions connect macro- and micro-politics, examine highly emotional movement-staged public events and address the role of attempts to express, regulate and ignore emotions within social movements. Above all, this volume contributes to the general understanding of how emotions work in a social context. Comprising three main sections, the work focuses on theoretical frameworks, movements that challenge states and state policies and movement consolidation and demise.

Sociologists and political activists around the world will find this volume to be of great interest given its wide-ranging approach and its heretofore unique emphasis on the role of emotion in protest, dissent and social movements.

Helena Flam is Professor of Sociology at Leipzig University. In addition to co-initiating a Network on Emotions with the European Sociological Association, she has held posts at the Max Planck Institute for Social Research and the University of Konstanz. **Debra King** is Lecturer in Sociology at Flinders University, Australia. She has served as the learning adviser for Research Education at the University of South Australia and is on the editorial advisory board of the *Journal of Sociology*.

Routledge advances in sociology

This series aims to present cutting-edge developments and debates within the field of sociology. It will provide a broad range of case studies and the latest theoretical perspectives, while covering a variety of topics, theories and issues from around the world. It is not confined to any particular school of thought.

Emotions and Social Movements

Edited by
Helena Flam and Debra King

Routledge
Taylor & Francis Group

LONDON AND NEW YORK

First published 2005
by Routledge
2 Park Square, Milton Park, Abingdon, Oxon OX14 4RN

Simultaneously published in the USA and Canada
by Routledge
270 Madison Ave, New York, NY 10016

Routledge is an imprint of the Taylor & Francis Group

Transferred to Digital Printing 2006

© 2005 Selection and editorial matter, Helena Flam and Debra King;
individual chapters, the contributors

Typeset in Sabon by Wearset Ltd, Boldon, Tyne and Wear

British Library Cataloguing in Publication Data
A catalogue record for this book is available from the British Library

Library of Congress Cataloging in Publication Data
A catalog record for this book has been requested

ISBN 0-415-36316-0

Publisher's Note
The publisher has gone to great lengths to ensure the quality
of this reprint but points out that some imperfections in
the original may be apparent

Printed and bound by CPI Antony Rowe, Eastbourne

Contents

Notes on contributors

Tova Benski is Dean, Department of Behavioral Sciences, Rishon Lezion, Israel. Her co-authored book *Iraqi Jews in Israel: Social and Economic Integration* (1991) was awarded a prestigious prize in Israel. She has presented and published in the areas of social movements, gender studies, emotions and ethnicity.

Ron Eyerman is Professor of Sociology and Co-Director of the Center for Cultural Sociology at Yale University. He has researched and published in the areas of cultural and social movement theory, critical theory, cultural studies and the sociology of the arts.

Helena Flam has been Professor of Sociology at the University of Leipzig since 1993. She has written on organizations, social movements, East European states and emotions. She is the co-initiator of the Network on Emotions within the ESA and the initiator of the very first session on emotions held at the 32nd annual meeting of the German Sociological Association in 2004.

Debra Hopkins is Research Fellow in the Strathclyde Centre for Disability Research at the University of Glasgow. Her research interests include qualitative research theory and practice, ethics of care, professional discourses and practices of care, and chronic illness.

Bill Hughes is Head of Social Sciences at Glasgow Caledonia University. His current research interests include disability, impairment, the body and social theory. He is co-author (with colleagues at GCU) of *The Body, Culture and Society: An Introduction* (2000).

Debra King is a Lecturer in Sociology at Flinders University, South Australia. Her research and teaching is informed by over 15 years of feminist activism in community and peace organizations. She has researched and published in the areas of emotions, activist identity, social movements and work.

Jochen Kleres has a Diploma-degree in Sociology and Law and is a research assistant at the Institute of Sociology, University of Leipzig.

His Ph.D. work is on the demise of NGOs. He has published various articles and essays on the East German gay movement.

Linda McKie is Research Professor in Sociology at Glasgow Caledonian University and Associate Director at the Centre for Research on Families and Relationships. Recent research includes the book *Families, Violence and Social Change* (2004, Open University Press) and work on ethics and social care.

Silke Roth is Visiting Assistant Professor in the Sociology Department at the University of Pennsylvania. Recent publications: *Building Movement Bridges. The Coalition of Labor Union Women* (2003) and *Europas Töchter. Traditionen, Erwartungen und Strategien von Frauenbewegungen in Europa* (co-edited with Ingrid Miethe, 2003).

Erika Summers-Effler is an Assistant Professor at the University of Notre Dame. Her chapter in this volume is part of a comparative ethnography of two social movement groups. She has also done theoretical work on interaction, emotion, culture, gender and the self.

Nick Watson is Professor of Disability Studies, Strathclyde Centre for Disability Research, Department of Sociology, Anthropology and Applied Social Sciences, University of Glasgow, Glasgow.

Åsa Wettergren has a Ph.D. in Sociology. She is a research assistant at Karlstad University, Sweden. Publications include 'Like moths to a flame – Culture jamming and the global spectacle', in A. Opel and D. Pompper (eds), *Representing Resistance, Media, Civil Disobedience and the Global Justice Movement* (2003).

Guobin Yang (Ph.D., New York University, 2000) is an Assistant Professor in the Department of Sociology at the University of Hawaii at Manoa and a Research Scholar in the Department of Asian and Middle Eastern Cultures of Barnard College, Columbia University.

1 Introduction

Helena Flam in collaboration with Debra King

This book is about emotions *and* about social movements. Its contributors draw both on the sociology of emotions and theories of social movements. Both these sociologies date back to the mid-1970s – a time which witnessed the rise of many new sociological perspectives and special areas of inquiry. But whereas the development of the sociology of emotions was marked by anarchistic pluralism from its very beginning, research on social movements evolved much more like 'normal science'. It was clearly marked by deferential-referential dynamics constitutive of various schools of thought with their distinct approaches to social movements.

Until today the sociology of emotions has featured various competing perspectives on emotions. Even though both American and British sociologists have established special sections in their national organizations devoted to this field of sociology, and many edited and single volumes have come out which bear witness to the creativity, productivity and popularity of the sociologists of emotions, no single approach to emotions – with the notable exception of, perhaps, Arlie Hochschild's – has come to dominate this area of inquiry. Instead those interested in the sociology of emotions have practiced a happy eclecticism drawing on the perspectives worked out by Theodore Kemper, Randall Collins, Thomas J. Scheff, Peggy Thoits, Candance Clark, Cas Wouters, Norman K. Denzin, Eva Illouz, Jack Katz, Jack Barbalet, Francesca Cancian and numerous others who have brought their gift of creativity to this area of study. If the sociology of emotions keeps gaining momentum today, it is more due to its compelling nature than to any co-ordinated organizational or programmatic efforts. Without exaggeration it can be said that despite this lack of any co-ordinated or frontal assault many areas of sociological inquiry have begun paying at least some attention to emotions. Even the most ardent enemies of emotions, such as the rational choice proponents, have come to recognize that they are unable to explain the many anomalies which they encounter in their research without recourse to emotions. Research on social movements has also succumbed to emotions, albeit very recently.

From its beginning, social movement research has been marked by well-defined controversies which, after initial polarizing effects, have resulted in the introduction and diffusion of additional approaches to social movements. There are, of course, many founding fathers and mothers – Charles Tilly, Mayer Zald, John McCarthy, Doug McAdam, Myra Marx Ferree, William A. Gamson, Sidney Tarrow, David A. Snow, Robert D. Benford, Kim Voss, Verta Taylor, Nancy Whittier, Alberto Melucci, Alain Touraine and others – who compete with each other on the scientific market. However, a casual look at the numerous social movement readers and journals reveals that, although the qualitative 'Europeans' are granted definitely less presence, hardly any approaches are denied the recognition they deserve. Most of them feature chapters or articles devoted to what by now has become the standard approaches: the resource mobilization perspective, political opportunity structures, networks, framing, identities, subcultures, space and temporality, and so on. Yet, despite this flurry of unceasing, exciting research, one gains the impression of restlessness and dissatisfaction. It seems that social movement researchers and theorists, having explored various older approaches to social movements, are now looking towards new explanatory frameworks, including those that are more inclusive of emotions.

So far just two initiatives have acknowledged the importance of emotions in social movements in an explicit, focused and central manner: the first initiative was the publication of *Passionate Politics* (2001) and the second was to devote one special issue of the international journal on social movements, *Mobilization* (2002), to emotions. Singling out these two publications is not meant to deny that several well-known social movement theorists – mostly female – have addressed emotions in their earlier work or that recently quite a few separate articles have been published in refereed journals. The contributors to this volume repeatedly acknowledge many of these intellectual predecessors in their texts. This singling out is instead merely intended to underline that new – collective, organized, visible – interest is being taken in the specific area of emotions in social movements.

Both *Passionate Politics* edited by Goodwin, Jasper and Polletta and the special *Mobilization* issue guest edited by Aminzade and McAdam contributed to a better visibility of emotions in social movement research and bestowed the necessary legitimacy on research dedicated to emotions in social movements. It is, however, worth noting that unlike these editors we lean more heavily on the sociology of emotions to demonstrate that movement emotions and feeling rules produce both structural and action consequences. More specifically, contrary to the guest editors of the special *Mobilization* issue devoted to emotions, we believe that it is not too early to link movement-generated emotions to protest strategies or movement action repertoires in a systematic way.

Our undertaking also differs in several other respects from past efforts. We examine a wider range of emotions. In this volume not only the standard set of shame, pride, anger and solidarity is subject to analysis, we also make room for emotions such as loyalty, joy, hope, fear, contempt, sadness, distrust, empathy, compassion, altruism, outrage, gratitude and happiness. However, to prevent a cacophony of emotions, we offer several frameworks that aim to link them to each other in a systematic manner.

We go beyond simply introducing emotions to social movement research, we are further developing the field by:

- showing how emotions connect the macro-politics to the micro-politics of social movements;
- focusing on highly emotional movement-staged public events and the role of emotions in constituting not only the movement collective or its interactions with the opponents but also those with its public;
- bringing emotions into the analyses of the sustainability and demise of social movements;
- paying attention to the difficulties associated with attempts to express, regulate and ignore emotions within social movements.

The contributors to this volume do not see the exploration of emotions as merely opening up our eyes to new dimensions of social movements, but instead they grant emotions a definite causal weight. In essence, they propose a more theoretical approach to emotions in social movements, by either extending older theories of emotions based on data gained from social movements, or constructing new theories of emotions more appropriate to the study of social movements.

Furthermore, the present volume deals with both democratic and repressive political systems, emphasizing differences between the two. The empirical material presented here is truly international. It comes from Australia, Canada, China, re-united Germany, Israel, 'socialist' Germany and Poland, Serbia, the UK and the US. Among the contributors to this volume one finds both seasoned scientists and young researchers whose innovative scholarship has already been distinguished by numerous awards. Some are also activists who have brought their vast movement experience into their scientific work.

By paying attention to emotions as a key feature of society, the contributors move beyond the usual concern with cognitions, interests and strategies. By staking out this new thematic territory they also go beyond the burgeoning research in this area which mainly treat emotions as merely a mobilization resource or an object of management. Most significantly, this volume shows that there is much to be gained when the sociology of emotions and the sociology of social movements are explored together.

The structure of the book

The first section of this volume focuses on theoretical frameworks for the study of emotions and social movements. The second section – which also proposes further theoretical frameworks – portrays movements as challengers to the states, their policies and the market. It highlights the role of emotions in turning-point movement-staged events geared, among others, to the mobilization of the public. The third and fourth sections highlight the role emotions play in movement consolidation and demise.

Theoretical frameworks

The following chapters by Helena Flam and Ron Eyerman have a dual purpose. They describe the theoretical context within which interest in the role of emotions in social movements is currently developing. They also propose new theoretical and methodological approaches to the study of emotions in social movements. Helena Flam calls attention to what she names the normal distribution of 'cementing' emotions in society. She points out that emotions such as loyalty, anger, shame and fear, uphold social structures and relations of dominations in both democratic and repressive regimes, but they differ in their weight. She then argues that regime-dependent social movements counter these and construct new, subversive emotions. The research agenda she proposes emphasizes the emotional-institutional context within which social movements do their emotion work, and thus moves away from the tendency to treat emotions as a purely micro-level phenomenon. Flam's first focus is comprised of two elements. One is on the particular emotions and feeling rules which social movements construct to accomplish the emotional re-framing of reality, with the other being on the structural preconditions leading to individual emotional liberation. Her second focus is on emotions as a causal factor. Here she concentrates firstly on movement emotions towards opponents and then on movement emotions and feeling rules in order to persuasively demonstrate that these have significant structural and action consequences.

For Ron Eyerman emotion is an essential component of movement emergence, maintenance and, where it is lacking, decline. It is what puts the 'move' in movement. As with several other authors in this volume he proposes that to best analyze a social movement it is necessary to focus on the emerging movement, its opponent(s) and its public. His special purchase on these three is found in performance theory. Through performance theory, Eyerman links cognitive framing, narration and discourse to the practice of mobilization through emotion. Using the perspective of performance to examine the practice of demonstrations, Eyerman is able to highlight the corporeality of movement emotions and the place of the body in the emotional reframing of values and meaning. As he states, 'it turns our attention to the performance of opposition and the aesthetics of movement, to the very choreography of protest, as well as to the moral and emotional in mobilization'. More specifically Eyerman argues that protest events involve ritual practices, symbolic gestures and shared experiences of empowering, collective effervescence which affect the move from framed emotion to action and from individual to collective, narrative identity. In attempting to move their publics and opponents, movements rely on contentious gatherings and communication. When they stage their public self-presentation, they frame their struggle not only in a cognitive-narrative manner, but also become involved in the emotional, symbolic and dramatic 'performance of opposition' – opposition which is always performed in public spaces, often chosen precisely for their emotion-evoking symbolism.

Eyerman's discussion of the emotional dimensions of 'movement choreography', combined with Flam's insights into the work on emotion through which social movements encourage people's disengagement from dominant society, sets the scene for the following chapters. Each of the subsequent chapters, however, provides its own perspective on the study of emotions and social movements.

Social movements against states, state policies and markets

The next section is comprised of four chapters devoted to social movements which oppose the state, its policies or the market. Three of these chapters draw attention to an aspect of social movement research which has received much too little attention: the interaction between social movements and their onlookers. Taking a different approach is a chapter that analyzes a conflict between two movements about a government policy.

In an extraordinary display of patience, dignity, resilience and defiance, a group of Women in Black perform a monthly vigil on a roundabout in Haifa, Israel. The aim of their vigil is to link the effects of militarism and patriarchy through protesting against the Israeli occupation of the Palestinian territories. In so doing these women stage a spectacle that generates strong feelings in the public. Tova Benski's focus is on these feelings. She interprets the vigils as 'breaching events', a concept derived from Garfinkel's micro-level experiments demonstrating the importance of routines for the smooth operation of everyday social life and anchored in Durkheimian discussions of the social bases of social solidarity. A 'breaching event' is defined as an act of defiance that is performed in public which is composed of real and/or symbolic violations of accepted social practices, definitions and nominations of reality. Such an event necessarily invites negative emotional responses from the by-standing public. These responses express the anxiety, frustration and outrage that members of a society feel when their taken-for-granted cultural and political definitions of reality are violated. Benski analyzes five visual elements of the 'breaching event'– the location, the women's clothing, the signs held, the women's bodies and the time of the event. She shows that each element conveys a specific breaching message and provokes a specific set of reactions. They pose a strong challenge to the accepted gendered social order, the hegemonic definitions of the current phase of the Israeli-Palestinian conflict, and frames of the discourse over security issues in Israel.

In the next chapter, Guobin Yang uses a dramaturgical lens to analyze the 1989 Chinese student movement. He argues that in order to fully understand the dynamics and processes of collective action it is necessary to take account of 'critical emotional events' constructed in and by a movement. He focuses on three critical emotional events: the Xinhuamen incident which was sparked by the death of a sympathetic (and therefore demoted) party leader in which mourning students become drawn into a violent confrontation with the police, and in a spiral of anger and shame with the party leaders; the successful demonstration in Beijing which was accompanied by massive, enthusiastic and warmhearted citizen support; and, finally, the tragic hunger strike which evoked a general outpouring of sympathy and compassion, transforming the course of collective action and thereby affecting the future. These events brought movement activists, opponents and the public together in intensely emotional encounters in symbolic places. To understand how 'critical emotional events' transform the dynamics of collective action, Yang develops a dramaturgical approach that takes account of the emotional structures – both emotional schemas and immediately relevant context-specific emotions – of social movements. The dramaturgical perspective Yang proposes explores dramatic techniques or strategies of protest, the comportment of opponents, public responses, place and temporality. It provides a framework which brings together identities, interactions, rituals and emotions in a coherent manner.

Culture jamming is a form of symbolic contentious politics, directed at a capitalist, commercialized, undemocratic society within which we – without ever being consulted – are constantly inundated with visual messages that reinforce consumer capitalism. Åsa Wettergren's chapter on the 'Adbusters Media Foundation' (AMF) is innovative in focusing on visuals as a means of mobilization. The AMF is a significant culture jamming organization, founded in 1989 with the aim of subverting corporate logos and advertisements, and mobilizing a 'culture jammers movement'. Wettergren analyzes AMF's discourses, spoof-ads and uncommercials – which subvert the commercial messages conveyed by, for example, Benetton, Smirnoff and Calvin Klein – to reflect upon how culture jammers attempt to mobilize the public. She pays particular attention to the emotional processes involved in this mobilization. She shows how through the use of irony and moments of surprise, the visuals are intended to evoke emotions of pleasure, guilt, shame, anger and fear in the viewers. Wettergren argues that although the intended function of these visuals is to produce a dislocating shock and critical reflection in the viewer there is a risk that, since the necessary cognitive framing is left up to the spectator, the anger and disgust that are meant to be directed at specific products in particular and consumer culture in general, will instead be directed at the AMF, thus alienating potential adherents rather than mobilizing them.

Debra Hopkins and her co-authors depict two social movements – the Disability and the Feminist Movements – involved simultaneously in a conflict with each other and the British state about the concept of care. For several decades the Disabled People's Movement (DPM) in Britain has been campaigning against the professional and welfare discourses which construct disabled people as passive, helpless and pitiable, thus depriving them of a sense of dignity and pride. DPM revolted against the emotionalized, demeaning notions of the dependent needy and the heroic, self-sacrificing caregivers, and sought to institute the language of rights and interest. It aimed to extricate disabled people from the disempowering discourse of care by arguing for the removal of emotion from the care relationship through the development of direct payments for 'personal assistance'. In 1997 this battle was won. Feminists, in contrast, have placed value on care in human relationships, while expressing concern that carers, or 'personal assistants', often women who provide nurturing and caring services to uphold their gender identity, are being manipulated and exploited. Feminists argue that stripped of the reciprocity and the emotional components of care, such as devotion or trust, the care relationship may thus exist as merely a low paid economic commodity. They believe that removing the emotional component from care is misguided and perilous. The value of this chapter is not only to highlight the salient points of a movement controversy about a particular government policy and the stages of transition towards 'emancipatory care' which grants the disabled the right to (co-)define the feeling rules, but also to shed light on how movement discourses work towards both the cognitive-normative and the emotional (re-)framing of reality.

Movement consolidation: re-charging emotional batteries

Activists sense particularly strongly the tension between being embedded in the emotional culture of a particular social movement, being pressed upon by the values and emotions of broader society and developing one's own cognitive-normative and emotional frame. This often results in the need for activists to recharge their emotional batteries. They do so in a variety of ways. As Erika Summers-Effler demonstrates in her chapter dealing with a Catholic worker community in a large American city, *laughter* helps to release built up tension and downplay shame-evoking distinctions of status among movement members and those they want to help, while solidarity-ascertaining *rituals* help them to go on. Or, alternatively, activists may decide to become involved in one of many sensitivity-training and consciousness-raising *practices* on offer. Re-evaluation Counseling (also called co-counseling) is one such practice. As Debra King points out it allows Australian activists to sustain their hope for and participation in social change, while providing an opportunity to construct new ways of thinking and feeling which improve their capacity to co-operate with others. At the other end of the spectrum, Silke Roth's research on an American women's caucus deals with friendship and quitting and is presented in greater detail in the next section. Suffice to say here that it shows how important friendly, supportive and informative *networks* are for career-making within the male-dominated American union movement. Her analysis, which demonstrates the limits of these networks, adds a much needed sobering dose of reality which counter-balances an over-idealized view of activism-sustaining activities and bonds.

Both Debra King and Erika Summers-Effler highlight the difficulties of being engaged in intense movement activities questioning the dominant norms and relations at every possible level. As Debra King puts it, activists occupy the space between integration and de-integration, between the established and the questioned, and are thus subject to dissonance at both emotional and cognitive level. As Erika Summer-Effler points out, day-by-day activists are confronted with limited resources, conflicts, stress, ridicule and their own inconsistencies, while acting under pressure to sustain their solidarity with other activists and the groups they aim to serve. While King examines the emotion work involved in the process through which activists become capable of producing, and not simply reproducing, their subject positions, Summers-Effler investigates the value of rituals and laughter for sustaining hope and solidarity.

These chapters show that activism is not the result of a single, individual decision, but rather constitutes a long-term commitment which, however, is difficult to sustain without external support. This support can come from within the movement, or it can be accessed outside the movement, taking the form of a revitalizing practice, network, organization or event. It is an interesting research question why, as these chapters suggest, only some movements are capable of providing internal activism-sustaining activities; and whether it makes any difference for the consolidation of the movement if it relies on internal or external activism-sustaining practices. Finally the three chapters suggest that sustained activism is not a matter of a single moment of cognitive, normative and emotional liberation, but instead is best understood as a process which entails a series of choices about further – reinvigorating and commitment-deepening – involvements.

King's observation is that while Touraine provides a useful framework for examining this process through his concept of subjectivation – through which the Subject becomes social movement – his disregard of the emotions limits its relevance to social movement theory. In addressing this limitation, King relies on Hochschild's concept of emotional dissonance to explain the activists' need to engage in practices of emotional reflexivity to construct themselves as Subjects. Her empirical reference is to Australian activists relying on one type of organization that explicitly advocates such practices. King analyzes the kinds of emotion work activists engage in to achieve the level of reflexivity that enables them to align their ideals and actions. In critically engaging with Hochschild's concept of emotional labor, her research demonstrates that emotional reflexivity goes beyond the management of emotions. It also requires that activists reflexively engage *with* their emotions to disintegrate from hegemonic emotional and cognitive norms. Emotional reflexivity is therefore central to the process of subjectivation. It provides a means for activists to sustain hope and participation in social change; to re-examine those areas where there are discrepancies between their politics and their emotional attachment to dominant discourses; and for constructing new feeling rules that enable them to engage flexibly and creatively with other activists, their social movement organization and with the dominant discourses within which they operate. Emotional reflexivity therefore constitutes a key to sustained activism and thus to the continuation of social movements.

Erika Summers-Effler's starting point is that the field of social movements has acknowledged the significance of emotion for understanding social movement dynamics but, until this point, the emphasis has primarily been on the social construction of emotion rather than the impact of the structure of interaction on emotion. The two perspectives need not be mutually exclusive. In fact, a combination of the structure of interaction and social construction of emotion makes for a powerful theory of emotions in social movements. Summers-Effler shows that Catholic workers live in voluntary poverty in impoverished neighborhoods, sharing their home and other possessions with their neighbors, and that while voluntary material vulnerability allows these activists to bridge differences in social positions and create solidarity with people in their neighborhood, ritual and laughter are central to generating and maintaining solidarity within their community. In analyzing these aspects of the activists' lives, Summers-Effler focuses on the impact of the structure of interaction on emotion. Furthermore, she argues that only by highlighting both cultural and structural conditions can we understand how the structure of interaction and available interpretive frames create opportunities for bonding emotional experience.

Movement demise: quitting

The research on social movements still emphasizes the emergence and consolidation of social movements. To redress this imbalance, the last point on our research agenda is the much under-explored issue of movement demise. It is crucial to find out what sort of emotions lead to member withdrawal and movement demise for in understanding the disengagement we also gain insight into the grounds for engagement and consolidation. The contributions on re-charging emotional energies suggest that if the movement activists do not find some re-charging opportunities, at some point they may succumb to burnout, well-known from organizational sociology. Hirschman (1982) suggested that disappointment with enthusiastic engagement in any form of politics sets in when the load of personal labor and the duration of engagement over time keeps increasing without any visible positive effects. It is ultimately the failure to see that one's actions are effective, despite all efforts that have been made, that makes one disengage. An alternative, widespread interpretation suggests that when a movement's goals are achieved, its members leave, although this again is dependent on specific outcome-framing. As Kleres also informs us, several small and scattered studies suggest that the changing membership structures of social movements can explain movement demise.

Positing an alternative to these individualistic, goal-focused approaches, Jochen Kleres examines the impact of the reunification of Germany on the Saxon chapter of the Gay Association of Germany, today the core national gay and lesbian organization which was originally founded in the East. In particular, he analyzes the emotional consequences of the intra-movement distribution of power. He attributes demobilization within this organization to Westernization in the wake of the reunification of Germany in 1989 and organizational expansion to the West. It was through this process that Western activists, who had joined the organization in 1990, managed to seize increasing influence within it. He shows why, when newcomers take over the control of an older, but expanded organization, the old-timers may decide to withdraw rather than fight for their due share of resources and power. His compelling argument emphasizes the role that shame plays in preventing the old-timers from asserting themselves in relationship to the power-usurping newcomers whom they, at first, uncritically admire and respect. His study supports the view that the distribution of resources and power has to be equitable in order to produce emotions which keep an organization going. In contrast to Polletta (2002), Kleres shows that those excluded from power and mutual affective regard do not necessarily respond in an assertive way – instead they just abandon the movement which proves itself incapable of providing them with emotional nourishment and a legitimate share of power. Kleres constructs a convincing argument about how the emotion of shame exercises a decisive causal power. He shows that we have to grasp emotions in their historicity because their intensity, and thus their motivational strength, depends on the substance of interactions which develop over time in a changing macro-context.

The problem of finding ways of integrating new and old members into an organization was also highlighted by Silke Roth, who focused on the role of friendship. Although some feminists have argued that bureaucratic organizations are anti-feminist per se because women prefer a less rationalized emotion culture, Roth's research suggests that friendship can play an important role even in a bureaucratic women's organization. In examining the Coalition of Labor Women (CLUW), Roth found that membership in CLUW made it possible to meet women from other unions and develop friendships. Most members joined it because they felt isolated in a male-dominated labor movement. Emotional support, exchange of knowledge and expertise, as well as network connections were intertwined. Women who developed friendships within CLUW, were part of support networks, and held leadership positions at the local, regional, and national level, tended to stay in the organization. At the same time their participation in CLUW helped them move up the union ranks and to influence the agenda of labor unions. As Roth shows, however, existing friendships and informality also had pronounced negative effects. They presented an obstacle to integrating new members and satisfying members who turned into 'pressed-for-time' union leaders. As with Polletta (2002), Roth shows that friendships and informality may alienate not only their new but also their old, albeit efficiency-oriented, members. However, in contrast to Polletta (2002) and more like Hirschman (1970) Roth shows that, even if dissatisfied with their organization, these members do not necessarily quit. Loyalty to 'their' organization keeps them within its boundary. Roth argues, finally, that CLUW's long-term beneficiaries achieved a lot, but did so at the expense of the excluded, non-unionized women and internal democracy. CLUW constituted a case of exclusionary solidarity in more than just one sense.

Two key themes

There are two specific themes to which we would like to draw special attention of the reader. In our view, research on social movements focuses too much on the movement mobilization per se and too little on the reactions of the public to this mobilization. One of our particular interests in this volume is in the role that emotions play in movement mobilization directed at a public, and in public reactions to this mobilization. By amplifying some of the contributions, we want to give additional weight to this, as yet, little explored research area. The second research theme concerns emotions in transnational movements. In part because some of these movements constitute a very new phenomenon and in part because research on these movements has only just begun, we have not been able to include any contributions which address this theme. By reviewing some recent attempts to tackle the issue of emotions in the transnational movements in this introduction, we want to stress its importance and show the direction in which current research is moving.

Movements' work on onlookers' emotions

Several essays in this volume are united in their concern with movements' work on onlookers' emotions. Social movements often wish to affect and mobilize by-standers whom they hope to entice over to their side. Some movements work on the emotions of the public, even when they 'only' provide commentary on the 'dry' statistics, and even when they are not aware of it. The very fact that the scientific material is usually meant to alarm, shock or warn of impending dangers implies that it has *emotion-evoking* potential. Such material might aim to move the public to sense fear and shock and, possibly, distrust other information provided by business or the authorities. Other movements, like the adbusting movement Åsa Wettergren analyzes in this volume, may specialize in creating emotion-evoking images, giving a slight twist to reality. They may, for example, employ extremely shocking pictures of cancer or war victims, tortured animals, abused children or dead forests to evoke a gut-level movement-supporting response. Social movements as an aggregate employ a wide range of media to evoke specific emotions in their public and possibly persuade people to join. Some seek to give an emotional twist, others an emotional u-turn to reality. Finally, while some work mainly with cultural artefacts others, such as those analyzed by Benski and Yang in this volume, put their own bodies and minds on display in the service of protest.

The protest movements which Tova Benski, Åsa Wettergren and Guobin Yang portray in this volume stage events which question central symbols, societal institutions and interaction modes. These events differ profoundly in their emotional substance. While the Adbusters hope to provoke shocked amusement, sadness or shame, Women in Black – whether they want to or not – provoke frustration, anxiety and anger. In contrast to both, the protesting Chinese students are met with an outpouring of sympathy, compassion and respect. In one respect, however, the three contributions agree: social movements wish to shock the onlookers out of their everyday routine compliance or indifference, cynicism and resignation. They all offer a radically different *emotional (re-)framing* of reality.

One research question that can be raised is whether this emotional (re-)framing of reality is effective. The Adbusters wish to cause laughter or sad reflection to force their on-lookers to engage with their ironic viewpoint. They hope for a gestalt switch (frame transformation), but we do not really know what they achieve. Wettergren suspects that cynism rather than outrage may be the result. Benski does not tell us what intentions Women in Black pursue by staging their infuriating, unbearable 'breaching events' which generate extremely strong feelings in the public. However, the outraged, defensive reactions to these events suggest that they presumably fail to provoke a gestalt switch. The protesting Chinese students of 1989 create 'critical emotional events', put on a tragic, heroic drama far removed from the resignation and boredom of everyday life, yet it still falls well within the mainstream of the Chinese history and culture. They hope for and indeed achieve both a gestalt switch and a deep emotional engagement of the public on their side. Although we need much more research of this type to reach any reliable conclusions, these three examples suggest that neither ironic nor 'breaching protest events' achieve their purpose, while the 'critical emotional events' do.

It is interesting to recall Yang's (2000) earlier text to work out the contrast between successful but differing – dramaturgical and satirical – protest forms. The protesting Chinese students made their bodies the carrier of revolution against the intransigent power-holders, the most dramatically and tragically so, when some opted for death through starvation (and, later on, some thousands of them remained on the Tiananmen Square, even though they knew that they would be attacked). But long before the protest ended on this tragic note, they resorted to song, poetry, recitation, declamation and declaration to bestow symbolism, pathos, honor and 'out of the ordinary' depth on their protest (Yang 2000). As the protest moved towards its tragic conclusion, not only the intransigence of the authorities, but also the weakening bodies of students who decided to starve themselves to death in protest were on display for everyone there to see. Their deeply upset parents and peers, some begging them to stop (but to no avail), were also in plain view. Most onlookers felt spontaneous sympathy for the protesters and could not resist a chance to partake in this extraordinary emotional event which constituted a much desired form of departure from the daily routine. Once drawn in, they joined others in a move upwards on an emotional spiral.

There could be no greater substantive emotional contrast than with the carnivalesque protest forms which mushroomed in the 'socialist' regimes of Poland and East Germany in the 1980s and came to full bloom in Belgrade in 1996–1997. Satire, humor, comedy served in these cases as an alternative means of pulling the by-standers into the protest in repressive regimes. Arguably the protesters not only amused the passers-by but also ridiculed the system, the elites and their moral standards. They managed to persuade the by-standers to shed their fears and join the protest (Flam 2004a). For example, the Polish Orange Alternative [*Pomarańczowa Alternatywa*] which emerged as a protest movement in about 1983–1984:

> ... brought some fun into the street scenes. Starting with the colorful clothing (often orange or red), paper decorations (the 'Aurora' cruiser), posters, masks, gremlin hats, and banners ... (such as *We are For!, Love the People's Police!, Long Life to the Undercover Agents!*) the organizers attracted onlookers' attention, offering them an attractive form of happening, laughter and mockery of the entire system. Common plays, chants and dances became the constant element of the street life. The intervening police did not encounter any opposition, and the protesters peacefully loaded the police cars, kissing the officers and inviting them to play ... While it was not difficult to pack the demonstrators into the police cars, it was impossible to have them convicted or penalized ... In 1987 the Orange Alternative had organized 15 different events: 'The Parade of the Casseroles' ... 'Gremlins in People's Poland' ... 'Rockmelon in the Mayonnaise' ... 'Toilet Paper – the Second Edition' ...
>
> (Misztal 1992: 63)

The Polish Orange Alternative perhaps did not, but the successful 1996–1997 protests against falsified election results in Milošević's Serbia certainly qualify as 'critical emotional events'. In this case street festivals legitimated the public presence of the masses. In one street people participated in a chess or football game, listened to a concert or watched ballet or a theatre piece. The popular 'pet-walking' played the same legitimatory role. Among the pets one could find parrots, guinea pigs, aquarium fish, cats, birds in cages and one particularly popular horse. Inseparable from carnival were noise, laughter and play:

> Here laughter had the function of punishment [of the dictatorial and corrupt power-holding elite], but at the same time its function was to remove the burden of fear and exaggerated respect for authority ... laughter is always a powerful weapon when confronted with deadly serious and dull authority.
>
> (Petronijević 1998: 274)

Satirical and carnivalesque protest forms are also found in Western democracies. These mobilize through amusement and attack through irony. In the past they seem to have been devoid of the fear-diluting and anger-managing element that their counterparts in repressive systems possessed. However, as Åsa Wettergren pointed out (e-mail, February 17, 2004), when confronted with repression and direct police violence, even protesters in democracies experience fear and 'experiment with ways to become "funnier" and more "ironic". In the demonstrations against WTO and World Economic Forum ... [protesters resorted to] the "white overalls" ... shields covered with photographs of babies, street party, etc'. Even though they take place in old democracies formally bent on the protection of human rights, EU-related protests seem singularly exposed to repression and violence, whether they take place in Copenhagen or Gothenburg. Quite possibly as the EU-meetings continue, we will see a corresponding explosion of 'innocent' carnivalesque protest forms anticipating repression and violence.

The examples cited here show that social movements develop a variety of protest forms in an attempt to disengage or shock the onlookers from the daily routine. They resort to irony and humor, drama or the grotesque. Relying on these different instruments, they hope to gain not only the attention, but also the emotional engagement of the onlookers. The exploration of these different protest forms and their dependence on various movement characteristics and the emotional-institutional context in which they emerge promises not only to constitute an exciting research area but would also contribute to our understanding of movement effectiveness.

Emotions and 'global movements'

Although this new century has, from its very beginning, witnessed a remarkable resurgence of transnational movement activity in the form of 'global movements' such as Attac, the European Social Forum or Global

Peace, this volume contains no contribution on emotions in this type of movement. In large part this is due to the fact that research on this topic is in its early stages. In this introduction we draw on the work in progress to indicate the ways in which emotions play a role also in this type of movement. In this way we hope to invite more systematic research of this kind.

A small-scale German research project concerned with mobilizing for the international counter-summit to the G-8 summit in Genoa in July 2001 showed that local and regional groups in Saxony could not agree on anything apart from a shared title on a leaflet persuading others to join and the logistic-technical details concerning travel and accomodation in Genoa (Ullrich 2002). The leaflet featured the common title, followed by a number of differing slogans and programs representing various local groups. Attac actually encourages this minimalist search for a common denominator when it stresses diversity, democracy and self-determination. The participating organizations decide to what extent they will develop a shared programmatic profile while seeking to persuade each other and those as yet unorganized to join the protest. The same study points out, however, that in a different part of Germany groups preparing for participation in the Genoa counter-summit managed to reach a substantive regional agreement about their shared goals. This suggests that while there is often reluctance, there is also variability in the extent to which local groups are willing to transfer even part of their identities and emotions to larger, supra-local organizational and programmatic units.

Donatella della Porta's (2005) research on the participants in the first European Social Forum which was organized in Florence in early November 2002, also suggests that, although participants of transnational movement meetings closely identify with, may even feel passionate about and/or gain an exhilarating feeling from membership in a movement critical of globalization, the movement remains dominated by local activists. Between local organizations and transnational coalitions of social movement organizations there is a national void. A glance at the attitudes of these remarkably heterogeneous activists confirms that, although most do not doubt the existence of a single movement with which to identify and are enthusiastic about this movement's diversity, their actual identification is ultimately very narrow. It is limited to concrete action objectives, a few groups in which they simultaneously participate, and an unprecedented openness to group-multilogues generating new values. Their intense emotions seem curiously split between the vision of the participatory future and the small-scale projects in which they are engaged. Their disappointment in and mistrust for governments and parliaments, which far exceed the average for their co-nationals, sharply contrast with their shared, intense desire to build a new type of participatory, deliberative polis – 'instinctive, joyous, celebratory, [and] practical' (della Porta, 2005: 254). This desire unites them in their expressive, anti-neo-liberal and anti-professional action.

While the counter-summit in Genoa in 2001 and the first European Social Forum in Florence in 2002 point to a reluctance to identify and organize along national lines, deep emotional identification with one's nation sets limits on the transnational peace and global solidarity movement. Whether in the form of collective memory of the hurt or limited nationalist inclusivity, nationalism prevents bonds of solidarity from developing across national borders. The following overview of two research projects illustrates these problems.

During the 2003 Iraqi War, North Korea announced its wish to withdraw from the Treaty on the Non-Proliferation of Nuclear Weapons and the American President Bush called Iran, Iraq and North Korea the Axis of Evil (Nomiya 2004: 7). These two events caused deep anxiety in the Pacific region about the imminence of war against North Korea. In this context a major coalition of movements within the Japanese-based World Peace Now approached a key anti-war and peace movement coalition in South Korea to establish a grand coalition for peace among countries surrounding the Pacific Rim, such as South Korea, the US and Japan. However, these two movements could not even agree on just three shared demands. Nomiya (2004: 8) argues that the collective memory of hurt felt about the Japanese violent annexation of Korea in the early twentieth century constituted one of the main obstacles to co-operation. Given the past Japanese record the South Korean group, interested in white-washing North Korea for the sake of much desired unification, questioned the right of the Japanese movement members to criticize North Korea for its human rights violations. Nomiya's research highlights how this particular initiative failed, even though both peace movements are connected to the World Peace Now – a global coalition for peace.

Nomiya (2004: 10–11) stresses the limitations that collective memory about past national hurt imposes on co-operation between particular national movements within the worldwide peace movement. He further contends that even where co-operation exists, it remains superficial. Contrary to those who uncritically praise the internet, Nomiya notes that World Peace Now's reliance on the internet promotes both 'surface interaction' and an 'only-at-this-time' orientation to communication. While this form of interaction helps to create a global movement since it prevents the past from casting its shadow on the present, it also minimizes the articulation of differences about the present. In both these ways it creates an appearance of unity in the World Peace Now Movement. The actual unity is, however, extremely superficial. It has nothing to do with mutual understanding but rather with technical possibilities of creating co-operation and co-ordination in its absence. For these reasons 'an image of "global citizens" participating and nurturing global collective identity seems ... misleading' (Nomiya 2004: 11). Not for the first time in modern history, citizens seem unable to escape their nationalisms to create a peace movement in true defiance of national borders.

Similarly, Goodman's research explores 'the place of the national in transnational movements' (2004: 1). Against globalist rhetoric which heralds the rise of crossnational social movements to prominence in the international arena and ignores the obstacles which these encounter in finding co-operative partners and exerting political influence (see also Flam 2002; 2004b), he stresses that national identity constitutes one of the major obstacles to the emergence of global solidarity. Goodman investigates the Australian citizen movement of solidarity with refugees who have been detained or refused admission to Australia. His purpose is to show that this movement wavers between 'humanitarian norms and national identity, between borderless cosmopolitanism and reconstituted nationalism' (2004: 1, 4–5). Recounting several heartbreaking or exhilarating demonstrations of solidarity between detainees/refugees and Australian citizens (including some members of the riot police and navy), Goodman pinpoints the role of extraordinarily intense and moving emotions in open displays of border-defying humanity. As he further argues, however, the very same outpouring of solidarity reproduces positive national identity. It shows that 'not all Aussies are heartless bastards' (Goodman 2004: 4). It (re-)constitutes them instead as a compassionate, generous, caring people with a long tradition of hospitality. Goodman also shows that when reason comes to moderate this seemingly inexhaustible outpouring of solidarity, it creates 'bounded emotionality': arguments about the criteria that should best be used to distinguish between acceptable 'legal' and undeserving 'illegal' refugees which recreate fences the very minute these are torn down. Goodman lists numerous public persons, campaign groups and citizen initiatives that sought to unite reason with emotion (2004: 5–7). They work to improve the admission criteria and the conditions in the detainee camps for the refugees. They are moved by their belief in the Australian nation and its capacity to combine humanism with nationalism. Advocates of globalist refugee solidarity who reject nationalist inclusivity with its search for a 'just' refugee program by their very existence delineate the limits of this particular perspective on the refugee problem. They instead demand open borders. And boundless emotions.

This brief overview of ongoing research on transnational movements suggests that emotions play an important role in these movements, perhaps even constitute a key to understanding why it is so difficult to realize the goal of global solidarity. In their own right the four research projects imply rather paradoxical results. While the first two suggest that local identities and emotions are not transferable to regional or national collectivities but can be paralleled by a strong but abstract emotional identification with the transnational movement, the second two suggest that it is national identities which keep the transnational solidarity movements within the limits of 'bounded emotionality'. Positing these research projects against each other constitutes a puzzle that needs to be solved. This task we leave to future research.

References

Aminzade, R. and McAdam, D. (2002) 'Emotions and contentious politics', Special Issue on Emotions and Contentious Politics, guest edited by R. Aminzade and D. McAdam, *Mobilization*, 7(2): 107–9.

della Porta, D. (2005) 'Multiple belongings, flexible identities and the construction of another politics: between the European Social Forum and the Local Social Fora', in D. della Porta and S. Tarrow (eds) *Transnational Protest and Global Activism*, Lanham: Rowman and Littlefield.

Flam, H. (ed.) (2002) *Pink, Purple, Green – women's, religious, environmental, and gay/lesbian movements in Central Europe today*, East European Monographs. New York: Columbia University Press.

—— (2004a) 'Anger in repressive regimes: a footnote to *Domination and the Arts of Resistance* by J. Scott', Special Issue on Anger in Political Life, guest edited by M. Holmes, *European Journal of Social Theory*, 7(2): 171–88.

—— (2004b) 'Whose civil society anyhow? On TNGOs, NGOs, SMOs, and value imperialism', paper presented in the Thematic Session 'The Role of NGOs in Social Movements: U.S. and European Contrasts', at the 99th Annual Meeting of the American Sociological Association, San Francisco, August 14–17, 2004.

Goodman, J. (2004) 'Social movements and refugee solidarity: breaking the borders or remaking "the nation"?', paper presented at the 36th World Congress of the International Institute of Sociology in Session 17 on Social Movements and Collective Action in the Era of Globalisation, Beijing, July 7–11.

Goodwin, J., Jasper, J.M. and Polletta, F. (eds) (2001) *Passionate Politics*, Chicago: Chicago University Press.

Hirschman, A.O. (1970) *Exit, Voice and Loyalty*, Cambridge, MA: Harvard University Press.

—— (1982) *Shifting Involvements*, Princeton: Princeton University Press.

Misztal, B. (1992) 'Between the state and Solidarity: one movement, two interpretations – the Orange Alternative Movement in Poland', *British Journal of Sociology*, 43(1): 55–78.

Nomiya, D. (2004) 'Linking local-historical memories to global movements: the World Peace Now Movement in Japan', paper presented at the 36th World Congress of the International Institute of Sociology in Session 17 on Social Movements and Collective Action in the Era of Globalization, Beijing, July 7–11, 2004.

Petronijević, E. (1998) 'Streets of protest: space, action and actors of protest 96/97 in Belgrade', *Polish Sociological Review*, 3(123): 267–86.

Polletta, F. (2002) *Freedom is an Endless Meeting: democracy in American social movements*, Chicago: The University of Chicago Press.

Ullrich, P. (2002) 'Gegner der Globalisierung. Organisation und Framing der Proteste gegen den G8-Gipfel in Genua', Magisterarbeit verfasst beim Institut für Kulturwissenschaften an der Universität Leipzig.

Yang, G. (2000) 'Achieving emotions in collective action: emotional processes and movement mobilization in the 1989 Chinese Student Movement', *The Sociological Quarterly*, 41(4): 593–614.

2 Emotions' map
A research agenda[1]

Helena Flam

In this chapter I outline a research agenda for the study of emotions and social movements. This agenda draws on the steady advances in the sociology of emotions in the past 30 years as well as on the bourgeoning research on emotions and social movements. The research agenda proposed here introduces many new research themes and conceptual tools in order to broaden the perspective on social movements and the emotion work they do. This contribution argues that research on emotions and social movements should start with macro-politics. We must map out emotions which uphold social structures and relations of domination to then show how social movements work to counter them. Most social movement researchers so far have focused on the role of mobilizing emotions or on how social movements transform and manage the feelings of their members. In contrast, the following research agenda contends that emotions do not exclusively belong in the realm of the micro-politics of social movements and that we need to more systematically connect the micro-politics of social movements to the macro-politics. It cautions about treating emotions in a narrow, instrumental-functionalist manner, as social facts with functions or as a new type of resource that movements can use.

In this volume emotions are understood as social, cultural and political constructs (Hochschild 1979; 1990; 1993). Of interest are the many ways in which social movements re-define dominant 'feeling rules' about their own members, their opponents and other relevant aspects of reality. The primary focus is on the emotional re-framing of 'reality', which often pre-dates and inevitably accompanies its cognitive-normative re-framing. As challengers to the *status quo*, social movements re-interpret specific aspects of social reality, call for new, obligatory emotions and feeling rules and wish to draw on these to mobilize individuals for collective action whose aim it is achieve social change.

The research framework that I am proposing starts with the routine distribution of *cementing emotions* in society. From these it is possible to derive the *subversive counter-emotions* which movements have to generate in order to be persuasive and win new members. This differs from the usual approach to social movements in that it does not single out the moments of emergence, growth and decline understood through the prism of networking, mobilization or organization as the keys to understanding social movements dynamics.

Instead, the new framework identifies gratitude and loyalty as the most important *cementing emotions.* These are reinforced by the *sanctioning emotion* of anger. Underpinned by fear and shame, these emotions hold society and its relations of domination together. The movement-proposed *subversive counter-emotions* are those which social movements attach to their own members and direct towards their opponents. Most important among those directed towards the opponent is not only hate, as is often assumed, but also distrust and contempt. These very subversive emotions cause disaffection from the system.

Another emotion often directed at the opponent is anger. Since it normally constitutes the prerogative of the powerful, social movements have to re-appropriate the right to feel and display this particular emotion by their members. For reasons explored in this chapter, this is often rather problematic in democratic systems and implies heightened repression risks in repressive regimes or contexts. Nevertheless, as Gamson (1992: 31–2) pointed out long ago, inequities may cause cynicism and/or resignation, emotions which demobilize. In contrast to cynicism and resignation, moral outrage or anger directed at the opponent mobilizes. That is why re-appropriating anger seems crucial for mobilization. Hope plays a similar, activating role.

Social movements striving for recognition (engaged in identity politics) face additional difficulties when trying to recruit and mobilize members. They have to generate pride as a self-oriented emotion to replace such demobilizing feelings as shame or guilt before anger at the opponent can be felt. And, finally, movements emerging in repressive contexts or systems have to overcome the additional barrier of fear.

Interestingly, successful feeling rules which impose subversive counter-emotions, such as hate, contempt, anger and/or hope directed towards the opponent carry specific implications for collective action repertoires. The research agenda proposed in this chapter constitutes the first attempt to connect dominant societal emotions with different, movement-generated subversive emotions and with protest strategies which they imply. Contrary to Aminzade's and McAdam's argument (2002: 109) it is not too early to make this connection. The research agenda proposed here also demonstrates that collective emotions and feeling rules pertaining to movement collectivities produce significant action and structural consequences. It demonstrates that collective emotions and feeling rules are of interest not only because they expand our research horizon but because they possess a great explanatory power.

Normal distribution of routine emotions in society

In this section my point of departure is the social structures and relations of domination. I ask what sort of emotions cement and uphold them. This sets the context for proceeding to the question of what social movements have to accomplish in order to weaken and counteract these cementing emotions and thus cause disaffection of individuals they seek to mobilize in protest.

Loyalty

Georg Simmel (1999: 652–70; Flam 2002: 18–20) singled out loyalty and gratitude as the two emotions which cement social relations converting them into permanent institutions. These two emotions, he argued, keep the interactions going long after the initial emotions, such as love or mutual sympathy, which bound individuals together, are gone. Max Weber associated loyalty more closely with legitimate systems of domination. He posited loyalty as a key emotion which links the powerless to the powerful. Weber argued that loyalty to the powerful is at the base of every legitimate form of domination and that it, together with fear, constitutes a magnetic field which shapes obedience.

Loyalty seems to pervade every nook and cranny of modern society. In fact most prominent social scientists attribute great significance to its binding role. Jürgen Habermas (1987: 320), for example, argued that modern political-adminstrative units are systems which exchange administrative achievements and political decisions for loyalty and taxes. More recently, Mabel Berezin (2002: 38) pointed to the exchange between the democratic nation-states and their citizens in which states deliver security and receive confidence and loyalty in exchange. This also applies to other social institutions and settings. Fordism, now in demise, involved an exchange of employment, work security and career for hard, disciplined work and loyalty to the bosses (Goldthorpe 1969). In addition, Albert Hirschman (1970) argued that organizations, such as firms, voluntary associations, political parties and even states, do not collapse, even when their products deteriorate, because their members and customers, rather than abandoning them, sustain them for the sake of the loyalty they feel towards them. And, as Simmel pointed out, loyalty and gratitude play a key role in cementing couples and marriages long gone sour. Conversely, Arlie Hochschild (1993) demonstrated that when the domestic political economy of gratitude does not work, love is undermined and the way is paved for conflicts, separation and divorce.

Anger

Other-directed anger is not spontaneously or easily felt in Western democracies (Flam 2004). Social superiors expect, and usually see on display, the positive emotions of their subordinates (Hochschild 1983; Collins

1990). Positive feelings flow up and negative feelings flow down social hierarchy. We find the same pattern in corporations and in gender relations. Corporate feeling 'rule number one' is that subordinates should not display anger, since it is a power prerogative and an instrument of power of the bosses (Hearn 1993). In relationships between men and women, anger is a male privilege (Hochschild 1983: 163; Taylor 2000: 288) and therefore, arguably, their instrument of power. From this it follows that social inferiors, corporate subordinates or women who display anger easily become targets of negative sanctions. Well aware of this, socialization agents such as parents, teachers or peers, put a lot of effort in instilling a *habitus* of obedience in the children destined to play subordinate roles when they grow up (Flam 1998: 239). They teach them to swallow their feelings of humiliation and anger which come up in daily encounters with superordinates who deny the subordinates their autonomy (cf Scott 1990). As a result, the overt display of rebellious anger is in fact rare in the West. The habit of obedience is so deeply ingrained in the powerless that they lose the capacity to display the level of anger required for rebellion.

Theodore Kemper (1978; 1981) argues that we experience anger as a 'real emotion' when we are confronted with power that seriously limits our autonomy and we attribute the blame for the loss of autonomy to the power-holder. But he also argues that anger will not be shown when we expect punishment for its expression. For this reason even if our 'real emotion' is anger, we put on indifference or feign positive feelings. To sum up, then, in liberal democracies anger is a prerogative of the powerful which the powerless find hard to display.

Shame

Shame is a multifaceted phenomenon, but here I will name only two of its multiple functions and effects. First, most of us feel shame when we fail to live up to our own and/or the internalized societal standards (Simmel 1992: 141–7; Flam 2002: 21–5). Shame in this sense is best understood as a self-control mechanism which, nevertheless, can be triggered in us by others when they want to achieve our compliance. This mechanism operates not only in families or institutions of education, but also in corporations. Superiors as well as peers play the role of reinforcement agents who shame non-conformist individuals back into the ranks of the pliant. One is shamed into obedience.

Second, shame is applied to fortify systems of domination and stratification (Kemper 1981; Neckel 1991: 195–213). Those less powerful are confronted with classification systems that force them to think of themselves as inferior in terms of morals, skills, appearance, and so on. Since these classification systems are internalized by a great number of people, they become played out in daily interactions over and over again: at work, in the supermarket, at home.

Theorists also speak of shaming, ridiculing and laughing at as strategies which the powerful elite or status groups use to scare away the undesired aspirant outsiders and to bring conformity among the deviant members of their own group (Parkin 1971; Kemper 1981; Neckel 1991; Flam 2002: 149–65). The powerful also rely on shaming, ridiculing and scornful laughter to keep the protesting powerless down – only when this does not work do they take to repression. Shaming, ridicule and scornful laughter are only effective when the individuals at which they are directed share norms with those applying these sanctions. Making another person feel ashamed or ridiculous is one of the most effective means of intimidation. Imagine the feelings of a lesbian confiding in a good friend that she would like to adopt a child, and the friend then responding by snorting in derision. Or imagine what a child feels like who approaches its playmates to play with new kindergarten toys and is told: 'We do not play with Jews'.

Since World War II it has been mostly such social groups as women, homosexuals, disabled and ethnic minorities which, on the one hand, have been confronted by powerful discursive images and interaction patterns classifying them as inferior, and, on the other hand, have organized in movements to challenge these images. Many have claimed and won societal recognition and new feeling rules towards their members, in some cases codified in law. At least in public they can now expect respect and expressions of solidarity from their 'community of love'.

Fear

In Max Weber's concept of domination, fear is inherent in every form of legitimate domination. In liberal democracies this fear concerns one's life chances. Whether in relationships between social superiors and inferiors, super- and subordinates, or between genders, as long as those more powerful are in a position to decide the life chances of those less powerful, the latter will obey and conform for fear of putting those life chances into jeopardy. In repressive systems the fear for life chances is joined by the fear for one's physical freedom and life. Sociologists have long argued that fear about losing one's job and forfeiting career chances, motivates conformity and obedience on the job in liberal democracies, even when an individual would prefer to quit or criticize the firm for which he or she works (Terkel 1972; Jackall 1988; Flam 2000: 49–67). Since most people spend the majority of their waking lives on the job and, since these jobs provide a financial basis for their entire life constructs, job-related fears can be said to be the pillar on which these very constructs rest. Many people who have become extremely critical of the corporations for which they work, in fact do not dare to criticize them for fear of losing their jobs or career chances. Fear keeps them glued to the organizations of which they have become critical.

Above I have proposed that loyalty, shame, anger and fear are the key emotions which support social structures and relations of domination. But these do not exhaust the list of such emotions. For example, I did not give love its due place, although it is another emotion which sustains social structures and relations of domination. It binds the individuals to their countries, people, governments, armies, parents, spouses and partners. Another emotion which plays a key role in macro- and micro-politics is hate – an emotion which is sadly as widespread as it is under-analyzed in the literature. When either love or hate are redirected or the entities to which they are directed expand or decrease in scope, we can be certain that a social movement is at work. That is why both these emotions deserve separate treatment. But my main purpose is to initiate the task of mapping out emotions relevant to social movement mobilization, while leaving for the future research the completion of this task. Let me now move on to point out another interesting research niche.

The emotion work that social movements do

Now what new social movements attempt to do, is to *re-socialize* their (potential) members and the larger public. They teach their members to work on emotions directed towards themselves and their opponents. Movements attempt to suppress self-defeating feelings which came with the socialization processes and instead propose new, assertive emotions as appropriate for their members and the general public – they thus propose new 'feeling rules' (cf Hochschild 1983). These feeling rules parallel an 'alternative ideological account' which shifts blame from the individual to the system and its moral standards (Britt and Heise 2000: 256).

Sowing distrust

It has to be more widely recognized that the 'framing activities' of a social movement never exclude a strong emotional component (Taylor and Whittier 1995; Taylor 1996; Jasper 1998). Every cognitive frame implies emotional framing. Diagnosis involves not only telling people that there is a problem and who is responsible for it but also that they should feel angry about it. Prognosis tells people what action they should take and what the future prospects are, but it also implies that hope for change or destructive hate are called for.

For example, many West European anti-nuclear movements of the 1970s became involved in scientific, debating and reporting activities in order to counteract the official image of nuclear energy as clean, cheap and safe (Flam 1994). As their government and public utility opponents rightly claimed, relying on counter-arguments, pictures and statistics, movement activists spread fear of nuclear energy while simultaneously sowing distrust of, and anger at, the authorities/utilities and their policies in an attempt to achieve massive disaffection away from the nuclear energy programs. In several European countries they were quite successful and managed to compel their governments to depart from their hitherto unwavering support for the use of nuclear energy for civilian purposes.

Social movements attempt to shake people out of their routine trust in the authorities and out of their everyday assumption that authorities work towards the public good and therefore deserve their loyalty. This fits nicely with two recent perspectives on the state. On the one hand, it has been argued that the democratic states are best understood as a composite of a community of love and a secure state. In Mabel Berezin's rendition:

> Security with its attendant feelings of confidence and comfort is the emotional template of the major form of modern political organization – the democratic nation-state. The territorially bounded state inspires confidence and loyalty in its members, citizens, by providing internal (police) and external (military) security. In exchange citizens develop an emotional bond that makes them willing to defend the security of the state under threat and to forfeit income to taxes. Patriotism and civic nationalism are the positive descriptors of this feeling of attachment . . .
>
> (Berezin 2002: 38)

On the other hand, a general argument has been advanced that Western states have monopolized responsibility for public security, extending the security concept to matters of industrial safety, environment, public health, etc. By gaining control over standards and/or provision of public health and safety these states have acquired new sources of legitimacy, but at the same time they also created new grounds of de-legitimation for themselves (Kearl 1995: 11–17). They have made themselves more vulnerable to new types of criticism and mistrust. Every food scandal and each fatal epidemic can escalate into distrust directed against the government. In this general context, social movements play a prominent role as social agents who try to *instigate fear, suspicion, distrust and anger – a distrust of and anger at authorities, and the fear of their policies and their results.* Government officials who start comprehensive inquiries, change policy programs or resign indicate that such movements have succeeded in pressing their demands.

Social movements not only trade in anger, distrust and fear about state policies, but also debate about which principles and feeling rules should apply in a given policy sector. For example, issues of emotionality versus reserve, dependency versus equality run through the British debate about the care for the disabled today. Feminists advocate the humanizing virtues of loving care which the care-takers provide for the disabled, while the disabled movement argues for pure, equalizing exchange of services for money. Social movements can develop a powerful stake about feeling rules which, from their point of view, should prevail in a policy sector (see

Debra Hopkins *et al.* in this volume). When successful, they make a lasting contribution to severing policy sectors, bureaucracies and citizens from the routine ways of doing things.

Re-appropriating anger

Much current research tells us that social movements engaged in identity politics and striving for societal recognition for their members teach women, gays or members of various other minorites to see anger and its expression as legitimate (Taylor 1996; Hercus 1999: 36–7; Britt and Heise 2000: 256–9; Gould 2002: 185; cf Holmes 2004). In effect, they reverse one important social norm or 'feeling rule' which constitutes anger as a prerogative of the powerful and labels it as deviant when displayed by the powerless. Social movements try to teach the powerless to reconquer or *re-appropriate* this emotion for themselves.

In the as yet modest, Western literature on emotions and social movements, anger directed at the opponent is seen as a valued commodity. It is seen as the very currency of protest: anger at the opponent is to replace the hitherto felt self-destructive, immobilizing feelings of vulnerability, guilt and shame.

Building on her earlier research, Verta Taylor (2000: 272) showed how in the course of the 1980s and 1990s the American post-partum depression movement changed its view on women's role in society. It abandoned the ideal of happy motherhood and diagnosed the problems of 'unloving' or hostile mothers as caused by a male-dominated society in which mothering is a responsibility solely of women while absolving men. With each others' help, movement members converted their feelings of frustration, guilt, shame and depression into anger. In groups of mutual help and in the media they openly displayed pride about having survived a situation which had led others to suicide or infanticide. They did not hesitate to show their anger about unrealistic societal expectations, negligent husbands and indifferent and patronizing obstetrician-gynecologists who, even today, refuse to treat the postpartum depression and psychosis as illnesses. Similarly, Debbie Gould (2002: 183) showed that when the ACT UP activists re-framed AIDS, from 'death by virus to murder by government neglect', they simultaneously lifted the burden of shame about 'deviant' sexual practices attributed to homosexuals, evoked government-directed anger, and defined 'angry, militant activism the object of lesbian and gay pride' (Gould 2002: 184–5). Gould's analysis pinpointed the exact historical, contingent moment in which ACT UP finally managed to turn the US government into the object of righteous anger for its unwillingness to define AIDS as a top public danger which required immediate intense counter-measures and vast sums of research money. In both studies pride, anger and solidarity are signs of newly emerging collective identities and a precondition for coordinated collective action for social movements striving for recognition. In contrast, Britt and Heise (2000) proposed a reversed causal chain for times of routine gay mobilization. They argued that the American gay movement instills fear of homophobic policies and violence among its members to replace the existing self-shame to then whip up anger which induces participation in gay parades which in turn generates pride. Even this argument pairs pride and anger with public collective action and displays of solidarity.

Anger is of key importance because it constitutes a key antidote to the fear of repression. Whistleblowers in private and public corporations in several Western democracies, just like dissidents in Czechoslovakia, reported that they overcame their fear and sustained their critical stand in face of direct repression because they felt raging anger about the transgressions against the public good that the firms/authorities allowed themselves (Glazer and Glazer 1999: 289–91). Peer support helped to sustain them in their struggle.

While speaking of anger as a prerequisite for protest, it is perhaps necessary to devote a few words to earlier studies. Barrington Moore, Jr (1978), a renowned American historian, focused on the importance of anger. He was concerned with the question of 'how human beings awake from anesthesia, how they overcome the sense of inevitability and how a sense of injustice may take its place' (Moore, Jr 1978: 461) and argued that the emergence of moral outrage cannot be taken for granted. Neither human suffering as such, nor injustice in itself, makes people angry. Instead the change in the very principles of distribution of social rewards paired with the realization that the cause of change is human makes people angry (Moore, Jr 1978: 455). But mobilizing moral anger emerges first when a complex, contingent and time-consuming process of developing new standards of injustice and condemnation comes to its conclusion (Moore, Jr 1978: 338–9, 461–2, 469, 476–7).

In a seminal article Fireman *et al.* (1979) similarly showed how precarious and contingent the emergence of collective protest is. In contrast to Moore, Jr, they demonstrated that some individuals react with disbelief, anger and disgust to the very first transgressions of authorities. Based on research involving three watershed encounters and 33 laboratory experiments they, like Moore, Jr, emphasized that it nevertheless takes many contingencies, such as the development of leadership, alternative framing, organizing and bonding, before a rebellious collective emerges and defines its course of action (Fireman *et al.* 1979: 18–29).

Several social movement theorists, including Gamson (1992: 7, 31–2) argued that collective action is impossible without a sense of injustice which he equated with moral indignation or hot cognition. A sense of injustice cannot emerge without a new diagnosis of the situation and a conviction that existing conditions are unjust. In themselves inequities do not cause anger-powered mobilization, only hot cognition of injustice does:

Different emotions can be stimulated by perceived inequities – cynicism, bemused irony, resignation. But injustice focuses on the righteous anger that puts fire in the belly and iron in the soul. Injustice ... is a hot cognition, not merely an abstract intellectual judgment about what is equitable. The heat of moral judgement is intimately related to beliefs about what [concrete] acts or conditions have caused people to suffer undeserved hardship or loss.

(Gamson 1992: 31–2)

On this version of the concept, first when the perception of inequities joins hands with a concretization of its source, a mobilizing sense of injustice, such as is powered by righteous anger, will invariably appear.

Suffice to say that at the theoretical level the recognition of anger as an emotion necessary for mobilizing in protest has a long and noble pedigree. However, newer research posits anger as an object of study in its own right and reveals that not only social movements (Taylor 1996; Hercus 1999: 36–7; Britt and Heise 2000: 256–9; Gould 2002: 185) but also elites rely on anger to mobilize the masses (Ost 2004). Research also shows that movement anger is ambivalent and unruly. It may actually resist the desired feeling rules which suppress issues and conflict articulation, ultimately splitting instead of, as intended, uniting the movement (Holmes 2004). Recent work on anger therefore goes beyond seeing it as one of the many preconditions of protest. It underlines that much is to be gained by defining anger as a social, cultural and political construct, investigating its discursive components and organizational preconditions to then assess its various consequences for the movements and larger political contexts.

To summarize, in the West social movement activists as well as movement theorists believe that the powerless should re-appropriate anger. They trust that open anger will both go unpunished and push social change in the desired direction (see Flam 2004). This belief seems to be deeply rooted in the democratic framework in which law constrains the employment of repressive violence against the protesting masses and in which the legitimating principle of great numbers often brings power-holders to heed the claims of the masses.

The contrast to repressive regimes or contexts is extensive. Even though activists in these societies call for civil courage, they rarely try to foster anger. On the contrary, they seek to limit its expression. They fear that open, angered opposition would lead to bloody confrontations with the power-holders and their representatives, cause harm to bodies and lives, and spell ultimate defeat. Instead they try to inspire hope and/or contempt and, if at all possible, develop frames and (inter)action patterns which help to manage fears.

Countering fear

Successful social movements help to manage or reduce the double fear, the fear of repression and the fear about one's life chances. Flam (1998; 2000) writing about 'socialist' Poland and East Germany before 1989 argued that the fear of repression and the fear for one's life chances attach people to those with decision-making powers. Only individuals who succeed in managing this double fear are able to act upon their critical views and move to swell the ranks of the pioneer dissenters. Oppositional movements in less repressive systems have a good chance of developing 'symbolic worlds' – which propose new role models, while reversing status hierarchies and values – which help critical individuals to manage their fears, join the opposition and persevere as dissidents. This is more difficult to achieve in systems of absolute control which leave no space for the development of dissident counter-cultures (cf Scott 1990).

A related problem is that of managing the fear of repression that is likely to develop prior to, or during, public demonstrations. Guobin Yang (2000), focusing on the Chinese student revolt in Beijing in 1989, shows how students counteracted their own fear of what they believed was an impending death by preoccupying themselves with writing proclamations, songs, poems or their last wills. They also pledged to each other to face impending death with honor. The dramatization of these individual and collective declarations helped to lock protesters into an honorable course of action. Similarly, Petronijević (1998) analyzing several months-long demonstrations against Milošević and his clique in Belgrade in 1996/1997 focused on carnivalesque protest forms in general, and shouting and banging in particular, as fear-management devices. Flam (2004), comparing several East European movements prior to 1989, argued that carnivalesque, satirical protest forms in repressive systems help to manage fear – one's own and that of the public – while trying to dilute the anger of police and the authorities. Goodwin and Pfaff (2000) identified six fear-management mechanisms in their comparison of the US civil rights movement of the 1950s and 1960s with the East German civic movement before and during 1989. Interestingly, the authors pinpointed not only the identification with the movement, shaming, mass meetings and speeches, but also shouting, cheers, chants, and songs. In paying attention to how such cultural elements help to manage fears their analysis reinforces that of Yang and Petronijević: movement participants resort to many different types of rhythm and loud sounds, as well as invest a lot of effort into the creation of dramatic acts, repeated pre-demonstration motivational 'pride and anger' speeches and even entire elaborate discourses, in order to activate and sustain the process of fear management among movement members.

Shame and shaming out

So long as they believe societal myths, members of routinely downgraded groups, such as ethnic minorities, women, gays or people with a disability, live with the shame of having characteristics defined as inferior by societal norms. They are expected to swallow insults and have more or less vicious jokes poke fun at them. Sometimes they even contribute jokes of their own. Prototypical here are anti-semitic or anti-women or anti-gay jokes, told and sometimes invented by the members of the minority group themselves. A self-assertive social movement attempts to destroy societal myths hurtful to their group and to reverse the feeling rules of the affected group about itself. It calls for pride to replace shame. This new feeling rule manifests itself in the refusal of Jews to hear yet another anti-semitic joke or comment, the insistence of Malcolm X and his followers that 'black is beautiful' and the open organizing of the Gay Pride Parades. But the re-socialization does not stop at changing the feeling rules about oneself and one's collectivity.

Shaming, ridiculing and laughing at are two-edged weapons. Social movements re-appropriate these strategies of social control, just like they re-appropriate anger, and re-direct it against their opponents. The pressing emotions of growing disappointment with, and contempt for, the hitherto respected elites generate a u-turn from being ashamed to shaming out. Contempt for the other implies asserting oneself and one's own moral standards. It implies a feeling of superiority towards the other who claims more than deserved status and/or power. Contempt as a compelling emotion puts one in a position to laugh and shame at the other out (Berger 1997: 157–9; Kemper 2000: 66; Scott 1990). Although simply asking a policeman confronting protesters 'Aren't you ashamed of yourself?' or saying 'Shame on you' are good examples of shaming activities (Goodwin and Pfaff 2000: 297), ridicule and satire are ways of creating even more advanced shaming activities directed at the established elites. All represent attempts to shame the opponent back into moral conduct. To provide just one example: In 1996–1997 when crowds protested against Milošević and his clique in Belgrade, the walking masses regularly showered the parliament, the city hall and the television building with eggs and red paint (Petronijević 1998: 272–3). Since in Serbian the word 'thieves' is a derivative of 'egg', the symbolic meaning of the red egg showers was very clear. Similarly, one held one's nose or threw toilet paper on the buildings in which Serbian press and television were housed. One day, flowers were deposited in front of the Palace of Justice, while condoms and some constitutional law books were placed outside the Supreme Court. This last example shows that the bitter disappointment and scathing contempt, as collective emotions felt towards a powerful opponent, influenced the use of shaming, ridiculing and laughing at as the most likely form for collective protest. We need to find out more about how these emotions emerge at the collective level in contemporary societies (cf Scott 1990) and how movements go about instilling these emotions among their members.

Structural factors facilitating disaffection and transfer of loyalties

Apart from the question of what movements do about emotions to detach individuals from the established institutions, organizations, and cognitive and normative patterns, more research on the preconditions facilitating movement mobilization is needed. The literature on the preconditions facilitating disaffection – or loyalty detachment and transfer – is sparse. One basic argument is that ascribed identities, such as gender, class, religion, ethnicity or nationality, often hinder the process of individualization as well as movement participation since they provide lenses through which these are perceived as 'other' or 'anti-traditional' (Kriesi 1988: 359–60). Ascriptive identities are frequently reinforced and stabilized by established institutions: even when passive, they maintain the status quo (Barnes and Kaase 1979: 455–69, 516–17).

Rainer Lepsius refines this argument. To explain differences in the timing and intensity of enthusiasm about the Fascist movement in Germany, he proposes the 'immunization' thesis (Lepsius 1993: 51–79). The key question is whether and what kind of social recognition, influence and representation each group wishes to find and, in fact, finds in the national community. Beliefs do not suffice to immunize against new ideologies. A social group or a class is only immunized when it possesses leaders and organizations which sustain and protect its sub-cultural values, beliefs and self-images while at the same time providing a desired form of social recognition, influence and representation. Groups which have little, indirect or no influence and representation, and which are granted little social recognition, are the most open to new movements when these offer to provide them with both.

Finally, Flam (1992; 1993) proposes three different contexts in which individuals become more open to protest: a) when societal ties weaken, that is, when mass organizations meant to represent and institutions meant to bind neither represent the interests nor bind the emotions of their members; b) when long-term life projects are blocked and these cannot be pursued due to the absence of opportunities (blocked educational and/or few job/career opportunities; suffocating gender or family relations; stifling bureaucratic controls or destructive market interventions, etc.); and c) when social pressures and social controls make the playing out of multiple, at times contradictory, identities impossible. In these three contexts individuals start a long process of *emotional liberation* which involves detaching loyalties and other positive emotions from the institutions and organizations to which they were hitherto attached. Emotional liberation includes one's emotional transformation, relaxation and cutting of the old emotional attachments, and the construction of new emotional bonds. This prepares ground for what political scientists name a transfer of loyalties. The processes involved in emotional liberation also make individuals more open-minded to negotiations about joining like-minded social movements. Flam (1993: 86–7) contrasts this concept with McAdam's *cognitive liberation* which movements help along when they postulate a new target for blame attribution and spread a belief in their own efficacy (McAdam 1988). Flam argues that both must run parallel in order for individuals to join and stay with social movements. Debra King (this volume) shows, moreover, that the cognitive-emotional liberation is not to be understood as a single moment of enlightenment but rather constitutes a never ending process for many activists. They consciously choose movements or movement-practices in which they become involved and so keep crafting the contours of their own liberation.

Movement emotions toward opponents and their action consequences

The construction and display of emotions directed toward an opponent constitutes another important aspect of movement work which movements undertake. I showed earlier that research has identified anger as the main emotion directed at opponents in Western democracies. I also pointed out that social movements spread distrust and fear of the state and/or contempt for the ruling elites. Another opponent-directed emotion that social movements often generate is hate. Hate is the opposite of love – an emotion which is normally expected to be felt towards one's country and, by extension, towards its government.

Some movements go self-consciously about imposing hatred of the opponent as the obligatory rule for their members, while for others this kind of hatred emerges as a result of *interactions* with opponents (della Porta 1991; 1995: 152–8, 161). Although the difference between the *state- or regime-evoked emotions* and *movement-evoked emotions* is sometimes very subtle, below I argue that the characteristics of a state (openness or closeness to protest), as well as concrete government/political elite actions (repression or tolerance/negotiations), are the keys to understanding the prevailing emotional orientation of the movement.

Hatred

In her study of the extreme left and right in Italy and Germany between about 1965 and 1975, della Porta (1995: 158–61) showed that the 'traumatic', 'shocking' and 'outrageous' recollections of police brutality, of the state's authoritarianism, and of the routine employment of violence against demonstrators, the underground movement members and the prisoners, enraged left-wing activists, who, in both countries, developed 'an image of a "violent" and "unfair" state'. This image, which in each country became embroidered by past- and turning event-related symbols, helped to reinforce the intense hatred of the state and to legitimate one's own reliance on the 'defensive' and/or 'revolutionary' counter-violence. In della Porta's study, contrary to the expected direction of causality, the violence of the state caused left-wing movements to respond with violence. The movements did not have to do much work on the emotions of activists to cause disaffection from the system and hatred towards the state. The state, which supposedly stands for law and order, in taking to unjustified violence did this work for them.

Hope and fear

Della Porta's work deals with the radical left and the radical right. But what are the feeling rules in movements which are situated between these two extremes? How do social movements who define the state as an opponent feel about it? I would like to suggest that hope mixed with fear, and contempt mixed with hope, also constitute frequent emotional mixes directed towards an opponent. They run parallel to the expectations concerning the openness of the state and its elites to protest. They have differing action consequences and influence the forms and the general tenor of protests.

Let me offer some illustrations. In their analysis of the anti-nuclear movements, researchers (Kitschelt 1986; Flam 1994) distinguished between more and less confrontational movements. Confrontational movements believe that they deal with a 'closed' political system and its intransigent representatives. They set up hatred of the opponent as the feeling rule. Hatred implies the wish to destroy the opponent and thus the employment of violence. In the contrary case, when movement activists believe that their opponent is open to negotiations, and the political system creates opportunities for co-shaping the policy agenda, these beliefs will go along with the hope that the opponent will realize movement demands and with anxiety that it will not.

As *States and Anti-Nuclear Movements* (Flam 1994) shows, interactions with the opponent often lead movements to debate and re-think their feeling rules, so that the same movement can move from extreme hatred to hope and from hope to disappointment and hatred. The movement emotions also change much over time. In 'socialist' Poland in the summer of 1980 we can find the familiar emotional combination of hope and fear among protesting dockside workers whose actions ended with the emergence of Solidarity a few months later. When these prepared their famous list of 21 demands for the Polish party-state, they hoped to be heard, but feared that they would not be (Flam 2004: 177–8). They turned euphoric once their demands went through and the trade union movement was accorded official recognition. When the party-state resorted to repression in the end of 1981, the feeling of euphoria turned into intolerable frustration, hatred and fear.

The foolish mixture of contempt, hope and fear

The emotion of contempt mixed with hope has quite distinct action consequences. This emotional mixture is contradictory. Contempt implies that the moral standards of the opponent are judged to be beyond repair, while hope implies that the opponent is seen as reformable. Yet this emotional mixture is common and has its own action consequences. Protesters simply cannot resist the 'foolish' hope that, against all odds, the corrupt and/or cruel power-holders will reform themselves under their moral pressure. This mixture generates more self-assertive, scathing and aggressive symbolic protest forms than pure hope or hope mixed with fear, but it stops short of physical violence in contrast to hatred. The protesters deliberately use comedy, folly, irony and/or satire for the purposes of attack directed against institutions and the elites (Berger 1997: 158). Satire is best interpreted as an aggressive, militant irony. It involves an assertion of a moral point of view, targets the opponent, and relies on the use of (often grotesque) fantasy (Frye in Berger 1997: 158–9). As Scott (1990) showed the repeated, yet anonymous-protective, employment of satire, grotesque and/or carnivalesque protest forms has had a long historical tradition among the masses in the systems of total control. It always bordered on, and sometimes even turned, revolutionary. The satirical, carnivalesque protest forms mushroomed in Poland and East Germany between 1980 and 1989 (Flam 2004). They provided comic relief from the tensions of everyday life in grey, repressive systems, but they also laughed and shamed the powerful out, while their apparent innocence diluted the anger of the very same group. This protest form seems more frequent in repressive than in liberal contexts.

As these sketches of the emotions directed towards an opponent imply, social movements which hope for reform engage in pleading, appealing or demanding. Movements which are moved by a mixture of contempt and hope, engage in unmasking, shaming and laughing at. Finally, movements which hate, destroy. This means that the emotions that social movements harbour or develop towards their opponents have very strong action consequences – they decisively influence the forms of protest.

Collectivities, their emotions and feeling rules, and their action consequences

Several researchers have already demonstrated that collective emotions and feeling rules have serious structural and action consequences which affect the fate of the entire movement. Since this is where much explanatory power lies, future research should further explore the variable connections between emotions, feelings rules and their consequences.

Donatella della Porta's (1995) study of right and left-wing radicalism in Italy and Germany between about 1965 and 1975 shows that the affective dynamics of a movement may have unintended, clearly undesired, consequences. Left-wing activists, involved in both legal and terrorist groups, characterized relationships in their groups as warm and caring, based on good feelings, generosity and everyday solidarity, the most often used metaphors being that of a 'family' or a 'merry brotherhood' (della Porta 1995: 177–9). Reinforced by a sense of absolute loyalty and responsibility towards each other in the underground these emotions intensified. The unintended upshot of this emotional constellation was that both the free and the already imprisoned militants, although they wanted to quit, felt that they could not. Solidarity and loyalty to the other group felt obligatory. Each group continued its form of struggle for the other. The imprisoned activists felt that those outside risked their lives to free them, while the free activists, who risked death by staying, did not want to surrender or escape abroad in order not to abandon those who were in prison. Quitting would have amounted to betrayal. Only once the activists met together to face a trial, could the collective decision to quit be taken.

Solidarity and mutual love for movement members as obligatory feeling rules have also been shown to have other undesired consequences. These professed feeling rules stifled open conflicts about real issues and reinforced white, middle-class, heterosexual women's domination within the American and New Zealand's feminist movements (Polletta 2002: 151, 259 note 2; Holmes 2004).

In her nuanced article on the unruly and disruptive emotion of anger Mary Holmes (2004) questions the utility of the concept of the 'feeling rules' for understanding the emotional dynamics of social movements. She shows that feminists active in New Zealand's 'second wave' women's movement between the late 1970s and the early 1990s saw anger as unruly and ambivalent. When unleashed against men in a 'healthy', 'dignified' and 'restrained' manner, disruptive anger was emancipatory. It helped to fight against guilt, resentment or shame which kept women enslaved. When, however, it was unleashed amongst women, it was counter-productive. Since the feminists wished to see themselves as the egalitarian and caring alternative to the hierarchical, power-hungry, violent and egoistical patriarchal society, they condemned unrestrained, personalized expressions of anger in their own midst as a form of false consciousness. Yet a repressive rule forbidding expressions of anger between 'good' feminists failed. When some feminists argued for the recognition of anger, conflict and negotiations as healthy and constructive, the fear of schism led to the insistence on consensual decision-making, even though differences of opinion remained. Lesbian and Maori feminists felt increasingly frustrated since they sensed constant, disrespectful pressure to fit in against their better judgment or else to risk exclusion. They felt angered by the dominance of the white, heterosexual women within the movement. Ultimately they left or came to openly argue for the exit option. Their anger also forced the dominant feminists to grant recognition to social divisions and conflictual issues within the movement. It led to more self-criticism and self-reflection.

In her study of several American social movements, Polletta (2002) focused on the relationship between strong friendship ties and experiments in participatory democracy. She showed that although the Student Non-violent Coordinating Committee (SNCC), Students for a Democratic Society (SDS), Women's Liberation and related women's groups differed in their interaction and decision-making styles, these relied on strong friendship ties. The friendship ties, accompanied by deep mutual trust, respect and affection, developed spontaneously over the years of shared struggle and so differed from the obligatory feeling rules discussed earlier. Yet they had similarly important action consequences. They initially favored participatory decision-making as well as programmatic successes and organizational growth of each organization, but when newcomers joined these organizations, they showed themselves unable to sustain participatory democracy (Polletta 2002: 4, 14–26, 45–8, 78, 83–4, 105–10, 124, 139–44, 158–65). This is so since friendships are by definition exclusive and so little effort is put into incorporating newcomers on equal terms. These are treated with indifference or even animosity which alienates them. 'Newcomers' social marginality may translate into political marginality ... And veterans ... realize that they have been exclusive only when newcomers attack them for their insufficient commitment to participating in democracy ... ' (Polletta 2002: 140). The emerging new conflict line between veterans and newcomers aggravates existing problems and conflicts, and leads to power struggles which – through centralization or formalization – terminate experiments in participatory democracy. As Kleres (this volume) shows a conflict develops only if both veterans and newcomers are self-assured. Shame-ridden newcomers do not assert themselves. They instead take the exit option and the last hope for internal democracy with them.

These few examples suffice to demonstrate that emotions and feeling rules developed by the movements have serious consequences for the social movements which range from the unconditional commitment through conflict and secession, to the termination of experiments in participatory democracy.

Conclusion

The research agenda outlined in this chapter opens up exciting new directions for the study of emotions and social movements. It draws our attention to those emotions which social movements (de-)construct or redirect to achieve an emotional re-framing of reality. Moreover, it proposes that emotions allow macro-politics to connect to the micro-politics of social movements. In particular, exploring the cementing emotions, such as, loyalty, fear, shame or anger, which uphold social structures and relations of dominations, allows us to better understand which counter-emotions movements construct. Asking which organizational and discursive dynamics lead movements to generate a particular set of emotions and feeling rules constitutes another interesting area of inquiry.

Research suggests that we should broaden our understanding of the emotions that social movements direct towards themselves as well as towards their opponents. The number of emotions that social movements construct cannot be reduced to two emotions – solidarity reserved for one's own group and anger directed at the opponent. Instead many other emotions have to be put on our research agenda. We must recognize that they are constructed but neither as disciplined nor as consensual as some movement members wished they were. Some emotions may just remain unruly. They resist attempts to become rule-bound and have their intensity, direction or duration prescribed.

Avoiding stereotypes and pet ideas about such emotions as solidarity and anger is crucial. Research shows that solidarity – a much praised collective emotion or feeling rule – far from shielding the individual and/or collectivity actually reinforces hurt or schisms. Similarly, attempts to forbid anger directed at co-activists, when juxtaposed against divisive issues and hierarchies, are bound to fail. The minority view that anger should not be avoided and can actually be constructive even when directed against other movement members should be heeded also in our research. Finally, research suggests that not only anger, but also fear, hope, hatred or contempt can be generated towards the movement opponent and that, interestingly, these have differing action consequences. While, for example, contempt implies the use of scathing satire as a protest form, hatred implies a destructive use of violence. While it seems that in democratic contexts social movements have to counteract shame or guilt among their members in order to mobilize them, in repressive contexts fear has to be managed instead. To sum up: social movements produce a variety of emotions and feeling rules which have various, sometimes counter-intuitive, structural and action consequences. These, as well as their macro- and micro-preconditions, are well worth exploring.

Note

1 I am indebted to Jochen Kleres for his criticism and assistance. I would like to thank Donatella della Porta for supplying me with two great texts and many more good ideas, and Debra King, Åsa Wettergren and the members of Donatella della Porta's seminar at the European University Institute for their critical suggestions. Debra also kindly corrected my English.

References and consulted sources

Aminzade, R. and McAdam, D. (2002) 'Emotions and contentious politics', Special Issue on Emotions and Contentious Politics, guest edited by R. Aminzade and D. McAdam, *Mobilization*, 7(2): 107–9.

Barnes, S.H. and Kaase, M. (1979) *Political Action: mass participation in five western democracies*, London: Sage.

Berezin, M. (2002) 'Secure States: towards a political sociology of emotions', in J. Barbalet (ed.) *Emotions and Sociology*, Oxford: Blackwell Publishing and The Sociological Review.

Berger, P. (1997) *Redeeming Laughter: the comic dimension of human experience*, New York: Walter de Gruyter.

Britt, L. and Heise, D. (2000) 'From shame to pride in identity politics', in S. Stryker, T.J. Owens and R. White (eds) *Self, Identity, and Social Movements*, Minneapolis: University of Minnesota Press.

Collins, R. (1990) 'Stratification, emotional energy, and the transient emotions', in T.D. Kemper (ed.) *Research Agendas in the Sociology of Emotions*, Albany, NY: State University of New York Press.

della Porta, D. (1991) 'Die Spirale der Gewalt und Gegengewalt: Lebensberichte von Links- und Rechtsradikalen in Italien', *Forschungsjournal Neue Soziale Bewegungen*, 4(2): 53–62.

—— (1995) *Social Movements, Political Violence, and the State: a comparative analysis of Italy and Germany*, Cambridge: Cambridge University Press.

Fireman, B., Gamson, W.A., Rytina, S. and Taylor, B. (1979) 'Encounters with unjust authority', in L. Kriesberg (ed.) *Research in Social Movements, Conflicts and Change*, Volume 2, Greenwich, Conn.: JAI Press.

Flam, H. (1993) 'Die Erschaffung und der Verfall oppositioneller Identität', *Forschungsjournal Neue Soziale Bewegungen*, 2: 83–97 (a re-worked excerpt of a paper presented in the 'East European Movements and Social Movement Theory Session' of the First European Conference on Social Movements which took place in Berlin in October 1992).

—— (ed.) (1994) *States and Anti-Nuclear Movements*, Edinburgh: Edinburgh University Press.

—— (1998) *Mosaic of Fear: Poland and East Germany before 1989*, East European Monographs, New York: Columbia University Press.

—— (2000) *The Emotional Man and the Problem of Collective Action*, Frankfurt a.M.: Peter Lang.

—— (2002) *Soziologie der Emotionen: eine Einführung*, Konstanz: UVK Verlagsgesellschaft.

—— (2004) 'Anger in repressive regimes: a footnote to *Domination and the Arts of Resistance* by J. Scott', Special Issue on Anger in Political Life, guest edited by M. Holmes, *European Journal of Social Theory*, 7(2): 171–88.

Gamson, W.A. (1992) *Talking Politics*, Cambridge: Cambridge University Press.

Glazer, M.P. and Glazer, P.M. (1999) 'On the trail of courageous behavior', *Sociological Inquiry*, 69(2): 276–95.

Goldthorpe, J. (1969) *The Affluent Worker in the Class Structure*, Cambridge: Cambridge University Press.

Goodwin, J. and Pfaff, S. (2000) 'Emotion work in high-risk social movements: managing fear in the U.S. and Eastern German civil rights movements', in J. Goodwin, J.M. Jasper and F. Polletta (eds) *Passionate Politics*, Chicago: Chicago University Press.

Gould, D.B. (2002) 'Life during wartime: emotions and the development of ACT UP', *Mobilization*, 7(2): 177–200.

Habermas, J. (1987) *The Theory of Communicative Action*, Volume Two: 'Lifeworld and System', Boston: Beacon Press.

Hearn, J. (1993) 'Emotive subjects: organizational men, organizational masculinities and the (de)construction of "emotions"', in S. Fineman (ed.) *Emotion in Organizations*, London: Sage.

Hercus, C. (1999) 'Identity, emotion, and feminist collective action', *Gender & Society*, 13(1): 34–55.

Hirschman, A.O. (1970) *Exit, Voice and Loyalty*, Cambridge, MA: Harvard University Press.

—— (1982) *Shifting Involvements*, Princeton: Princeton University Press.

Hochschild, A. (1979) 'Emotion work, feeling rules, and social structure', *American Journal of Sociology*, 85: 551–75.

—— (1983) *The Managed Heart: the commercialization of human feeling*, Berkeley: University of California Press.

—— (1990) 'Ideology and emotion management: a perspective and path for future research', in T.D. Kemper (ed.) *Research Agendas in the Sociology of Emotions*, Albany, NY: State University of New York Press.

—— (1993) 'The economy of gratitude', in D. Franks and E.D. McCarthy (eds) *The Sociology of Emotions*, Greenwich, Conn.: JAI Press.

Holmes, M. (2004) 'Feeling beyond rules: politicising the sociology of emotion and anger in feminist politics', Special Issue on Anger in Political Life, guest edited by M. Holmes, *European Journal of Social Theory*, 7(2): 209–27.

Jackall, R. (1988) *Moral Mazes: the world of corporate managers*, New York: Oxford University Press.

Jasper, J. (1998) 'The emotions of protest: affective and reactive emotions in and around social movements', *Sociological Forum*, 13(3): 397–424.

Kearl, M.C. (1995) 'Death and politics: a psychosocial perspective', in H. Wass and R.A. Neimeyer (eds) *Dying: facing the facts*, London: Taylor & Francis.

Kemper, T.D. (1978) 'Towards a sociology of emotions: some problems and some solutions', *The American Sociologist*, 13: 30–41.

—— (1981) 'Social constructionist and positivist approaches to the sociology of emotions', *American Journal of Sociology*, 87: 336–62.

—— (2000) 'A structural approach to social movement emotions', in J. Goodwin, J.M. Jasper and F. Polletta (eds) *Passionate Politics*, Chicago: Chicago University Press.

Kitschelt, H. (1986) 'Political opportunity structures and political protest: antinuclear movements in four democracies', *British Journal of Political Science*, 16: 57–85.

Kriesi, H. (1988) 'The interdependence of structure and action: some reflections on the state of the art', in B. Klandermans, H. Kriesi and S. Tarrow (eds) *Research on Social Movements, Conflicts and Change*, Greenwich, Conn.: JAI Press.

Lepsius, R.M. (1993) 'Extremer Nationalismus: Strukturbedingungen vor der nationalsozialistischen Machtergreifung', in his *Demokratie in Deutschland*, Göttingen: Vandenhoeck & Ruprecht.

McAdam, D. (1988) 'Micromobilization contexts and recruitment to activism', in B. Klandermans, H. Kriesi and S. Tarrow (eds) *Research on Social Movements, Conflicts and Change*, Greenwich, Conn.: JAI Press.

Moore, B., Jr (1978) *Injustice: the social bases of obedience and revolt*, White Plains, NY: M.E. Sharpe.

Neckel, S. (1991) *Status und Scham. Zur symbolischen Reproduktion sozialer Ungleichheit*, Frankfurt a.M.: Campus.

Ost, D. (2004) 'Politics as the mobilization of anger: emotions in movements and in power', Special Issue on Anger in Political Life, guest edited by M. Holmes, *European Journal of Social Theory*, 7(2): 229–44.

Parkin, F. (1971) *Class Inequality and Political Order: social stratification in capitalist and communist societies*, London: MacGibbon & Kee.

Petronijević, E. (1998) 'Streets of protest: space, action and actors of protest 96/97 in Belgrade', *Polish Sociological Review*, 3(123): 267–86.

Polletta, F. (2002) *Freedom is an Endless Meeting: democracy in American social movements*, Chicago: The University of Chicago Press.

Scott, J.C. (1990) *Domination and the Arts of Resistance: hidden transcripts*, New Haven: Yale University Press.

Simmel, G. (1992) 'Zur Psychologie der Scham', in H.J. Dahme and O. Rammstedt (eds) *Schriften zur Soziologie*, Frankfurt a.M.: Suhrkamp.

—— (1999) *Soziologie. Untersuchungen über die Formen der Vergesellschaftung*, complete edition, Volume II, edited by O. Rammstedt, Frankfurt a.M.: Suhrkamp.

Taylor, V. (1996) *Rock-a-by Baby: feminism, self-help, and post-partum depression*, New York: Routledge.

—— (2000) 'Emotions and identity in women's self-help movements', in S. Stryker, T.J. Owens and R.W. White (eds) *Self, Identity, and Social Movements*, Minneapolis: University of Minnesota Press.

Taylor, V. and N.E. Whittier (1995) 'Analytical approaches to social movement culture: the culture of the women's movement', in H. Johnston and B. Klandermans (eds) *Social Movements and Culture*, London: UCL Press.

Terkel, S. (1972) *Working: people talk about what they do all day and how they feel about what they do*, New York: Pantheon Books.

Yang, G. (2000) 'Achieving emotions in collective action: emotional processes and movement mobilization in the 1989 Chinese Student Movement', *The Sociological Quarterly*, 41(4): 593–614.

3 How social movements move

Emotions and social movements

Ron Eyerman

Introduction

The recent cultural turn has re-opened discussion of emotions in the academic study of social movements (Goodwin *et al.* 2001). The replacement of the collective behaviour approach, which conceptualized social movements along a scale of irrationality (Aminzade and McAdam 2002), by the hyper-rationality of resource mobilization has now been rectified, at least partially, by this turn to culture (Zald 1996). Along with the inclusion of feminist perspectives, this has helped put emotions back on the agenda, not as irrational forms of behaviour, but as an essential component of all human action, collective as well as individual. On the epistemological level, these changes have been accomplished with the aid of social constructivism, an approach which focuses on cognitive framing, narratives and performance. My own work on social movements from a 'cognitive perspective' (Eyerman and Jamison 1991; 1998) has followed and contributed to these developments, a process I hope to continue here.

Historically, the study of emotions or affective experience has been divided between those stressing physiological and biological aspects on one side and those stressing social relations and environmental conditions on the other (Hochschild 1983). Regarding the study of social movements, one would include in the latter the focus on group and crowd behaviour of the collective behaviourists who developed symbolic interactionism, like Herbert Blumer (1939) and, later, Ralph Turner and Lewis Killian (1987). As Aminzade and McAdam point out this 'earlier work typically equated emotions with irrationality and assumed that emotions and rationality were incompatible' (2002: 107). To the generally recognized, largely negative, emotions such as fear and anger discussed in this tradition, more recent studies of social movements influenced by these new developments have added shame, pride, love, hate, awe and wonder, in their analysis of how emotions are constituted and reproduced in everyday social interactions (for an example see Kim 2002; Gould 2002; Taylor and Rupp 2002).

In addition to the dichotomy between the social and the physiological, human emotions have primarily been studied from the point of view of the individual; Richard Wollheim's *On the Emotions* (1999) can serve as an exemplar. For Wollheim 'an emotion is a kind of mental phenomenon' within which one can differentiate mental states from mental dispositions (1999: 1). There are exceptions to this focus on individual disposition, the collective behaviourists mentioned above viewed certain emotions as emergent collective phenomena. From the point of view of collective action, two problems can be imagined: (1) how individually-based emotion is transformed in social movements and (2) how new emotions are created through the collective (see the discussion in Aminzade and McAdam 2002: 20ff). This latter was the starting point for the collective behaviour school, which was grounded in the Durkheimian belief that an explanation of *collective* behaviour required a social, rather than individual starting point (Eyerman and Jamison 1991). The developments pointed to above have opened paths to bridging the gaps between these perspectives. The role of social movements in this process can now be explored in light of these new theoretical developments and the current volume represents an important contribution towards this end.

With its focus on rationality and institutionalization and its underlying model of the actor, much of contemporary sociology has failed to sufficiently recognize that modern societies are composed around conflicting values and alternative structures of feeling. It is here that social movements, with their capacity for collective articulation can play a central role. As social forces grounded in values (and not merely organizations or networks) social movements articulate structures of feeling, as Raymond Williams (1977) called those deeply rooted dispositions and sensibilities which organize and define a way of life. In this sense, movements can be said to be emerging cultures, transforming as well as articulating values, and in the process, creating new and alternative structures of feeling. Seen this way, emotions (among other things of course) are the feeling side of values, and as such are an important link between values and actions. Emotions provoke responses which lead to action (this is the focus of Åsa Wettergren's chapter in this volume) or to reaction, (which is the focus of Tova Benski's chapter) or to its opposite, a sense of being unable to act, being paralyzed by fear or dread. Both of these, the impetus to act and the fear of acting, are aspects linking emotions to social movements and other forms of collective action. Emotional responses can move individuals to protest and to contend and, once in motion, social movements can create, organize, direct and channel collective emotion in particular directions, at particular targets. Emotions are part of the dynamic of movements, internal conflicts within a movement, stimulating anger and frustration, may spur fractionalism and even a new movement. This was at least part of the explanation for the emergence of the women's movement in the early 1970s, as the growing awareness of the way women were treated by male leaders raised anger and created grounds for sensitivities, feeling and forms of consciousness and for gender-based organizing.

More generally, and by way of overcoming some of the dichotomies which have plagued the understanding of social movements, participating in movement events and activities can be exciting and pleasurable. These are forms of emotion which invite continued participation. Even the experience of fear and anxiety, not uncommon in the midst of protest, can be a strong force in creating a sense of collectivity and be an attractive force in collective actions. Anger may motivate activism, shame may prevent it, just as moral concerns and good intentions may circumscribe a series of protest events. Once in motion, however, movements are necessarily strategic and practical, as well as expressive. Like the old distinction between reason and emotion, the dichotomy between expressive and instrumental forms of action does not hold.

All movements are emotional and strategic, combining and balancing good intentions and good results. In addition to being a source of instability and unpredictability (Flam 1990) the force of emotion is an essential part of what keeps a movement moving and its lack helps explain its decline. If those structural, organizational and institutional approaches which have dominated the analysis of social movements have now been radically modified – if not transcended – by more dialogic, cultural approaches, the place of emotions is still left to be clarified. The focus on reasoned calculation and the efficient use of resources in structured settings has given way to the role of narration and performance, to framing and expressivity, but the tension between the expressive and instrumental still defines the field. It is here that performance theory can be helpful.

Emotions and movements: performing opposition

Social movement is a form of acting in public. Movements are political performances which involve representation in dramatic form, as they engage emotions inside and outside their bounds while attempting to communicate their message. Such performance is always public, as it requires an audience which is addressed. Following Goffman (1971) and others (for example, Schechner 1985; 2002; Hetherington 1998, Apter n.d., Alexander n.d.), the application of a theory of performance allows one to call attention to the place and space of movement, as well as how opposition is performed. Performance, as methodology in the term's broad meaning, focuses on corporality, presence and (though not exclusively) the pre-discursive. Performance theory gives central place to emotion and emotions, as both actors and audiences must be moved if a performance is successful. The adoption of performance theory allows us to better address questions concerning what happens when people enter a movement, how this affects their actions and the actions of others, and to ask how social movements move. While Goffman focuses primarily on individuals in their everyday social performance, the cultural pragmatics of Alexander and Apter offer a collective perspective, calling attention to social drama performed *en scene* and to the long-standing and deeply rooted frameworks of meaning which structure contemporary performances.

In analysing how opposition is performed and what movement means, it is necessary to separate at least three distinct, yet interrelated arenas or social spaces in which opposition is performed: an emerging social movement, its opponents and, finally, the general public. A social movement emerges when groups of disparate and ever changing individuals sense they are united and moving in the same direction. People and organizations move in and out of social movements but this sense of collective movement, continuous over time and place, is what makes a movement what it is. To achieve this, forms and feelings of collective identity and solidarity emerge through processes which mark off those inside the movement from those outside. Who 'we' are defines and distinguishes who are not us, at the same time as it identifies what 'we' are against. Framing this Other, is part of the emotional process of movement formation, as that which a movement moves against. Finally, movements address and attempt to influence, to move, the general public. In this way, movements help to form and to affect public opinion, both distant and invisible and, as Benski in this volume shows, local and visible.

While social movements may create a We and Them, they do so as a form of symbolic interaction, with mutual expectations involved, and they do so in front of an audience of potential supporters who must also be addressed and moved, not least of which includes taking a political stance regarding the movement itself. To do this a movement must express and communicate – express common grievance and communicate discontent – to protest and, in the best case, to effect changes in attitudes and practices of those inside and outside the movement. When the latter occurs, society itself may be said to have moved. Social movement in other words, involves many levels and dimensions of movement, mobilizing and affecting opinions, engaging emotions, changing laws, preventing some actions while encouraging others. The various levels of movement include the bodies, minds and emotions of those inside and outside what has come to be identified as the movement; the physical, geographical aspects of staging and managing collective actions; the decisions and practices which are incorporated in the process of changing established societal practice, the norms, rules and laws which form the basis of society. All of these aspects and sorts of moving and being moved are fused with emotion.

Inside the movement

Social movements move by transforming identities and emotions, by focusing attention and by directing and coordinating actions. Movements are often spurred into existence by cognitively framed emotions, anger, frustration, shame, guilt, which move individuals and groups to protest, to publicly express and display discontent, engaging in what McAdam *et al.*

(2001) call contentious actions and protest events. Such an occurrence may contain and collect enough energy and coherence to generate similar events in the future, as well as recall the memory of those in the past. This sequence of events can set in motion a process of collective will formation whereby individual identities and biographies are fused into a collective characterized by feelings of group belongingness, solidarity, common purpose and shared memory, a movement in other words. Once in motion, this process has both situational (manifest) and long-lasting (latent) affects, a sense of moving together, of changing and being changed through participating in a large social force. This sense can emerge in context, through participation in collective actions. However, this sense of movement may move beyond the situational, becoming incorporated into individual biography as significant experience and memory, as well as objectified in representational form in cultural artefacts or more structurally in networks and organizations, 'free spaces' (Polletta 1999), which can preserve and transmit this feeling of movement, its cognitive praxis, its distinctive structure of feeling, between protest events. One can be moved, in other words, before, during and after the fact, as one recalls a situation through hearing a piece of music or viewing a film or a photograph, which represents an event, as well as the movement itself becoming objectified in organizations and networks, which one may be moved to join or support. In this case, movement has moved from interactive experience to a narrative connected with individual and collective memory, from event to metaphor (Amin 1995). With this, symbolic gestures and performative action are an added value in both the practice and the understanding of collective action, in that, as Alexander (2004: 91) puts it, 'explicit messages take shape against background structures of immanent meaning'. It is here that performance theory, with its focus on drama, staging and scripts, as well as actual performing, is a valuable analytical frame.

The notion of movement can be used as both verb and noun, a performance perspective however, calls attention to an experience of moving and of being moved and to the centrality of ritual and the emotion fusing of identities. A sense of movement can be attributed to forces greater than one's self, individual will or rational choices. Randall Collins (2001) links such an experiential process to Durkheim's notion of collective effervescence, where individual identities are temporarily transformed into a group identity. In this process, according to Collins, an emotional transference occurs, which produces a charged, collective emotional energy, a sense of belonging to some greater force than oneself. An empowering can take place, especially as cognitive shifts occur, and clarity of vision and purpose give direction to the sense of movement. Cognitive framing and ritual performances are important mechanisms in such processes, I would add. Cognitive frames, in the form of narratives structure, focus and direct emotion/energy and actions in particular directions. Within social movements this means in collective, political directions. Narratives are stories containing rhetorical devices, storylines, which link a particular occurrence/experience to others, broadening their meaning beyond the situational, imposing a higher order of significance, thus orchestrating and amplifying both the emotional experience and the meaning of the event, as individuals fused into a collective, with a purposive future and a meaningful past.

From inside, social movement involves the move to protest, from framed emotion to action, in addition, it involves the transformation of an individually-based, diffuse experience into a focused, collective one. A central mechanism here is a set of ritual practices which are performed as part of collective protest. Public displays of commitment and solidarity often build around collective voicing and parading, ritual practices which are also transformative in that they help blur the boundaries between individual and collective and help fuse a group through creating strong emotional bonds between participants, while at the same time permitting new and often 'forbidden' emotions to emerge (Taylor 1995). The repeated experience of ritual participation produces a feeling of solidarity – "we *are* all here together, we *must* share something"; and lastly, it produces collective memory – "we *were* all there together"' (Berezin 2001: 93). A collective story emerges, linking places and events together and a metaphor, the movement, is applied. We are here now, we were there then and we will be together in the future. We are a movement. This is not to say that the original 'move', is necessarily individually-based, for the framed emotion which led to protest may well have been aroused and supported through dialogue and interaction with others, in friendship networks for example (Diani 1995; Polletta 1999), the point is that even such networks move through the ritual practices of collective protest.

Ritualized or not, collective practices within movements are important not only in creating a sense of collectivity, but also of overcoming fear and giving courage. The affective reaction to and the tactical selection of symbols is also important in creating and sustaining movement. In what must be one of the most brilliant and compelling analyses of movements from the participant/observer perspective, Norman Mailer writes this about the difference between the anti-war protests at the Pentagon in Washington, DC in October 1967 and the protests at the Democratic Party Convention in Chicago less than one year later:

> The justifications for the March on the Pentagon were not here. The reporter [Mailer] was a literary man – symbol had the power to push him into actions more heroic than himself. The fact that he had been marching to demonstrate against a building which was the living symbol of everything he most despised – the military-industrial complex of the land – had worked to fortify his steps. The symbol of the Pentagon had been a chalice to hold his fear; in such circumstances

his fear had even flavored his courage with the sweetest emotions of battle.

(1968b: 140)

Even rational choice theorists would accept that fear must be overcome in taking the step across the threshold to participation in protest activity. Mailer, however, moves us much beyond simple calculation in helping us understand the role of emotion in social movements. Take for instance his analysis, in conjunction with the March on the Pentagon, of moving not only beyond fear, but also overcoming prior socialization, image plantation, accomplished through schooling and mass media:

> Anyone who has passed through the educational system of America is in unconscious degree somewhere near half a patriot.... The brain is washed deep, there are the reflexes: white shirts, Star-Spangled Banner, saluting the flag. At home is corporation land's whip – the television set. Who would argue there are no idea-sets of brave soldiers, courageous cops, great strength and brutal patriotic skill in the land of authority? Obvious remarks, but it is precisely this huge and much convinced unconscious part of oneself which a demonstrator has to move against when he charges with his small part of an army into a line of MPs (military police) close-packed, arms locked; anxiety washes the will with its dissolving flood ... on moves unarmed into men who hold clubs and rifles. One does not know the guns are unloaded.... It was not so easy, therefore, when the moment came to charge into the Pentagon.

(1968a 265–6)

With all this to overcome, a strong will and surging collective emotion was necessary.

Outside the movement

Social movements address and interact with others, opponents, as well as that broad mass we call 'the public'. These others must be 'moved'. Charles Tilly (2003: 45) has pointed out that in making their contentious claims 'political actors follow rough scripts to uncertain outcomes as they negotiate demonstrations, humble petitions, electoral campaigns'. In these actions, collective actors must find ways to express that they are 'worthy, united, numerous and committed'. A social convention which we know as the demonstration was invented for just this purpose, opening a material basis for opposition and creating a performative space. On Tilly's (2003: 203ff) account, the term demonstration was first heard in the 1830s and had become a recurrent phenomena in Britain and the US by the 1850s. As social process, the demonstration merged two established forms of public display (1) the procession, where groups would collectively march to a common meeting place and (2) the presentation of a collective petition to some authority. The size of a demonstration, the number of participants, has often been thought to speak for itself, thus making reporting the numbers involved a constant source of conflict and controversy. Important as well in this reporting was the appearance and behaviour of those involved, as the numerous also had to reveal themselves as worthy, yet at the same time committed and determined, at least to the extent they sought acceptance and inclusion into the larger political community. Other demonstrative performances may seek different ways to express protest and opposition, which do not include being worthy, but still committed, something which can be a cause of tension between the various coalitions which make up a demonstration.

Demonstrations are now accepted forms of political action and in democratic societies are protected by law and even encouraged as important forms of political socialization and societal renewal. However, demonstrations do not speak for themselves, they are performances which must be rehearsed and put in play, as well as seen and interpreted. A demonstration, following Tilly, involves (1) gathering deliberately in a public space – preferably one which combines visibility with symbolic significance, (2) display both membership in a politically relevant population and support for some position by means of voice, print or symbolic objects, (3) communicating collective determination by acting in disciplined fashion in one space and or moving through a series of spaces. Demonstrations became a more or less conventional means of 'drawing forbidden or divisive issues, demands, grievances, and actors into public politics' (Tilly 2003: 204). It became in other words, both an expression and an extension of democratic principles, the right to free assembly and to free speech. Demonstrations however involve a great deal of emotion and their performance is not merely the expression of principles or rights, but of anger and solidarity, of fear, anxiety and hope. More like spaces and scenes, demonstrations are stages where an emotionally charged performance of opposition can occur.

The notion of 'framing' (Snow *et al.* 1986; Snow and Benford 1988) is an important concept in recent social movement theory and an important middle step in bridging past dichotomies. Framing calls attention to the cognitive processes of making sense and the often contentious struggle of defining a situation, but it can also involve dramatization, placing an event, a demonstration for example, within a narrative which lifts it from being a single occurrence and gives it wider significance through connecting it to others (Zald 1996; Hercus 1999 adds emotions to this perspective). In a sense, framing flows into ideology (Jasper 1997: 157). Social movements articulate frames as much as they may make use of them as resources in mobilization, in that activists make sense of their own protests through already existing narrative frames (Eyerman 2002). Affective (as well as effective) performance on the other hand is what gives this story life, adds drama and activates emotion, through *mise en scene*. If social movements articulate frames of understanding, the performance of protest actualizes them. As mentioned earlier, performance focuses on corporality and presence; performance is what makes a movement move and helps it move others. The performance of opposition dramatizes and forcefully expresses a movement through designed and stylized acts, communicating protest beyond the movement itself.

Performance theory adds a new dimension to the study of social movements in linking cognitive framing, narration and discourse with the practice of mobilization, and thus emotion. Performance theory calls attention to corporality and presence, to acting and acting out, to the role of drama and the symbolic in movement activity. It turns our attention to the performance of opposition and the aesthetics of movement, to the choreography of protest, as well as to the moral and emotional in mobilization. Looking through the lens of performance also brings forth the tension between the expressive and the strategic which I believe to be characteristic of contemporary social movements.

On a collective level, strategic performance is part of a social movement's representation of itself, a collective self-presentation. Leaders and activists in the various phases of the American civil rights movement, for example, chose different symbolic means to express and exemplify their 'movement'. In the early 1950s, when movement aims focused on acceptance and integration and a progressive narrative framed self-understanding, the ideal of the 'good Negro' was adopted as a form of collective self-presentation. Exemplary representatives like Martin Luther King, Jr and Ralph Abernathy often appeared at the head of marches and demonstrations in newly bought or pressed bib-overalls and work shirts, when they were not wearing the more traditional suit and tie of the minister-community leader and 'race man'. In the later Black Power phase, the black leather jacket and beret became prominent and expressive of a younger, urban generation's striving for autonomy and distinction. An entirely different type of verbality and gesture accompanied this performance of opposition, which sought to demonstrate both an opposition to the dominant white society and, at the same time, to the 'integrationist' mode and practice of other movement leaders. These forms of symbolic expression were guided by scripts and narratives, those of an earlier black nationalism and a 'redemptive narrative' (Eyerman 2002), which give them wider meaning by connecting them to a collective past, as well as the present situation. The latter is especially conditioned by strategic aspects, since performance is aimed at moving others by presenting consciously chosen evocative images. Strategic performance is designed with affect in mind. It must also be effective, and there is always an element of chance and risk involved. The aim, after all, is to move emotion and cognition in a particular direction, but how a performance will affect others cannot be entirely predicted, and this uncertainty regarding reception is only amplified through the intervention of mass media.

Collective self-presentation is part of the process of collective identity formation. As Goodwin *et al.* (2001: 8–9) points out, the notion of collective identity is often used to point to a cognitive process of boundary drawing, demarcating 'them and us', leaving out the emotional side of this process. The inclusion of performance theory, which focuses on bodily presence, on moving, the emotive and evocative, is an important corrective in this regard. However, performance can also be interpreted as non-emotional or strategic role playing, a doing without feeling or real engagement. While tactics and strategic actions are central to all forms of collective political action, social movements move because they engage emotion and values. Group solidarity is an emotional as well as cognitive experience. They must contain, therefore, non-strategic performances which motivate and move actors because they believe in what they are doing, that what they are doing is the right (moral) thing to do. How is this affected? What is it that in the midst of a demonstration, for example, creates a sense of belongingness that would move one demonstrator to come to the aid of another under attack from the police or opponent?

Creating an emotional bond is part of what is meant by collective identity and social movements must bond desperate individuals, even those who may already form some sort of network, together in an emotional way. The demonstration is one form which creates the possibility for such bonding. In the space opened through a demonstration, making the boundaries between them and us visible and real, these processes can be set in motion. Collective acts, such as singing, shouting slogans and so on, are means employed. But it is not simply or merely *in situ* that this occurs, for art and music can carry the strong emotional content which makes such bonding possible even between such protest events as demonstrations. Demonstrations, after all, are only one form of collective protest and while visible and dramatic, not the most common.

Creating and evoking moral empathy is part of what makes a movement. It is part of demarcating We and marking off Them. Demonstrators will rush to aid a fallen comrade, but it is unusual and requires a widening of the zone of empathy when they do the same for a fallen policeman in the same situation. Empathy, strongly felt identification with another, is first of all created through presence, through being there, when participation is an expression of side-taking and thus belonging. We are all together on this occasion against Them. Empathy, as well as belonging, can also be represented and reinforced through markers and symbols, buttons, pieces of clothing, flags, placards and so on, infused with symbolic value. These represent Us, to participants, as well as marking off this group for and against Them. In this sense, demonstrations are processes of identity and empathy formation re-enacting narrative dramas, as public practices, a form of ritual street theatre. This relates both to the demonstration as a collective practice in itself and to the more consciously arranged and performed plays and pieces which occur within them. In this expressive dramatization, the values, images and desires, of the movement are revealed and membership solidified.

In the midst of demonstrations, even those involving violent confrontation, there are attempts to communicate over the boundaries of We and Them. Norman Mailer describes such an attempt in Chicago, 1968 as demonstrators gathered outside the Hilton Hotel, site of the Convention and living quarters for most of the delegates:

> The kids were singing. There were two standards which were sung. An hour could not go by without both songs. So they sang 'We Shall Overcome' and they sang 'This Land is Your Land', and a speaker cried up to the twenty-five stories of the Hilton, 'We have the votes, you have the guns' (a reference to a recent poll showing popular support for the anti-war faction of the party) ... and then another speaker, referring to the projected march on the ... next day, shouted, 'We're going to march without a permit – the Russians demand a permit to have a meeting in Prague', and the crowd cheered this. They cheered with wild enthusiasm when one speaker, a delegate, had the inspiration to call out to the delegates and workers listening in the hundreds of rooms at the Hilton ... 'Turn on your lights, and blink them if you are with us. If you are with us, if you are sympathetic to us, blink your lights, blink your lights'. And to the delight of the crowd, lights began to blink in the Hilton, ten, then twenty, perhaps so many as fifty lights were blinking at once ... And the crowd cheered. Now they had become an audience to watch the actors in the hotel. So two audiences regarded each other, like ships signalling across a gulf of water at night, and delegates came down from the hotel; a mood of new beauty was in the air ...
>
> (1968: 153–4)

As this evocative description suggests, the articulation and objectification of the movement can occur through speeches as well as through scripted and costumed performance, death masks representing the bodies of people or animals killed by 'capitalists', who are themselves represented as 'fat cats with cigars', and so on. Through such performances a movement not only expresses what it stands for and what it stands against (representing and demarcating itself), binding participants together, but also creates an emotional bridge, a widening of the zone of empathy, to those non-present others who are represented as the victims of the forces that should be stopped. This is a process of emotional movement, a widening of We beyond the bounds of the present situation, as it represents those 'not here, yet still with us', if only symbolically. Part of a movement is its representation and expression of something transcendent, greater than 'I' and the 'here and now' of the current event. The movement thus moves itself and its participants to another level of experience, the experience of solidarity with unseen, unknown others, and at the same time adding an emotional charge through moving (expanding) the range of moral empathy. The expressive performance that is a demonstration aims at evoking and representing this in visible form. These acts of representation are amplified and diffused to much wider and broader audiences when they occur on camera, broadcast through mass media, exposing the movement to non-present viewers. This enlarges the audience of potential supporters and opponents, who also may be moved by what they see and hear.

Opposition is performed in public spaces, some of which are chosen for their particular symbolic significance and their media accessibility, with the 'whole world watching', as the popular movement chant would have it. This *mise en scene* is central to how social movements move. There is a setting, a stage and a script, performers and audience. Movements, as coordinated series of protest events, are scenes through which opposition is performed and attention, both inside and outside, is focused on a particular problematic: globalization, or women's rights, the environment, family values, and so on. This focus intensifies, highlights and dramatizes, an issue or a cause making it visible and multiplying its emotional intensity. But it does not determine its reception. Viewing a televised pro-(Vietnam) war demonstration while working at JFK airport in the 1960s, one of my work-mates was moved to tears by all the 'Americans' he saw in the flags carried by demonstrators. Even though I was myself moved in an opposite direction, the issue of national identity was brought clearly into focus for both of us by this event. As in a dramatic theatrical performance, the protest event, and the movement making it happen, highlighted an issue and focused our attention. The audience was moved, just as those on stage were moved to action. Social movements move even those who view them from afar, but whom they move and in which direction is not something easy to predict or control. The world that is watching is multifaceted and the media which mediates the message adds its own refraction. Mailer on Chicago again:

> The demonstrators were afterward delighted to have been manhandled before the public eye, delighted to have pushed and prodded, antagonized and provoked the cops over these days with rocks and bottles and cries of 'Pig' to the point where police had charged in a blind rage and made a stage at the one place in the city ... where audience, actors, and cameras could all convene, yes, the rebels thought they had a great victory, and perhaps they did; but the reporter wondered, even as he saw it, if the police ... had not had instructions from the power of the city, perhaps the power of the land, and the power had decided, 'No, do not let them march another ten blocks and there disperse them on some quiet street, no, let it happen before all the land, let everybody see that their dissent will soon be equal to their own blood; let them realize that the power is implacable, and will beat and crush

and imprison and yet kill before it will ever relinquish the power. So let them see before their own eyes what it will cost to continue to mock us, defy us and resist'.

(1968b: 167–8)

Whichever message was received, it is clear that movements move, albeit in differing directions, through evocation and provocation: that is, through emotion.

Conclusion

This chapter discussed the role of emotions in social movements with the aid of performance theory. The notion of performance often brings to mind role-playing, a detached, contrived way of acting which follows a prescribed script. If there are emotions involved they are also scripted, called for and not really felt, merely acted out. This in fact has been some of the criticism brought against Erving Goffman's dramaturgical perspective and its application to gender in the work of Judith Butler. The same can be said of the idea of strategic performance discussed above: in order to convince or defeat an opponent actors play a role, they present themselves in a particular way, not because they really are that way or are really committed to what they say but because they *are* being strategic and any display of emotion, as in a theatrical performance, is bound to be contrived. The performance of opposition in social movements, in practice, can certainly be said to have aspects of this.

However, performance theory implies something more. It calls attention not simply to role playing and acting but to narrating and dramatizing, to the cognitive practice of framing opposition within a meaningful storyline as well as to the acting out in practice, that is, through performance. These storylines are of a different character than the scripted performance of the theatre in that they are embedded in a life world, part of lived or common culture and are thus closely connected to values. The performance of opposition in social movements, while different in this sense from theatre, can be similar to the latter however in that they condense lived culture by focusing on one theme, one question, one belief. For example, while activists in a contemporary political demonstration are most certainly complex modern individuals, with various identifications and commitments, in participating in a demonstration they may well focus on only one aspect. Like a theatre piece, a demonstration, focuses attention to a limited range of issues, framing and bracketing out many others. This has the effect of dramatizing as well as lifting or foregrounding this particular question and this particular side or commitment of the persons involved. It does not mean that they no longer believe in or are not committed to other aspects of their lives or identity. It may also be the case that this dramatization involves role playing in the strategic sense and within the course of a demonstration actors may do things they would not normally do or accept, as collective behaviour theorists have long since demonstrated. None of this means that this implies non-commitment or role-play in the detached sense. On the contrary, the emotions involved are very real, and even unintended actions may have real emotional content.

While a sociologically informed performance methodology can help us understand how actors call upon narratives and images in the performance of social life, emotions are what give this force, providing the energy for the performance and the reaction/response on the part of observers. One could speak of the force of emotion in performance, both in theatre and in real life. In the performance of opposition, the demonstration provides a scene, a space, which is turned into a place as actors act out before an audience. This occurs because already existing narratives and traditions of opposition and protest are given life as they are acted played out. Such narratives are not simply scripted stories, but powerfully coded and contested interpretive frames out of which emotionally charged social drama unfolds.

References

Alexander, J. (n.d.) 'Symbolic action in theory and practice (1): the cultural pragmatics of performative action', unpublished manuscript, Yale University.
—— (2002) 'The social construction of moral universals', *European Journal of Social Theory*, 5(1).
—— 'From the depths of despair: performance, counter-performance, and "September 11"', *Sociological Theory*, 22(1): 88–105.
—— (forthcoming) 'The cultural pragmatics of social performance: between ritual and rationality', *American Sociological Review*.
Amin, S. (1995) *Event, Metaphor, Memory*, Berkeley: University of California Press.
Aminzade, R. and McAdam, D. (2002) 'Emotions and contentious politics', *Mobilization*, 7(2): 107–9.
Aminzade, R., Goldstone, J., McAdam, D., Perry, E., Sewell Jr., W., Tarrow, S. and Tilly, C. (eds) (2001) *Silence and Voice in the Study of Contentious Politics*, Cambridge: Cambridge University Press.
Apter, D. (n.d.) 'The symbolic uses of politics', unpublished manuscript, Yale University.
Berezin, M. (2001) 'Emotions and political identity: mobilizing affection for the polity', in J. Goodwin, J. Jasper and F. Polletta (eds) *Passionate Politics*, Chicago: University of Chicago Press.
Blumer, H. (1939) 'Collective behavior', in R. Park (ed.) *An Outline of the Principles of Sociology*, New York: Barnes and Noble.
Cockburn, A., St. Clair, J. and Sekula A. (2000) *5 Days That Shook the World*, London: Verso.
Collins, R. (2001) 'Social movements and the focus of emotional attention', in J. Goodwin, J. Jasper and F. Polletta (eds) *Passionate Politics*, Chicago: University of Chicago Press.

Diani, Mario (1995) *Green Networks: a structural analysis of the Italian environmental movement*, Edinburgh: Edinburgh University Press.

della Porta, D. and Diani, M. (1999) *Social Movements*, Oxford: Blackwell.

Eyerman, R. (2002) *Cultural Trauma*, Cambridge: Cambridge University Press.

Eyerman, R. and Jamison, A. (1991) *Social Movements: a cognitive approach*, Cambridge: Polity Press.

—— (1998) *Music and Social Movements*, Cambridge: Cambridge University Press.

Flam, H. (1990) 'Emotional "man": 1. the emotional "man" and the problem of collective action', *International Sociology*, 5: 39–56.

Gerhards, J. and Rucht, D. (1992) 'Mesomobilization: organizing and framing in two protest campaigns in West Germany', *American Journal of Sociology*, 98: 555–95.

Goffman, E. (1971) *The Presentation of Self in Everyday Life*, New York: Doubleday.

Goodwin, J., Jasper J. and Polletta F. (2001) *Passionate Politics*, Chicago: University of Chicago Press.

Gould, D. (2002) 'Life during wartime: emotions and the development of ACT UP', *Mobilization*, 7(2): 177–200.

Hall, M. (2000) 'Unsell the war: Vietnam and antiwar advertising', in W. Hixson (ed.) *The Vietnam Antiwar Movement*, New York: Garland Publishing.

Hercus, C. (1999) 'Identity, emotion, and feminist collective action', *Gender & Society*, 13(1): 34–55.

Hetherington, K. (1998) *Expressions of Identity*, London: Sage.

Hochschild, A.R. (1983) *The Managed Heart*, Berkeley: University of California Press.

Ignatieff, M. (1999) *The Warrior's Honor*, London: Vintage.

Jamison, A. (2001) *The Making of Green Knowledge*, Cambridge: Cambridge University Press.

Jasper, J.M. (1997) *The Art of Moral Protest*, Chicago: University of Chicago Press.

Kemper, T. (1978) 'Toward a sociology of emotions: some problems and some solutions', *The American Sociologist*, 13: 30–41.

Kim, H. (2002) 'Shame, anger, and love in collective action: emotional consequences of suicide protest in South Korea, 1991', *Mobilization*, 7(2): 159–76.

Klandermans, B. (1988) 'The formation of mobilization consensus', in B. Klandermans, H. Kriesi and S. Tarrow (eds) *From Structure to Action*, Greenwich: JAI Press.

Klandermans, B. and Tarrow, S. (1988) 'Mobilization into social movements', in B. Klandermans, H. Kriesi and S. Tarrow (eds) *From Structure to Action*, Greenwich: JAI Press.

Klein, N. (2001) *No Logo*, London: Flamingo.

Mailer, N. (1968a) *The Armies of the Night*, Harmondsworth: Penguin.

—— (1968b) *Miami and the Siege of Chicago*, Harmondsworth: Penguin.

McAdam, D., McCarthy, J. and Zald, M. (1988) 'Social movements', in N. Smelser (ed.) *Handbook for Sociology*, Newbury Park: Sage.

McAdam, D., Tarrow, S. and Tilly, C. (2001) *Contentious Politics*, New York: Cambridge University Press.

Mishal, S. and Sela, A. (2000) *The Palestinian Hamas*, New York: Columbia University Press.

Polletta, F. (1999) '"Free spaces" in collective action', *Theory and Society*, 28: 1–38.

Schechner, R. (1985) *Between Theater and Anthropology*, Philadelphia: University of Pennsylvania Press.

—— (2002) *Performance Studies*, London: Routledge.

Smith, P. (2000) 'Culture and charisma: outline of a theory', *Acta Sociologica*, 43: 101–11.

Snow, D. and Benford, R. (1988) 'Ideology, frame resonance, and participant mobilization', in B. Klandermans, H. Kriesi and S. Tarrow (eds) *From Structure to Action*, Greenwich, Conn.: JAI Press, 197–218.

Snow, D., Rochford, B., Worden, S. and Benford, R. (1986) 'Frame alignment processes, microbilization and movement participation', *American Sociological Review*, 51: 464–81.

Somers, M. (1994) 'The narrative constitution of identity: a relational and network approach', *Theory and Society*, 23: 605–49.

Sontag, S. (2003) *Regarding the Pain of Others*, New York: Farrar, Straus, and Giroux.

Taylor, V. (1995) 'Watching for vibes: bringing emotions into the study of feminist organizations', in M. Ferree and P. Martin (eds) *Feminist Organizations: harvest of the New Women's Movement*, Philadelphia: Temple University Press.

Taylor, V. and Rupp, L. (2002) 'Loving internationalism: the emotion culture of transnational women's organizations, 1888–1945', *Mobilization*, 7(2): 141–58.

Tilly, C. (2003) *Collective Violence*, New York: Cambridge University Press.

Turner, R. and Killian, L. (1987) *Collective Behavior*, Englewood Cliffs: Prentice-Hall.

Vetlesen, A.J. (1992) *Perception, Empathy and Judgement*, unpublished Ph.D. Dissertation, University of Oslo.

Wennerhag, M. (n.d.) 'Globalism and national sovereignty in the globalization movement', unpublished manuscript, University of Lund.

White, H. (1978) *Tropics of Discourse*, Baltimore: Johns Hopkins University Press.

Wollheim, R. (1999) *On The Emotions*, New Haven: Yale University Press.

Zald, M. (1996) 'Culture, ideology and strategic framing', in D. McAdam, J. McCarthy and M. Zald (eds) *Comparative Perspectives on Social Movements*, Cambridge: Cambridge University Press.

4 Breaching events and the emotional reactions of the public
Women in Black in Israel[1]

Tova Benski

'Have you no shame? How can you do this in our country? You are disgusting.'
'Anti-Semites, Israel haters.'
'Traitors, disgusting traitors.'
'Everybody in this country hates you.'

This is just a small sample of the responses shouted by drivers passing by the roundabout in Haifa, where WIB hold a vigil each Friday to protest the continued occupation of the territories by Israel.

> I think that we have accomplished a great thing. We have become an institution on this roundabout. At one o'clock in the afternoon, when there are only two of us, and we hadn't even taken out our signs and posters yet, the drivers are already cursing us. This roundabout has become a place. We are known here. It is an important accomplishment, don't you agree?
>
> There are people passing by, that have never seen us or heard of us before; they see our vigil and they ask what this is? And I don't care whether they are angry at us or are pleased with us. The main thing is that they are confronted with this phenomenon; somebody is saying the things that we are saying. I think that it is of real importance for people to realize that there are other opinions.

The second set of quotes demonstrates both the mixed feelings of the women to the comments, and the importance that they attach to spreading their message and to the reactions that they receive from the public. They also stress the difficult and angry nature of these reactions.

Both sets of quotes demonstrate the drama that I witnessed each Friday afternoon, during my participant observations of the vigil of Women in Black (WIB). However, both social movements and emotions theories have neglected the reactions of the public to protest and vigil acts.

In social movement theory, the public has been acknowledged as forming an integral part of protest events, primarily as forming a pool of potential 'opposition' or 'recruits/supporters.' Turner used the term 'by-standing public' to refer to non-adherents 'whose concern with the aims of the movement is minimal, but which reacts to the disruptions and inconveniences to which people who are not directly involved are subjected because of the struggle' (1970: 152).[2] However, beyond this statement, no attention has been directed to the actual street level reaction of the public while the act is performed. The content, manner and character of these reactions have yet to be studied systematically.[3] In a similar vein, the emotions that movement vigil acts arouse among spectators have yet to be addressed directly. Instead, the recent rise in attention to emotions in the study of social movements and collective action has tended to focus on emotions as an important factor in the emergence, recruitment and sustenance of movement activity and culture (Hercus 1999; Cadena-Roa 2002; Gould 2002; Perry 2002; Taylor and Rupp 2002).

The present paper is aimed at linking social movement perspectives and emotions theory by proposing an analysis of the vigil in terms of a 'breaching event' which includes examining the emotional nature of the public reactions to vigil, while the action is occurring. The concept of a 'breaching event' is modeled on Garfinkel's (1967) 'breaching experiments,' defined here as a publicly performed act of defiance that is composed of actual and/or symbolic violations of accepted social practices and definitions. The explanatory power of the term 'breaching event' to portray the messages of the vigil and explain the negative emotional reactions of the by-standing public will be demonstrated at the theoretical and empirical levels.

In his discussion of the emotional bases of society, Collins (1990) draws parallels between Durkheim's (1912/1954) macro-level analysis of the bases of solidarity in society and Garfinkel's (1967) micro-level 'breaching' experiments. He claims that both theories attempt to expose 'the conditions that uphold a social fact by revealing the opposition that occurs when it is broken' (Collins 1990: 30). In Durkheim's theory, rituals produce sacred objects. The moral sentiments that are attached to sacred objects form the bases of social and moral solidarity and of the integration of society. Violation of these sacred symbolic objects reverses these sentiments of moral solidarity into righteous anger that is directed at violators and their actions. Garfinkel is concerned with the social construction of routine, mundane reality at the micro-level. He contends that our mundane social order rests on the unquestioning acceptance of common assumptions and cognitive constructs. Garfinkel's breaching experiments revealed how deeply rooted these tacit common assumptions are. The emotional reactions of the subjects of his experiments to violations of these assumptions were dramatic. The most common reactions expressed were surprise and anger at the violations of the taken-for-granted world, and outrage against the violators. Thus, Collins (1990) contends that if we rephrase Garfinkel's experiments in Durkheimian terms, conventional social reality becomes the 'sacred object,' with experiments showing that violating the sacred object, produces the same effects as deviance and suicide in Durkheim's theory.

In light of the above discussion, some contemporary social movements can easily be interpreted as representing/constructing 'breaching events.' Melucci (1985; 1996) portrays contemporary social movements as posing a symbolic challenge to the political, cultural and social order. His often quoted assertion 'Medium is the message' neglects the end of his sentence which is 'and action sends back to the system its own paradoxes' (1985: 812). Thus, some movements are portrayed as questioning the 'definition of codes' and *'nominations* of reality' revealing 'what every system does not say of itself, the amount of silence, violence, irrationality which is always hidden in dominant codes' (1985: 812). They present 'to the rationalizing apparatus questions which are not allowed' (1996: 610) and some are even portrayed outright as involving 'a *breach of the limits of compatibility* of the system of social relationships in which the action takes place' (Melucci 1996: 24, emphasis by Melucci). These challenges that breach the limits of the system are presented through visual means, in the upsetting of cultural codes (Melucci 1996: 9). This is very much in line with Durkheim's perception of the violations of societal 'sacred objects' and Garfinkel's breaching experiments. I also claim that they are presented in public in the form of 'breaching events.'

Melucci does refer to reactions to the challenges posed by these social movements; but being concerned with the macro-consequences of the NSMs for the political system he only delineates the cognitive response of the system. He claims that:

> The system ... knows only two kinds of communication: on the one hand identification denoting incorporation into dominant codes, fusion with the power that denies diversity, and on the other hand separateness which establishes difference as exclusion from all communication.
>
> (Melucci 1996: 142)

In these formulations there is no reference to emotional underpinnings of the responses of the system, and no reference to the responses of the public the, 'audience,' who witness the upsetting of the cultural codes.

Three analytical components can be inferred from these theoretical statements: a 'breaching event' (the medium in Melucci's terms), the message that is communicated via the 'breaching event' medium, and a societal response. Melucci has characterized the general medium as being composed of visual acts that upset cultural codes; the message being the challenge to the hegemonic social order; and the responses of the system as composed of a binary model of inclusion – exclusion. This seems to leave a gap in our understanding of the responses of the by-standing public to the 'breaching event' and their emotional tone. However, a perspective of 'breaching event' can close this gap. Such an event, in line with both Durkheim's and Garfinkel's analyses, exposes the underlying forces and assumptions that hold society together and draws societal and public negative reactions, mostly in the form of 'righteous anger' (Collins 1990). Thus it is clear from the discussion above that the reactions of the by-standing public would be of strong negative emotional character, and directed at the event itself, the message and the performers of the event.

This chapter examines WIB vigils as a 'breaching event,' which constitutes the medium and the message and examines the responses of the public. Data has been collected through participant observations in the vigils of WIB in Haifa between February 2002 and April 2003, together with group interviews and discussions with women both at the vigil and on other occasions.[4] The analysis of this data highlights the emotional character of the reactions of the public to the event, the message, and the women.

Women in Black – a descriptive account

Women in Black (WIB) is an international feminist peace movement that is organized in the form of a network of vigils. It has won four international prizes for peace activism and was nominated for the Nobel Prize in 2001 (the Israeli and Serbian WIB). Established in Jerusalem in January 1988, a month after the outbreak of the first Palestinian uprising but soon spread to locations all over the country and all over the world. At the peak of its mobilization, WIB counted some 30 vigils in Israel. Following the Oslo Peace Accord, most of the vigils stopped in 1994, but resumed activity in 1998 when it became clear that the peace process was crumbling. The present vigils represent a second wave of WIB activism. According to WIB reports there are 15 vigils in Israel and over 250 vigils all over the world.[5]

Israeli WIB consists of silent vigils in central locations. Each vigil is conducted on a regular weekly basis, every Friday afternoon between 13:00–14:00. Participants wear black and hold signs in the form of a hand that is copied from the traffic 'stop' sign. The hand is black and on it, in white ink, is the slogan 'Stop the Occupation' in three languages: Hebrew, English and Arabic. This has become the identifying slogan of the movement. However, in Haifa participants also hold additional posters with different messages voicing protest at the continued oppression of the Palestinian people and the vicious circle of violence in the Israeli-Palestinian conflict, with its negative consequences for Israeli society.[6]

The Haifa vigil takes place at a roundabout situated at the bottom of the Carmel Mountain in front of the lower entrance to the Bahai Gardens, the major tourist attraction of Haifa. It is composed of both women and men (this is a change introduced in October 2000). During the research period, vigil size varied between 20–39 women and 2–7 men. The women hold a wide range of political attitudes prevalent in the Israeli peace camp

Figure 4.1 The Haifa Women in Black, 2002.

and various feminist identities. Many of them are also active in other peace groups. The vigil is heterogeneous as far as age is concerned, but highly homogeneous regarding education, occupation and ethnic origin. Most of the women have a university education (at least Masters degree) in the various social sciences, are in professional occupations, and are of European origin.[7] All these characteristics place the women at the heart of the hegemonic social order, in terms of both educational, occupational and class position but as we shall see, they are situated outside the hegemonic discourse.

The medium is the message: the 'breaching event'

The general message

In the case of WIB the vigil is the medium and the message is multi-layered. At the overt political level, the objective is to protest the ongoing occupation of the Palestinian territories, the violence and the injustice of the practices of the Israeli government within the occupied territories, and to express solidarity with the suffering caused by the continued occupation to both the Palestinian and Israeli people.

At the more covert, symbolic level, the message is one of defiance and rebellion, linking the issue of the occupation with feminist issues concerning the status of women in Israeli society and their exclusion from the central discourse in society – which concerns security issues. As one of the women in black stated:

> Women are fed up hearing all the time that 'these are security matters and you should shut up.' Women are not given the opportunity to express themselves politically.

Another more elaborate statement made by one of the women defines the military occupation as a major expression of patriarchal power structure in Israeli society:

> The occupation is not a phenomenon that exists only on the other side of the border. There is a social, cultural – normative system that has given rise to the occupation and is sustaining it. The very same system is the system of values and institutions that exploits women and is using the occupation to legitimate the oppression of women in Israel.... This is a masculine militaristic value system ... it sanctifies the state and security.... Without fighting the roots of the occupation, which is the Israeli expression of patriarchy, no attempt at the liberation of women in Israel can succeed.

In these quotes we find a combination of the basic components of the link made by the women between the occupation and the status of women in Israel: patriarchy, militarism, the occupation, the oppression of women, the centrality of the security discourse in Israeli society and the exclusion of women from this discourse.[8]

Simply put, the message of WIB reads as follows: women refuse to accept the militaristic, patriarchal gendered system with its exclusionary practices and power hierarchies as the central principle of social organization. They reject their exclusion from the central national discourse on security issues and insist on introducing their unique feminine voice into the discourse. In line with Melucci's (1996) portrayal of the women's movement in Western societies since the 1990s, in addition to the demands for equality and inclusion, these women are demanding the right to 'difference' without the power disparity that is usually attached to difference. This demand entails a radical challenge to the underlying logic of the social system and the structure of domination in a patriarchal, male dominated society. It strikes at the very bases of the hegemonic social order (Melucci 1996: 136). I would add here that the fact that these women, by virtue of their ethnicity, education, and occupational status, are an integral part of the hegemonic social order doubles the effect of their challenge since it seems to be posed from a place that is within the 'heart' of the hegemonic social order.

The 'breaching event' as the medium

As the medium, the vigil is composed of five visual components which, taken together, form the 'breaching event,' communicating both the overt and covert message of WIB:

1   The *central location* of the vigil – symbolizing the center of the stage, a place women have been traditionally excluded from. By standing in the centers of towns, women are symbolically appropriating the center from male domination and feminizing it for the hour of the vigil.

2   The *black color*. Being the traditional color of mourning for women in some Middle-Eastern and Western societies, black introduces feminine sentiments of bereavement and compassion into the violent conflict. Since it was originally adopted to signify the grief of both Israelis and Palestinians and is an expression of empathy with losses caused to both peoples, it blurs national distinctions and crosses lines of accepted definitions of national loyalties. However, it is also aimed at displaying feminine power, directly challenging gender power differentials, more specifically, the power of men.[9] As one of the women reminisced:

> Once the color was chosen, we started to think retrospectively about the various meanings of the color. According to most of the women it was the most salient, dominant color they could think of. We further found that in literature and folklore, the black color symbolized power and we identified with that part too. We were also very happy for the interpretation of the color as signifying dark forces. Witches. We are witches. Historically, who were the witches? They were very strong women. So we were pleased to adopt all these connotations. We used black to symbolize bereavement but also power, and certainly also because the color is very dominant.

3   The *signs* held by the women frame and define the ongoing Israeli-Palestinian conflict in terms of 'occupation.'[10] This frame is in direct contrast to the hegemonic framing of the situation in terms of a defensive war against Palestinian terrorism and terror acts aiming at ensuring the security of Israeli citizens, and in terms of 'a fight for our home' (the words of Prime Minister Sharon during his TV broadcast to the nation at the onset of the military operations against the Palestinian authority that started on April 2002). 'Protective Wall,' which is the name given to the recent Israeli military offensive (started on April 2002) is a further example of this hegemonic discourse frame. The word 'occupation,' with all its negative historical connotations, undermines the legitimacy of the presence of the Israeli Defense Forces and

the military actions in the territories of the Palestinian authority. More then that, this frame undermines the hegemonic conception of Israel's moral superiority in the conflict.

4   Women's *bodies*, which are displayed in the town square as a means of political expression, involve a very different use than the uses designated to the female body by the patriarchal system. This practice challenges the public/private division, traditional gender notions of women's place, and established definitions of political practices and expression.

5   The *time* – Friday lunchtime is the time when women are mostly engaged in their traditional roles of cooking and cleaning the house, preparing it for the Sabbath. By choosing this particular day and time when women should be engaged in the private sphere they are defying both traditional gender roles and national Jewish practices.

All these visual practices defy binary distinctions and ways of defining and perceiving reality. They challenge the framing of the hegemonic discourse on security issues in Israel, patriarchal definitions of women and femininity, and accepted notions of national loyalties and the boundaries of the national collective. It is thus the case that indeed the vigil forms an event of real and symbolic violation of cultural, social and national codes, a 'breaching event' that is performed visually, and is imposed on the public in a way that cannot be ignored.

More than that, the medium and the visual means chosen pose to society an inverted mirror of its own practices. The feminization of the public space places the women and femininity at the center of the stage. For this one-hour, they occupy the center, they are in charge of the situation, their voice is heard and their definitions and codes of conduct are the dominant in this situation. The public, mostly men, are relegated to the margins. Their voice is not heard, and most of the time, even when they shout their abuses, the women ignore them through their self-imposed silence (which is not always strictly kept). As one of the women said to me on one of the vigils: 'When I see the angry faces of the men in the cars, I either smile, which makes them even angrier, or ignore them completely and make them feel the way I feel each day of my life, being ignored.' This situation poses an extremely radical challenge to accepted definitions and loyalties, and is highly frustrating, to men in particular, who for a very brief moment are put in a position similar to the one in which women find themselves on a daily basis. Many men feel threatened by this feminine display of power and the inverted social order. And they react in the same manner that subjects in Garfinkel's breaching experiments reacted: with surprise, anger and outrage and attempts at re-establishing routine social order and power. Thus, the women, through the reactions of the men 'force the power into the open,' which in Melucci's (1996) opinion, is a very important accomplishment.

The responding public

Since the vigil is situated at a traffic roundabout, the public is mostly composed of drivers. Up until 5 April 2003, 548 negative responses (out of a total of 689) were recorded. The bulk of the negative responses (531) were by men. These form the basic data set for the analysis presented here.

Driving around the roundabout leaves the drivers little time to read the signs, absorb/understand their meaning and respond. As a result, responses are very brief conveying a very condensed message in a few words. It should be noted that these statements are actual 'gut-reactions' of passers-by and not answers to questionnaires designed by the researchers. They represent authentic phrases and the choice of words, slurs and images reveal the drivers' authentic, unsolicited and untamed reactions to the women, the vigil and the whole situation.

One of the shortcomings of the special situation is that I do not have any objective information about the drivers themselves. This is similar to the situation that Temkin and Yanay (1989) faced when analyzing anonymous hate-letters sent to one of the Israeli left-wing parties. However, some clues as to the characteristics of the members of the responding public were present. They could be inferred from their looks, dress, the type of car they were driving and whether they were or were not wearing a Yarmulke (skull cap). I can safely say that most of the negative responses were made by a wide cross-section of men, of various ages, class positions and Jewish ethnic origin, mostly non-orthodox Jews, and that most of them are definitely supporters of right-wing politics or take a 'security' stance in the political discourse of the Arab-Israeli conflict (Peleg 2002).

The emotional character of the responses

In light of the extreme challenge to the hegemonic discourse and power structure by the vigil of WIB, it is not surprising to find that the most salient feature of the responses of the drivers was their highly aggressive and emotional language. Since emotion words are very rare in ordinary conversations (Haviland and Goldstone 1992; Fischer 1995; Shields 2000), emotions can more readily be inferred from actions and threats (Lazarus and Lazarus 1994: 186–7). Indeed, most of the responses consisted of various acts, gestures, slurs, labels, swear words, suggestions, punishments, wishes in the form of 'death wish', insults etc. In addition, 73 of the responses also included the use of the following kinds of emotion words: shame, disgust, contempt and hate, often appearing in various different combinations within one statement.

The anger, hate, disgust and contempt that are expressed in these messages frame the general tone of the messages in terms of other-directed, 'nasty' (Lazarus and Lazarus 1994), 'negative' (Ben-Ze'ev 1998), 'hostile' (Izard 1977), 'dramatic' (Collins 1990) and, excluding hate, as 'moral' emotions (Rozin *et al.* 1993). Since various combinations of these emotions often occur together, endlessly merging into each other (Scheff 1990; Barbalet 1998), Lazarus (1991), and Lazarus and Lazarus (1994) refer to these as the 'emotion family' of anger. Indeed they claim that anger is 'the thread that unifies the nasty emotions' (Lazarus and Lazarus 1994: 13). In a similar manner, Hochschild also groups them together, characterizing them as originating in feelings of frustration, claiming that they all 'correspond to different patterns of focus on the cause of frustration and on my relation to this cause' (1983: 226). Thus, anger is felt when the individual feels more powerful than the other who is perceived as the cause of the frustration; '*Indignation* is a name for adding a focus on a thing that is disapproved of; *contempt* is a name for adding a focus on one's social or moral superiority' (Hochschild 1983: 226).

Having delineated the 'breaching event' as the medium, the message and the general tone of the responses, the question that needs to be addressed next is what exactly are these drivers responding to? I have shown how complex the medium is, composed of five visual elements with a specific message embedded in each element, and how these specific messages, taken together, convey the general breaching of national, gender and social order, as well as the dominant discourses in Israeli society. Thus the whole event can be treated as a spectacle, a text, conveying a complex, multilayered message with both overt and covert meanings. It would be unrealistic to expect that the responding drivers would grasp the whole message during the brief moments of their exposure to the whole spectacle. Moreover, media studies suggest that the idea that messages are self-evident and transparent is erroneous. To assume that all people interpret the same 'text' in the same way is too simplistic, since all texts 'are inherently "polysemic" – that is, capable of generating multiple meanings – and as a result, although the text might have a "preferred reading", it does not follow that it will be decoded in the same way by everyone.' (Hollows 2000: 24). Furthermore, the meaning of the event will be further constructed, by each responder, according to the significance that the responder attaches to the 'text,' and, to rephrase Melucci (1996), according to the interests that are being brought to bear on the situation or perceived to be threatened the most.

Next I turn to the analysis of the responses to the general spectacle of the vigil, to its different visual elements, and finally, to the general message of the vigil.

General emotional reactions to the 'breaching event' – the spectacle

Responses directed at the event itself show that while the basic emotion expressed by the responders was anger, the most salient reactions to the event were of extreme disgust at the whole spectacle. In the Hebrew language there are a number of words to express disgust. The simplest form is just to say, as some drivers did: 'this is disgusting.' Another form is the Hebrew expression '*goal nefesh,*' which is more severe and can be roughly translated into English as 'soul disgusting.' This expression is very much in line with the assertion that 'disgust is primarily a response to actual or threatened harm to the soul' (Rozin *et al.* 1993: 575).

One quite frequent, non-verbal reaction to the whole situation was the very offensive act of spitting at the women and into the roundabout. In fact, the frequency of the recurrence of this practice has led one of the women to name one of the spots on the roundabout, where she claimed that most of the spitting occurred, 'the spitting corner.'

Accounts of the cultural evolution of disgust trace its origins to food rejection (Rozin *et al.* 1993; see also Wierzbicka 1986; Rozin and Fallon 1987; Lazarus 1991). The most recent expansion of this emotion is claimed to be in the direction of socio-moral violations of social solidarity (Rozin *et al.* 1993). Thus, while spitting can be interpreted as the most 'primal' form of expressing disgust, the elicitor, as demonstrated in the following statement, represents the most recent expansion of the phenomenon:

'This is "*goal nefesh*" (soul disgusting) to do such things in our country, *tfu* on you' and the man spat at the roundabout.

'Shame on you, Jews murdering Jews, *tfu*', and the man spat.

The further accentuation of the message by vocally expressing the onomatopoeia *tfu* is an accepted practice in various cultures to discourage evil spirits and curses and to avoid contagion and contamination. Like in the Eastern European Jewish traditional culture, and among the Greeks for example, as was accentuated in the film 'My Big Fat Greek Wedding.' Looking at the practice through this lens, these responses make it clear that the whole situation is considered a 'social blasphemy,' a 'social abomination.' The act is perceived as evil and immoral, and the women are seen as evil, immoral persons. This is viewed as something one should distance oneself from (Hochschild 1983), something that anyone who is involved in should feel ashamed of. Shame in this context is mentioned in its social control capacity, suggesting both socio-moral and emotional deviance (Scheff 1990; Thoits 1990) and the spitting can be interpreted as a symbolic casting out of the women and the whole situation from one's system and from society.

One may ask why do these men feel that they are allowed to publicly spit at the whole situation and at the women? The answer lies in another emotion that is directed at the whole spectacle, that of contempt, as was evident in some of the statements that referred to the whole situation as 'contemptuous.' Contempt, disgust and righteous anger are the prerogative of the powerful and those who feel that they are morally superior (Collins 1990). It is thus the case that the power/status dimensions (Collins 1990; Kemper 1990) that are intertwined in righteous anger (Collins 1990) can be the answer. The men can afford to spit at the whole situation and at the women because men are more powerful than women in patriarchal society and they are not afraid of the possible consequences. The status dimension seems to be at the bases of the symbolic expulsion of the women from the collective (Collins 1990; Kemper 1990).

Reactions to each visual element of the vigil

The conflict over the physical space

It was clear from the responses, that the politicization and feminization of the square was very disturbing to some of the drivers, who attempted to depoliticize and defeminize that roundabout. These attempts consisted of both verbal and physical acts. Many of the drivers reacted by sending the women to a more appropriate, political space, such as: 'Take your protest to the prime minister's office.' Others were much more physically threatening. One intimidating incident, expressing extreme outrage consisted of a very respectable looking man, in his 60s, who drove his car twice around the square, his face all red, shouting at the top of his voice: 'If you do not leave here I will make a *pigua drisa,* I swear that I will do it. It will be a *pigua drisa.*' The hebrew word *Pigua*, does not have an equivalent in the English Language. It is roughly equivalent to 'terrorist attack' but it is more of a root word that when attached to other words it becomes a phrase that specifies the type of terrorist attack that has occurred.[11] '*Pigua drisa*' was a term coined to refer to a number of incidents in which Palestinian drivers drove their car into a bus station, killing some of the people waiting. Thus, this driver threatened to actually drive his car into the square and kill the women. This is very much in line with Darwin's suggestion that anger is the preact or prelude to killing (mentioned in Hochschild 1983: 212). In another case, extreme anger spilled over into disgust as a bus driver drove his bus onto the roundabout where the women were standing, shouting: 'there is a strange stench of decay coming off the square.'[12]

The defeminization of the space and the whole situation is achieved through two main tactics: through the use of male grammatical language forms and through statements that defeminize and even dehumanize the women. The Hebrew language is highly gendered. With but a few exceptions, nouns and pronouns are either masculine or feminine, and in addition, gender is also indicated in the grammatical rules of conjugation of verbs (Weil 1993). Thus, by using the grammatical form that is used to address men instead of the correct grammatical way to address women, the defeminization effect is achieved. For example, The words '*bogdim,*' '*magilim*,' '*oyvim*,' '*tipshim*,' '*antishemim*,' '*fashistim*,' are all grammatically masculine ways of expressing the slurs: traitors, disgusting, enemy, antisemites, fascists.

The second tactic consisted of defeminizing through statements that defeminize, even dehumanize the women. As is evident in the following statements:

'You ugly old cow.'

'These, you cannot sell them either bras nor hair color.'

'With tits like yours you should be standing in the cow-shed.'

Reactions to the black color

Quite a number of responses were directed at the black color of the dress. The most common consisted of various punishments and comments that focused on the word 'black' in its symbolic meaning of bereavement. It seems that many drivers interpreted the black color in terms of betrayal of national loyalties and sentiments, seeing it as a one-sided act of identification with the Palestinians, and therefore with the enemy. Thus, some drivers suggested: 'You should wear red, not black,' insinuating that by supporting the enemy, they share the responsibility for the bloodshed and the victims of terrorism in Israel and have blood on their hands. The punishments that were associated with the black color were mostly in the form of two main 'wishes' for the women. The most common was 'You should wear black for the rest of your life,' wishing them an eternal state of bereavement. The other 'wish' was for the women to have a hard and dark life, as reflected in the following curse: 'May you always see only black in front of your eyes.' These examples make clear the extreme hate that is being directed at these women, and the anger that these men feel about the betrayal of national loyalties that is assumed to be associated with the black color that the women are wearing.

Reactions to the signs

Of all the elements constituting the event, the signs were the most obvious and easiest to interpret. I think that for this reason, coupled with the highly subversive messages conveyed through the signs, we find the whole range of the emotion frame of anger appearing in response to the overt, written messages. A large proportion of the anger responses were directed at the repeated use of the word 'occupation.' Many drivers could not accept this definition of the situation and reacted in the same manner as the subjects of Garfinkel's experiments; surprise at this framing of the situation, anger, indignation, disgust, contempt and a refusal to accept such a definition. As is evident in the following statements:

'What do you mean "occupation"'? You daughter of a whore, *tfu* (spitting), you fuckers.'

'What exactly did we occupy? What is the matter with you? We are in our country.'

'Say stop the terrorist attacks, not stop the occupation, you whores.'

'Why aren't you saying "stop the terror?," Your citizenship should be revoked.'

The last two examples represent an attempt at reinstating hegemonic definitions of the situation in terms of defense against terrorist acts. The drivers are demanding that the women change the signs and put up signs with 'stop the *Piguim*,' which define the situation in terms of terrorist attacks on innocent Israeli civilians, or else, their citizenship and membership in the collective is in danger.

Another sign that attracted highly angry reactions was the one that read; 'do not say "I did not know" of the crimes committed in the territories.' This sign attacks one of the most sacred institutions in Israeli society, the military. The angriest reactions were as follows:

'You zeroes, you nothing, you shits. How dare you speak of the army soldiers who are getting killed in the territories to defend you?'

'You should kiss the soldiers' feet. You should be ashamed. This is disgusting to do such a thing in our country. *Tfu* on you' (spitting).

The extreme disgust, contempt and outrage expressed in these responses relegate the women into completely insignificant creatures. This demonstrates the extent of 'sacredness' of the military among the responders. The women, through what was perceived by the responders as disrespect and ungrateful attitude towards the army soldiers who are sacrificing their life to protect these 'unworthy women,' have violated a sacred symbol in the Durkheimian sense.

Reactions to the body display and the time and day

Displaying the woman's body in a political function, on Friday, defies the public/private binary gendered division of social spheres of action and traditional gender roles. Furthermore, it poses a threat to many men since it appropriates their control over the woman's body and labor (on Friday), an ancient male prerogative in patriarchal societies. The angry reactions of most of the men can be interpreted as an attempt to reclaim their control over the women's body and reinstate the gendered social order and power disparities, by pushing the women back into the private sphere and to their traditional gender roles. One of the men, a pedestrian, approached the women and started a dialogue that was not hostile but it demonstrates the logic behind many other hostile reactions. He said:

> Hi girls, isn't it a pity that you are wasting your time like this? Your vigil doesn't mean anything to anyone. What is it? You want to change the world? You will not change a thing. Go home for a rest, cook, clean the house. Everybody has a role. Go fulfill yours.

Other men were more emotional and shouted at the women, expressing their disgust at the breach of traditional gender roles:

> 'Go home, clean the house and cook some food for your husbands, if you have any.'

> 'Shame and abomination, go home and sit by the heater' (on a very cold day).

> 'It is Friday, go home and sweep the floor, cook for your grandchildren, you retarded bitch, you stupid cow.'

The slurs attached to these statements express both indignation for the breach of the gendered division of labor, and deep contempt. The driver in the last statement felt the need to express his strong feelings by a double slur. In addition, there are also elements of dehumanization and humiliation, which appear in many of the responses.

Reactions to the general message of the vigil and to the women

The reactions to each visual element only present a fragmented picture. In this section I draw all these strands together and look at the general picture of themes and emotions expressed in the responses.

The first theme is that of the challenge posed to the normative gendered social order. Gender was prominent in the reactions to the black color, the body display and the time and day elements. The general emotion frame was that of anger, and in many cases the power element discussed by Collins (1990) and Kemper (1990) was very salient in the order: 'go home.' This is an obvious attempt to restore the traditional gendered social order.

These responses are somewhat mild compared with the responses that included references to sexuality, in the form of sexual labels such as 'whores,' 'ass fuckers,' which turn the women into sexual objects. In addition there was a very frequent non-verbal response in the form of the very intrusive gesture of raising the middle finger, suggesting sexual act of penetration. In effect, these women are being symbolically raped in an attempt to subjugate them. Thus additional emotions associated with this dimension are condescension and contempt, combining both power and status elements.

The second theme, that of breaches of national loyalties and boundaries, was most prominent in reactions to the place, the black color and the signs held by the women. Since this is by far the most salient group of response to the event, I will turn to a closer look at this element.

When the vigil is perceived in terms of the national discourse, the emotional responses are varied. Anger is always there, at the background, but many of the responses were of the typical political hate types. Hate was straightforwardly expressed through statements such as: 'Everybody in Israel hates you.' But it was also evident in themes and labels that are objects of hate and anxiety among Jews all over the world. The Holocaust theme that was very prominent in the hate letters analyzed by Temkin and Yanay (1989) appears in a number of the responses in the form of the labels 'Anti-Semites,' 'Israel haters,' and 'Nazis,' and in statements such as:

> 'The one who didn't burn your parents in Auschwitz was an idiot, you traitors.'

> 'Your mother was a Kapo.'

Indeed, the traumatic experience of the Holocaust supplies symbols that are the 'personification of essential evil. For many Jews in Israel nothing symbolizes in a stronger manner than the Holocaust the fragility and vulnerability of the Jewish people, on the one hand, and the need for a strong Jewish state on the other hand' (Temkin and Yanay 1989: 476). The meaning of using these terms in Israel cannot be overstated in their gravity and the intense emotional collective hatred, anxiety and fear that are associated with the Holocaust symbols. Just as in Temkin and Yanay's analysis, they are turned here into verbal aggressive acts against those perceived as the enemy (1989: 477).

Another hate-disgust theme that appears very often is the theme of national betrayal and treason. Labels such as: 'traitors,' 'collaborators,' 'the enemy,' 'disaster to the state,' 'insane,' etc. All these labels appear in Peleg's analysis of the words used in the politically right-wing oriented press, to refer to the political left in Israel, the Oslo Peace process and to the late Prime Minister, Yitzhak Rabin, in the hate build-up process during the period of time that preceded his assassination in 1995 (Peleg 2002: 433). To accentuate the severity of the betrayal of the women, they are accused of double treason. They are accused of collaborating with the enemy, lending support and legitimating terrorism:

> 'You are legitimizing Arafat.'

> 'Because of you we have *piguim*.'

At the same time they are accused of endangering collective and national solidarity:

> 'Because of stupid people like you our country is in danger of disappearing.'

> 'Shame on you, instead of uniting with the people, you are splitting our nation.'

The deep hatred expressed in these statements is probably due to the fact that the vigil is performed by women who are an integral part of the hegemonic social order; otherwise they would not have had the power to split the nation.[13]

Statman (1997: 38) states that hatred includes the wish to cause severe damage, if not outright annihilation of the object of one's hatred. In view of the above analysis, it is not surprising to learn that the responding men express a desire to harm the perpetrator of this 'despicable act of treason.' Indeed the punishments are very severe and range from expulsion to death by terrorist acts, which are two of the most common in the responses:

> 'Leave the country, you shits.'

> 'Go to Ramallah.'

> 'Go and demonstrate at Arafat's place, there is no place for you in our country.'

In these responses the men are banishing the women from the Jewish Israeli collective in an attempt to rid society of the menace that these women present to the hegemonic discourse and to society. By sending them to the Palestinian authority, they are sending them to unite with the enemy with whom they are perceived to sympathize.

But the next group of statements shows a wish to annihilate the women:

> 'You should all be killed in the next *pigua*.'

> 'A terrorist should come and blow himself up right here, among you.'

The physical annihilation of the women is not limited to the wish that they should die in the hands of those they support. Other non-verbal responses implied that the responder himself is prepared to kill them, at least symbolically. These reactions were in the form of moving one's hand across one's throat, suggesting slaughter or the pointing of the finger at the women in a gesture that signifies shooting them with a pistol.

Finally, when the connection between the challenge to the gendered social order and national loyalties is made, the extremely sexist element is added to the equation of WIB = traitor + enemy. The labels and punishments are mostly of a sexual nature, militaristic and intrusive:

'You are Arab fuckers.'

And the punishments:

'Your cunts should be conquered.'

'I wish that you will be raped.'

And also, death by fire:

'I wish I had a match, I would have burnt all of you.'

'You should all be burnt alive.'

This is reminiscent of the ancient witch-hunts in medieval Europe and in the US practised against strong women who posed a threat to the traditional values of the community and to the rule of men. Historically, burning was also applied to heretics, rebels, and books. It can be interpreted as expressing a fear of the diffusion of the heresy or oppositional views, within society. Another use of fire was to prevent the spread of contagious disease, which also reflects fear and disgust.

Concluding remarks

In this paper I chose to analyze the data gathered for my larger study through the introduction of a new concept, that of 'breaching event.' I applied it to both the analysis of the vigil and to the responses, highlighting the emotion-provoking aspects of the vigil of WIB and the actual emotional responses of the public to the event. The analysis demonstrated the importance of the concept and the theoretical and empirical potential that this concept has for understanding the strong negative emotional responses of the public.

At the theoretical level, it was demonstrated that this concept forms a link between social movements theory and theories of emotions. It was shown that when social movements violate important accepted practices in society by staging what I call 'breaching events' these invite emotional responses of the negative 'family' type from the public. They elicit core negative emotions. These responses express the anxiety and frustration that members of a society feel when their 'taken for granted' assumptions and definitions are violated.

I have also shown that a 'breaching event' can be a rather complex phenomenon that can be understood as a message conveyed via a particular medium. In the paper I analyzed the vigils of WIB in terms of both. In particular I drew attention to the intended meanings conveyed by its location, visual elements (such as dress code, text sign and body display) and the time at which it was held. I then analyzed the actual responses of the drivers passing by the roundabout to the vigil. I demonstrated that these drivers responded to the 'breaching event' by verbal and physical attempts to cast the women as traitors of the nation as well as to defeminize them and re-marginalize them along with their anti-occupation message.

This paper contributes to the future development of a more fully fledged theory of 'breaching events' and their outcomes in the form of the effects that they have on the public. It is clear that the idea can be fruitfuly applied to many other Western societies. Åsa Wettergren's analysis of the Adbusters and culture-jamming practices (this book), comes very close to a 'breaching events' perspective. She shows how the movement is creating 'cognitive "mind bombs,"' constructed to produce strong emotions in the viewer, emotions that accompany the state of moral shock into which the viewers are being manipulated.

Clearly the nature and composition of the event, the type of breaches and challenges that it poses, the specific socio-cultural setting, and the saliency and importance of the issues contested through the event are all intertwined to produce certain effects in their public and will differ in different societies. Within the Israeli context, the dangers involved in staging such an event were very salient in the data. Even though this paper was not aimed at understanding public discourse within Israeli society, the analysis presented here adds to the growing literature concernimg the violent nature of the discourse on security issues in Israel (Temkin and Yanay 1989; Peleg 2002). It also lends support to Peleg's conclusion concerning the failure of public discourse in Israeli society. This leads to the dimension of the political culture and culture of public discourse within the particular society as a factor affecting reactions of the public and the extent of danger that is involved in performing 'breaching events' within particular societies at a given point in time. All these demonstrate the potential for developing new perspectives both in the study of social movements and in the study of emotions, in particular the understanding of the emotional nature, content, and form of the reactions of the by-standing public to different types of 'breaching events.'

Notes

1 I would like to thank professors Zeev Klein and Amir Ben-Porat, Dr. Amichai Zilberman, Dr. David Segal, and my faithful assistants, Mr. Oded Levy and Ms. Keren Friedamn for their valuable assitance, advice and encouragement. I owe a debt of Gratitude to Prof. Suzanne Vromen and Prof. Bronislaw Misztal who have read earlier drafts of this chapter, for their fruitful advice and support.

2 For a different definition see McCarthy and Zald (1987: 23–4).
3 However, for a discussion of by-standing public reactions not exactly while the act was performed, see Kim (2002).
4 For further details see methodological appendix.
5 Reported at the International WIB meetings in Marina Di Massa (2003).
6 For additional accounts of WIB vigils in Israel see: Emmett (1996); Shadmi (2000); Helman and Rapoport (1997).
7 This is very much in line with findings reported for the Jerusalem vigil by Shadmi (2000) and Helman and Rapoport (1997). However, in Haifa, a number of Palestinian Israeli women are also participating in the vigil.
8 For additional discussion on the connection made by Women Peace Movements in Israel between the oppression of women and of the Palestinians, see Sharoni (1995).
9 However, Shadmi, for example, interprets it as ridiculing the 'mysterious portrayal of women as a dark fatal force' (2000: 25).
10 The main slogan is: 'Stop the Occupation.' Examples of additional slogans are: 'Occupation = Terrorism,' 'Yes to Peace, No to Occupation,' 'Stop Dying for the Occupation,' etc.
11 Thus, there are expressions to refer to suicide terrorist attacks (*pigua hitabdut*), to stabbing terrorist acts '*pigua dkir*,' to terrorist attacks in which the number of casualties is very high (*pigua hamoni*), etc. Apparently this is a linguistic cross-cultural variation and this large variety of words for terrorist acts is probably more charateristic of societies where this phenomenon is very frequent and constitutes an integral part of their life. It was further suggested to me by Ami Pedahazur, a political scientist working on studies of terror and security issues at Haifa University, that the Arab language also has a great number of phrases referring to such incidents and in addition they also have an umbrella term for the idea of self-sacrifice.
12 Various analyses of disgust elicitors include in their lists the smells and odours of decay (Lazarus 1991; Rozin *et al.* 1993).
13 This interpretation was suggested by one of the women of the Haifa vigil during the presentation of my analysis to the women on 27 April 2003.

References

Barbalet, J.M. (1998) *Emotion, Social Theory, and Social Structure: a macrosociological approach*, Cambridge: Cambridge University Press.
Ben Ze'ev, A. (1998) *Emotions in Everyday Life*, Tel-Aviv: Zmora-Bitan Publishers (Hebrew).
Cadena-Roa, J. (2002) 'Strategic framing, emotions, and superbarrio – Mexico City's masked crusader,' *Mobilization*, 7(2): 210–16.
Collins, R. (1990) 'Stratification, emotional energy, and the transient emotions,' in T.D. Kemper (ed.) *Research Agendas in the Sociology of Emotions*, Albany: SUNY Press.
Durkheim, E. (1912/1954) *The Elementary Forms of Religious Life*, New York: Free Press.
Emmett, A. (1996) *Our Sister's Promised Land – women, politics, and Israeli-Palestinian coexistence*, Ann Arbor: The University of Michigan Press.
Fischer, A.H. (1995) 'Emotion concepts as a function of gender,' in J.A. Russell, J.M. Fernande-Dols, A.S.R. Manstead and J.C. Wellenkamp (eds) *Everyday Concepts of Emotion: an introduction to the psychology, anthropology, and linguistics of emotion*, Dordrecht, The Netherlands: Kluwer.

Garfinkel, H. (1967) *Studies in Ethnomethodology*, Englewood Cliffs, NJ: Prentice-Hall.

Gould, D.B. (2002) 'Life during wartime: emotions and the development of ACT UP,' *Mobilization*, 7(2): 177–200.

Haviland, J.M. and Goldstone, R.B. (1992) 'Emotion and narrative: the agony and ecstasy,' in K.T. Strongman (ed.) *International Review of Studies on Emotion*, 2: 219–46, New York, NY: Wiley.

Helman, S. and Rapoport, T. (1997) '"These are Ashkenazi women, alone, Arab's whores, do not believe in God, and do not love Israel": Women in Black and the challenge to the social order,' *Theory and Critique*, 10: 175–92 (Hebrew).

Hercus, C. (1999) 'Identity, emotion and feminist collective action,' *Gender & Society*, 13(1): 34–56.

Hochschild, A.R. (1983) *The Managed Heart – commercialization of human feeling*, Los Angeles: University of California Press.

Hollows, J. (2000) *Feminism, Femininity and Popular Culture*, Manchester: Manchester University Press.

Izard, C.E. (1977) *Human Emotions*, New York: Plenum Press.

Kemper, T.D. (1990) 'Social relations and emotions: a structural approach,' in T.D. Kemper (ed.) *Research Agendas in the Sociology of Emotions*, Albany: SUNY Press.

—— (1993) 'Sociological models in the explanation of emotions,' in M. Lewis and J.M. Haviland (eds) *Handbook of Emotions*, New York: The Guilford Press.

Kim, H. (2002) 'Shame, anger, and love in collective action: emotional consequences of suicide protest in South Korea,' *Mobilization*, 7(2): 159–76.

Lazarus, R.S. (1991) *Emotion and Adaptation*, Oxford: Oxford University Press.

Lazarus, R.S. and Lazarus, B.N. (1994) *Passion and Reason: making sense of our emotions*, New York: Oxford University Press.

Lewis, M. and Haviland, J.M. (eds) (1993) *Handbook of Emotions*, New York: The Guilford Press.

McCarthy, J.D. and Zald, M. (1987) 'Resource mobilization and social movements: partial theory,' in M. Zald and J.D. McCarthy (eds) *Social Movements in an Organizational Society*, New Brunswick and Oxford: Transaction Books.

Melucci, A. (1985) 'The symbolic challenge of contemporary movements,' *Social Research*, 52(4): 199–226.

—— (1996) *Challenging Codes: collective action in the information age*, Cambridge: Cambridge University Press.

Peleg, M. (2002) 'If words could kill: the peace process and the failure of the public-political discourse in Israel,' *State and Society*, 2(3): 421–43 (Hebrew).

Perry, E.J. (2002) 'Moving the masses: emotion work in the Chinese revolution,' *Mobilization*, 7(2): 111–28.

Ritzer, G. (1988) *Sociological Theory*, 2nd edn, New York: Alfred A. Knopf.

Rozin, P. and Fallon, A.E. (1987) 'A perspective on disgust,' *Psychological Review*, 94(1): 23–41.

Rozin, P., Haidt, J. and McCauley, C.R. (1993) 'Disgust,' in M. Lewis and J.M. Haviland (eds) *Handbook of Emotions*, New York: The Guilford Press.

Scheff, T.J. (1990) 'Socialization of emotions: pride and shame as causal agents,' in T.D. Kemper (ed.) *Research Agendas in the Sociology of Emotions*, New York: SUNY Press.

Shadmi, E. (2000) 'Between resistance and compliance, feminism and nationalism: Women in Black in Israel,' *Women's Studies International Forum*, 23(1): 23–34.

Sharoni, S. (1995) *Gender and the Israeli-Palestinian Conflict – the politics of women's resistance*, Syracuse: Syracuse University Press.

Shields, S.A. (2000) 'Thinking about gender, thinking about theory: gender and emotional experience,' in A.H. Fischer (ed.) *Gender and Emotion: social psychological perspectives*, Cambridge: Cambridge University Press.

Statman, D. (1997) 'On the negative value of hatred,' in A. Ben Zeev (ed.), *Hatred*, Tel-Aviv: Zmora-Bitan (Hebrew).

Taylor, V. and Rupp, L.J. (2002) 'Loving internationalism: the emotion culture of transnational women's organizations, 1888–1945,' *Mobilization*, 7(2): 141–58.

Temkin, B. and Yanay, N. (1989) '"I shoot them with words": an analysis of political hate-letters,' *British Journal of Political Science*, 18: 467–83.

Thoits, P.A. (1990) 'Emotional deviance: research agendas,' in T. D. Kemper (ed.) *Research Agendas in the Sociology of Emotions*, New York: SUNY Press.

Turner, R.H. (1970) 'Determinants of social movement strategies,' in S. Tamotsu (ed.) *Human Nature and Collective Behavior: papers in honor of Herbert Blumer*, Englewood Cliffs, NJ: Prentice Hall.

Weil, S. (1993). 'Women and language in Israel,' in Y. Atzmon and N. D. Izraeli (eds) *Women in Israel*, New Brunswick and London: Transaction.

White, G.M. (1993) 'Emotions Inside Out: The Anthropology of Emotions,' in Lewis Michael and Jewannette M. Haviland (eds) *Handbook of Emotions*, New York: The Guilford Press.

Wierzbicka, A. (1986) 'Emotions: Universal or Culture-Specific?' *American Anthropologist*, 88, 585–94.

5 Emotional events and the transformation of collective action

The Chinese student movement[1]

Guobin Yang

Introduction

Studies of social movements have focused on movement emergence and have tended to neglect 'the dynamics of collective action past the emergence of a movement' and 'the ongoing accomplishment of collective action' (McAdam *et al.* 1988: 728–9). In these endeavors, analysts tend to devote their attention to identifying the structural conditions of movement emergence. While such conditions are central to movement emergence, they cannot adequately explain the dynamics and processes of collective action (Melucci 1988). As McAdam (1982: 53) argues, the process of social movements involves a different set of causal dynamics than in their emergence.

Against this background, the recent revival of interest in the role of emotions marks renewed attention to the process of social movements and collective action (for an overview of recent studies, see Goodwin *et al.* 2000). This chapter contributes to this scholarship, first by emphasizing the integration of historical sociology with a dramaturgical approach to emotions, and second by applying this approach to an empirical study of critical emotional events.

Emotions are defined as self-feelings that are situational, interactional, and temporal (Denzin 1984; Yang 2000b; also see McCarthy 1989: 56). As such, emotions are happenings. In social movements and collective action, emotional happenings abound. Like all happenings, emotional happenings invite historical analysis. Yet, as Aminzade and McAdam (2002) recently note, the historical study of emotions is not a strong point in social movement studies. This chapter moves in this direction by introducing a historical sociology of dramaturgy for the study of emotions in collective action. The central concept in this approach is the 'critical emotional event,' inspired by Sewell's (1996) notion of historical events. In developing his theory of historical events as transformations of structures, Sewell defines a historical event as '(1) a ramified sequence of occurrences that (2) is recognized as notable by contemporaries, and that (3) results in a durable transformation of structures' (1996: 844). In its focus on the

sequence of events and its attention to historical contingencies and cumulative and interactive effects, Sewell's theory is a historical sociology of
events (Abrams 1982). Taking cues from Sewell's work, I define a critical
emotional event in collective action as a ramified sequence of emotional
occurrences that results in the transformation of the dynamics of collective
action. An emotional occurrence is a single instance of emotional expression. Such an occurrence may take various forms, such as narratives, facial
expressions, gestures and voices. In the flux of social action, it is rare to
find single-case emotional occurrences – they almost always come in
sequences and clusters. I will argue that just as critical historical events
may transform historical structures, so critical emotional events may transform the dynamics of collective action. They do so by dramatizing the relationships among movement activists, publics, and opponents. Such
relationships compel action.

The student movement in China undulated with the changing patterns of
emotional happenings over a period of 50 days from 15 April to 4 June,
1989. The entire movement was emotionally intense throughout. Yet three
emotional events were critical in shaping its course. Without them, the
movement would have been different. The first was the Xinhuamen incident,
a 'bloody incident' on 20 April during student-police confrontations in front
of the central government compound in Beijing. The second was the student
demonstration on 27 April, 1989, and the last was the hunger strike. Each
of these events changed the dynamics of the movement. The empirical part
of this chapter analyzes these three emotional events. My goal is not to
attempt a comprehensive analysis of the entire movement, but to illustrate
my arguments about the usefulness of studying critical emotional events.
The empirical analysis draws on the recently released two-volume Chinese-
language documents about the events in the spring of 1989 (Zhang 2001)[2]
as well as other primary (e.g. diaries) and secondary sources.

Emotional events and emotional schemas

Sewell's theory of historical events addresses both the origins of historical
events and their transformative effects. Regarding origins, he argues that
historical events are rearticulations of structures, which are 'composed
simultaneously of cultural schemas, distributions of resources, and modes
of power' (1996: 842). He continues:

> Cultural schemas provide actors with meanings, motivations, and
> recipes for social action. Resources provide them (differentially) with
> the means and stakes of action. Modes of power regulate action – by
> specifying what schemas are legitimate, by determining which persons
> and groups have access to which resources, and by adjudicating con-
> flicts that arise in the course of action.

> (Sewell 1996: 842)

Following Sewell, I argue that emotional events in the course of collective action also have their structural origins. The origins of emotional events lie in both context-specific emotions and more stable affective bonds and loyalties (Jasper 1998: 397). Context-specific emotions arise within a specific context of social interactions. Social movements, which often deliberately cultivate emotions such as anger (Flam 2004) and control others such as fear (Goodwin and Pfaff 2001), illustrate different kinds of context-specific emotions. Stable affective bonds and loyalties are components of what I will refer to as 'emotional schemas.' If cultural schemas are 'meanings, motivations, and recipes for social action' (Sewell 1996: 842), emotional schemas may be defined as emotional meanings, memories, and recipes for social action. Emotional schemas resemble the collective memory of emotions; they are shared emotional pasts (Mattley 2002). In addition, they are culturally specific, as evidenced by the many studies of cultures of emotion (Shott 1979; Stearns and Stearns 1986; Lutz 1988; Heider 1991; Clark 1997). An excellent example of an emotional schema is provided in Flam's analysis of how a literary past imbued with romanticism and heroism influenced activists in the pre-1989 Polish opposition. As she puts it:

> Sienkiewicz's books, in particular, *Trilogy*, were also part of the mobilizing 'psychic reality' for numerous opposition members even after World War II.[3] This 'psychic reality' comprised not only the association between honor and the struggle for the national independence against all odds but also between honor and specific 'noble' character traits. Among these traits courage and a sense of responsibility towards one's own nation occupied a prime place. Subjectively, then, the heroic Polish past, its literary glorification as well as the noble conduct standards served to counteract typical oppositional fears and to mobilize one's self to action.
>
> (Flam 1998: 161)

Why are historical events transformative? Sewell argues that once they occur, they may introduce new ideas, produce new events, transform social relations, and thus impart 'an unforeseen direction to social development' and alter 'the nature of the causal nexus in which social interactions take place' (1996: 843). Historical events have such transformative power because they are moments of 'heightened emotion' (1996: 865) and 'acts of collective creativity' (1996: 867). At such times, Sewell further suggests, 'ordinary routines of social life are open to doubt, the sanctions of existing power relations are uncertain or suspended, and new possibilities are thinkable' (1996: 867).

Critical emotional events are transformative for similar reasons. They are 'moments of madness,' in Zolberg's (1972) provocative language, or in Victor Turner's (1969) more neutral terms, liminal moments. They morally shock and emotionally move people to action (Jasper 1998; Eyerman, this volume; Wettergren, this volume). But exactly how do emotions move? I adopt a historical sociology of dramaturgy to analyze how critical emotional events move people and transform collective action. The theoretical significance of such an analysis lies in its integration of dramaturgy with historical sociology.

A historical sociology of dramaturgy

If social drama is one of emotion management (Hochschild 1983) and emotional achievement (Yang 2000b), a dramaturgical approach should be particularly appropriate for analyzing critical emotional events in social movements (see Benford and Hunt 1995; Eyerman 2004). The analysis of critical emotional events entails identifying their context-specific emotions as well as showing their deeper cultural sources. Understanding the deeper cultural sources of emotions requires an analysis of emotional schemas, as mentioned above. The analytical weight in a dramaturgical approach to emotional events, however, falls on the context-specific emotions, because these are the emotions that appear in the movement and directly affect its dynamics. From a dramaturgical perspective, the main factors to be analyzed are: 1) the manner of opponents; 2) audience responses; 3) dramatic techniques or strategies of protest; and 4) place.

Emotions unfold in temporal order (Denzin 1984; Gordon 1987; cf. Mattley 2002). Thus a dramaturgical approach must not be content with the analysis of the various elements of an emotional drama. To stop here would render the analysis static. To capture the dynamics of critical emotional events, the dramaturgical approach needs to be buttressed by a historical sociology. By this, I mean the analysis should follow the drama as an unfolding process. Such an approach would integrate the analysis of the various elements of drama into a temporal historical account. It is with this in mind that I outline below the main analytic elements in a critical emotional event. The empirical part, however, will present these various elements in an integrated historical account.

The manner of the opponents

In social movements, three types of actors, or *dramatis personae*, may be distinguished: the challengers (movement organizers and activists), the challenged (opponents), and audience (spectators and media publics). I argue that emotional events transform collective action by linking the three types of actors into heightened emotional relationships, thus compelling action. Opponents respond to the challenges of social movements in various ways. The manner of their responses triggers emotions among the challengers (Scheff 1997). In a study of political violence in Venezuela, Gude finds that 'one common mistake of governments under the threat of insurgency is to overrespond (1971: 272), because over-responding, such as repression, may force insurgents into a position where there is nothing they could do but 'fight to the death.' Revolution happens when there is 'no other way out,' as Goodwin (2001) provocatively puts it. The obverse of this problem is under-responding. Not responding to protest actions, especially those actions that call for response, may signify indifference on the part of the opponents. Challengers could perceive such indifference as insulting and respond with more radical forms of protest.

Audience responses

Audience plays a central role in all dramas, including the dramas of collective action (Benford and Hunt 1995: 93). In a study of football victory celebrations, Snow *et al.* (1981: 37) argue that 'spectators are structurally essential' and 'the relationship between spectators and task performers is reciprocal and frequently interdependent.' Their analysis distinguishes between two types of spectators, proximal and distal. Proximal spectators are those on the scene. Distal spectators 'indirectly monitor' (Snow *et al.* 1981: 34) the events. They may include the media, publics, and what Flam (1998) calls 'bystanders.' The attitude of the general public toward the movement may influence both movement participants and opponents. For participants, public support is a source of emotional strength, because it may help to build an atmosphere of effervescence to boost the morale and spirits of the activists. The more likely repression is, and the stronger the sense of fear among participants, the more important it is to have public support.[4]

Dramatic techniques and place

Strategies are crucial for movement mobilization (Gamson 1990). Where movement organization is weak, an effective strategy could help achieve mobilization. From a dramaturgical perspective, movement strategies may be understood as 'dramatic techniques' (Benford and Hunt 1995). Dramatic techniques produce dramatic effects, which are also emotional effects. In social movements, movement performers may 'offer facial and verbal cues as well as utilize props intended to define and evoke the appropriate emotion or mood' (Benford and Hunt 1995: 90). They may do so by creating scenes and situations to embarrass or shame the opponents. They may also target the emotions of participants and audience by staging emotionally stirring scenes.

Places have symbolic meanings. Some places are more permeated with historical and emotional memories than others and therefore may better 'express' the movement than others (Lofland 1995: 203). Movement organizers often choose to stage actions in places rich in symbolic meaning and emotional overtones in order to build the proper kind of emotions among participants and the public. The symbolic meaning of Tiananmen Square is as clear as it is strong. This at least partly explains why it has been the archetypal place for public protest in modern China.

Three emotional events in the Chinese student movement

Many different theories have been put forward to explain the momentous events in China in the spring of 1989. At the macro-level, the opening up of political opportunities and deepening sense of cultural crisis among Chinese intellectuals (Calhoun 1994) and the changing relations between state and society (Zhao 2001) provided important background conditions for the rise of the movement. At the meso-level, formal and informal social networks are crucial organizational resources for the rise of the movement (Lin 1992; Calhoun 1994). At the individual level, factors considered important to the development of the movement are the transformation of personal identities created by the experience of movement participation (Calhoun 1994), rational choices made under conditions of uncertainty and incomplete information (Deng 1997), theatrical elements in the middle of collective interactions (Esherick and Wasserstrom 1990; Niming 1990; Guthrie 1995), and students' emotional and moral aspirations (Yang 2000b). My analysis builds on existing explanations that emphasize identities, interactions, rituals, and emotions. The concept of emotional events outlined above captures these various elements in coherent form. I argue that by bringing the multiple parties involved in collective action into heightened emotional relationships, critical emotional events transform the dynamics of collective action.

The Xinhuamen incident

The student movement started with the death of Hu Yaobang on 15 April, 1989. Initially, it took the form of mourning activities in universities in Beijing and in Tiananmen Square. Although the government apparently disliked these activities, they did not have good reason to stop them, because historically mourning the death of a party leader was not only legitimate but sometimes even officially organized. Students could claim that it was out of a sense of patriotism that they mourned the loss of a national leader. Then a 'bloody incident' occurred on 20 April, which pushed the movement to a higher level of mobilization. The drama happened at Xinhuamen Gate, the entrance to Zhongnanhai, the central government compound near Tiananmen Square. Zhongnanhai was both the symbolic and real center of political power in China. Protest activities in front of this power center had great symbolic significance. On 19 April, students had begun sit-ins in front of Xinhuamen, demanding that government leaders come out to meet with them. Police had formed a blockade in front of the entrance. Confrontations between students and police happened in the early morning of 20 April. According to government reports, students shouted inflammatory anti-Party slogans and attempted to break through the police line, injuring four (Han 1990: 44). Witness accounts describe the confrontation as a 'bloody incident.' One account reported that police attacked students with batons and injured many (Ogden *et al.* 1992: 83–4). Immediately after the Xinhuamen incident, many emotional narratives appeared in the form of wall-posters in universities in Beijing. As one witness puts it, these posters 'expose the "bloody incident," call on people to rise up in protest, and demand that the offenders be punished and the facts be clarified' (Tianhua 1994). One poem published in a poster was titled 'Blood Stains – In Remembrance of 20 April' (Han 1990: 44). Another poster described how police beat up students and called on students to 'jointly boycott classes to protest the violence and demand punishment for the prime culprits' (Ogden *et al.* 1992: 85).

The Xinhuamen incident both resulted from and changed the dynamics of the movement. Government leaders had interpreted students' demand for a meeting at the Xinhuamen Gate as an act of 'unsurpassable shame' (Zhang 2001: 143). Thus instead of meeting the students' demand, police were ordered to disperse them (Zhang 2001: 135). Students considered government leaders' reluctance to talk with them equally shameful. Police brutality added anger to feelings of shame. At this initial stage of the movement, both the students and the government were uncertain about the directions of the movement, and the likelihood of immediate repression looked small.

Why did government leaders consider students' demand for a meeting an act of shame for them? And why did students feel equally shamed to be denied such a meeting? To understand why requires an understanding of the emotional schemas in Chinese political culture. At the risk of simplification, it may be suggested that Chinese political culture in the twentieth century has two diverging emotional schemas. First, political authorities expect compliance, respect, and loyalty from those under their rule. To induce compliance and mobilization for state-sponsored projects, Chinese communist authorities would resort to their own 'emotion work' as a strategy of psychological engineering (Perry 2002). Such emotion work is not always successful, of course, and authorities are especially sensitive to behavior that makes mockery of their emotion work, such as an open display of disrespect and disobedience. It hurts them to acknowledge such open disobedience by meeting what the disobedient demands. But then, as if to build opposition into the design of the political culture, China's political culture also elevates a set of emotional schemas that directly contradict those of the authorities. If authorities demand respect, ordinary people earn *their* respect not by obeying the authorities, but by challenging them. In other words, the 'feeling rules' (Hochschild 1979) for ordinary people are not to buckle under authorities but to demonstrate courage and heroism, whereas the 'feeling rules' for authorities are to expect respect and compliance. When these two sets of feeling rules are confronted with each other, the result is likely to be conflict and the intensification of emotions on each side.

The Xinhuamen incident was the first critical emotional event in the movement. It changed the course of the movement in three important ways. First, a deep sense of shame and anger prompted students to organize themselves in order to carry on the movement in a more organized fashion. Thus, immediately after the incident, the very first independent student organizations began to form (Shen 1990). Second, as soon as these organizations were formed, they declared a class strike on 21 April to protest the Xinhuamen Incident. Third, also as a response to the Xinhuamen incident, thousands of students ignored government orders to close the Tiananmen Square and camped in the Square on the night of 21 April to wait for Hu Yaobang's funeral the next day. The funeral would lead to further, more intensified emotional encounters between students and government leaders. In short, the emotional reverberations caused by the Xinhuamen incident decidedly changed the course of the movement. Thereafter, the movement became more organized, mobilization became larger in scale, and the relations between challengers and the challenged became more confrontational.

The demonstration on 27 April 1989

Faced with the rather unexpected escalation of the movement, the government decided to rein it in once and for all. At 6:30pm, 25 April, the Central People's Radio Station and the CCTV broadcast an editorial to be published in *People's Daily* the next day. Entitled 'It Is Necessary to Take a Clear-Cut Stand against Turmoil,' the editorial labeled the student movement as 'a planned conspiracy and a turmoil,' which, if unchecked, would lead to 'a chaotic and unstable China without any future' (Odgen *et al.* 1992: 117). This was the most important response made by the government so far in the movement. It was a cold narrative, written with a dry and intimidating tone and broadcast with raised voices. Judging from available documents (Zhang 2001), the government leaders who made the decision to brand the movement as a 'turmoil' had not anticipated the responses the editorial would provoke.

For students, it was a deeply humiliating narrative, more so than police brutality at the Xinhuamen incident, because it marked a complete about-face from the relatively mild position the government had taken up to that point. Government leaders had previously acknowledged that the movement was a patriotic one. The language of 'turmoil' (*dongluan*) compares the movement directly to the Cultural Revolution, which had been penned into history textbooks as 'ten years of turmoil.' From the very beginning, students had tried to distinguish themselves from the Cultural Revolution, and now the label was officially applied to them. Student responses to the editorial were rapid and emotional. One poster titled 'Denounce the *People's Daily*' opens with the following sentence: 'We are very angry after reading the *People's Daily* editorial' (Ogden *et al.* 1992: 118). Another poster ends by expressing anger and calling for action:

> The extremely negative tone of the editorial has really caused deep, deep shock, disappointment, and anger in the nation's citizens!
>
> Since the government is not taking any constructive action, our movement must continue to the very end!
>
> (Han 1990: 87)

Government documents indicate that demonstrations protesting against the editorial happened in Beijing right after the broadcast. At 6:45pm, 25 April, for example, several thousand students of People's University were already marching out of the campus (Zhang 2001: 201). Protest activities also happened in other cities that evening, including Changchun, Shanghai, Tianjin, Hangzhou, Nanjing, Xi'an, Changsha and Hefei (Zhang 2001: 202). Amidst these small protest activities, the newly-formed Federation of All Beijing College Students Union called for a general rally on 27 April (Shen 1990: 195; Zhang 2001: 214). Organizing the rally was not an easy thing, because there was fear of possible government repression. The student movement organization in Qinghua University even decided not to participate (Tianhua 1994). In the morning of 27 April, groups of students began to gather hesitantly in their universities, uncertain about what lay ahead for that day. By the end of the day, however, the biggest and most influential student demonstration up to then had taken place.

Many factors contributed to the success of this demonstration. For those who participated in it, the most decisive factor was the enthusiastic response of the citizens of Beijing, the bystanders in this emotional drama. One student thus explained the success of the demonstration:

> During the march, as we saw police lines broken through one after another, our [pounding] hearts gradually calmed down. Only the organizers of the march and those many people who went through the experience can know what it was like to feel such fear and overwhelming relief. Well, how were the police lines burst through? Almost all were broken through for us by citizens of the city! ... Every time we arrived at a key intersection, [supportive Beijing residents would crowd in toward the police and] banter with them, trying to make them understand why we were marching. They tried to persuade them with reason and to move them with emotion.
>
> (Han 1990: 93)

Niming (1990), a witness who later provides an astute analysis of the movement, remarks on the importance of the bystanders' support: 'this demonstration was much larger than those previously, and bystanders along its route expressed their support for the students for the first time. People gave money, popsicles, food, and drinks to the students.' (Niming 1990: 89). A participant in the demonstration notes in a diary entry: 'Everyone shouted, screamed, sang, waved the flags in hand' (Tianhua 1994).

A recently published two-volume document about the movement (Zhang 2001) contains some detailed descriptions about the responses of the bystanders. The following describes one such episode:

> The streets in Zhongguancun and in the neighbourhood of the Friendship Hotel as well as the Chang'an Avenue were crowded with people. Some had climbed onto roof-tops or trees. Whenever student marchers appeared, people would applaud and wave the V gesture, a symbol for victory. At such times, students would shout slogans such as 'Long Live the People!' 'Long Live Understanding [from the people]!'
>
> (Zhang 2001: 216)

Another interesting facilitating factor was the spatial features of the demonstrations. The demonstrations started from the university areas in the western part of Beijing. The destination was Tiananmen Square in the middle of the city, about ten miles from the university areas. At various points along the demonstration route were ranks of police planted in advance to block the progression of the demonstrators. The instruments of power were mobilized to stop the challengers. Both symbolically and in reality, the demonstration was a progression from the periphery to the center of power. The fact that the demonstration assumed such a progression was important for understanding the emotional drama that it brought forth. First, the 'theater' was large enough to hold as many 'performers' and spectators as there were. Second, the progression, like the ritual process studied by Turner (1969), allowed ample time and space for interactions between demonstrators and bystanders and for a sense of camaraderie to develop. Thus as the demonstrators marched on, their ranks expanded and the sense of fear at the beginning of the demonstration was dissolved by the cheers and kind words from bystanders until, at the end of the day, students concluded the demonstrations with relief and exhilaration. The emotional shift from uncertainty and fear to joy and solidarity typifies the transition from liminality to communitas in a ritual process.

The 27 April demonstration was an emotionally intense event. It brought movement challengers, opponents, and the public into heightened emotional encounters. These encounters won the public over to the side of the student demonstrators. Blockade after blockade of police dissolved in the face of the powerful emotional outpourings from the students and the bystanders. Once again, a critical emotional event changed the course of the movement. While the Xinhuamen incident led to larger mobilization and better organization, the demonstration on 27 April showed what large-scale mobilization could accomplish in the confrontations of emotions between the challengers and the challenged. As a result of the demonstration, the government backed down from its accusation of 'turmoil' and agreed to hold dialogues with student leaders. In the history of the People's Republic of China (PRC), this was almost unprecedented. Few leaders in power had changed their positions in response to popular protest. This point alone shows the significance of the achievement of the demonstration on 27 April. But its impact went beyond that. Crucial to the development of the movement, the success of the demonstration gave the students the confidence to push the movement to a new stage.

Hunger strike

From 13 May to 19 May, 1989, students staged a powerful hunger strike in Tiananmen Square. The demonstration on 27 April had mounted a daring challenge against political power. The hunger strike was to show that citizens could occupy the center of power. The Tiananmen Square, which hunger strikers and student protesters began to occupy on 13 May, 1989, was a large, carefully crafted public space for the open display of political power. It had been the venue for Mao's mass mobilization at the beginning of the Cultural Revolution. Deng Xiaoping, now the target of the protesting hunger strikers, had himself used the square to display his own political power in 1984 when he staged the massive military parade and celebrations on the 35th anniversary of the founding of the PRC. In the spring of 1989, the square became students' political theater for staging the most stirring and most widely watched emotional drama in Chinese history. In the words of one astute analyst, student encampment in these sacred spaces

> was the most effective means of de-facing the state.... By shifting their bodies and their icons in such an open vulnerable position opposite the picture of Chairman Mao, they shifted the world's attention from the government to themselves.
>
> (Gladney 2004)

The hunger strike started with several hundred students and at its height reached over 3,000 participants (Landsberger 1990: 171). As a key emotional event in the course of the student movement, the hunger strike heightened the relationships between the different parties. Students considered the hunger strike as a last resort to pressure the government and a final moral test for the government. It was a radical 'dramatic technique' to challenge the government to respond. The self-sacrifice of the fasting students aroused the sympathy and compassion of the general populace. The government's failure to respond to such public outpourings of emotions provoked widespread indignation, leading to higher levels of protest in all major cities in China as well as in Beijing. The narratives produced by hunger strikers had great emotional effects. This is shown in the following example, a student's farewell letter to his parents:

> If this time I am unfortunate and die, please do not think that my hunger strike was done from a sudden impulse.... Perhaps I will not be able to fulfill my filial piety. For thousands and thousands of parents and their children, I have tearfully made the choice to go on this hunger strike.
>
> (Han 1990: 202–3)

A student who did not participate in the hunger strike was moved by the hunger strikers to action:

> Today I, together with all the teachers and students who have remained at Tiananmen Square, and millions of people of the capital, pledged to the people of the entire country and the entire world: 'We shall sacrifice our blood and lives in exchange for freedom and democracy, and for the bright future of the Republic! What a glorious moment it was! What a magnificent sight!
>
> What is most moving are the acts of the students of the Central Academy of Drama, who have refused water and food for several days now. It takes exceptional courage and willingness to risk one's life to do this. I admire them from the bottom of my heart!
>
> (Han 1990: 212–13)

Several types of audiences contributed to the emotional drama of the hunger strike. First there were the crowds in Tiananmen Square, including volunteers who were helping the hunger strikers, citizens who were demonstrating to show their support for the hunger strikers, students who had formed a ring around the hunger strikers and camped there to protect them, and others who went there for a glimpse of the fasting students 'out of both curiosity and sympathy' (Han 1990: 203). Then there were the distal spectators (Snow *et al.* 1981). These included, first, the protesters and demonstrators in other major cities in China. One of the main slogans of these demonstrations was to 'voice support' (*shengyuan*) for the hunger strikers. Second, as the hunger strike continued, the Chinese media began to cover the events extensively, often showing citizens' emotional appeals to the government. As one witness reports,

> The main contents of TV news programs are now about the student hunger strike. Even those who go to work in the morning and seldom watch morning news now punctually turn on the TV, hoping to read news about peaceful solutions, though the result is always disappoint-

ing. In today's [17 May] morning news, several mothers were shown in tears, vehemently demanding the government to have an immediate dialogue with students in order to avoid the deterioration of the current affairs.

(Jiang 1997)

Third, international media also played an unprecedented role in these emotional events. In one of the earliest published analyses of the movement, Calhoun (1989) provides insights into how student protesters targeted a Western audience, which the Western media helped to reach. Because of Mikhail Gorbachev's visit and the Asian Development Bank's first meeting in China, the international press had gathered in Beijing in greater than usual numbers. Students seized this opportunity and directly spoke to and performed for the international press. The foreign press in its turn helped to mobilize international public opinion on the side of protesters against the government, spread word of the protests to other parts of China, and even brought the protest to an international audience of overseas Chinese.

What could hunger strikers do in front of all these enthusiastic and eager audiences? They had to carry on the show. The hunger strike lasted for an entire week and became the most transformative emotional event in the course of the movement. Esherick and Wasserstrom (1990: 840, 841) call it a 'stroke of creative genius,' 'a potent piece of political theater' that 'earned the protesters enormous sympathy.' As a result, movement mobilization reached its apex. From 16 May to 18 May, the crowds in the square numbered at about one million daily. As one analyst puts it, the movement 'seemed to be on the verge of crushing all obstacles and bringing down the hardliners' (Lin 1992: 87).

Emotional schemas

Earlier, I argued that emotional schemas matter to emotional events in the same way that cultural schemas matter to Sewell's historical events. Emotional schemas are cultural resources for emotions and feelings. They resemble a habitus, an embodied cultural and social milieu that shapes feeling and action in subtle ways (Bourdieu 1990). Practical action activates emotional schemas while at the same time being guided by them. What kind of emotional schemas mattered most to the emotional events analyzed above? I argue that one specific aspect of Chinese culture particularly important for understanding the enduring cultural foundations of the emotions demonstrated by Chinese students in 1989 was a heroic mode in Chinese culture.[5] Scholars of Chinese literature have often observed a 'heroic' mode in Chinese poetry (Lo 1971; Duke 1977). Among the various qualities of a Chinese hero lauded in the 'heroic' mode of poetry, Lo (1971: 58–60) mentions the following: outstanding sensibility, character, and talent; courage and wisdom; self-awareness of personal worth;

generosity and magnanimity; spontaneity and freedom from restraint; and personal integrity.

The heroic mode in Chinese culture is not confined to the poetic literature; it has its counterpart in popular culture. The popular tradition of *xia*, a term that has been translated as 'knight-errant,' represents the heroic mode in popular imagination. The character-ideal of *xia* was captured by Sima Qian in his *Records of the Grand Historian*: 'Their words were always sincere and trustworthy, and their actions always quick and decisive. They were true to what they promised, and without regard to their own persons, they would rush into dangers threatening others' (Quoted in Yang 1957: 294).

Great heroes in Chinese history serve as moral exemplars from generation to generation. Their words and deeds are lauded throughout the ages and sink into the public memory through literature and folklore. The exemplary society that China is (Munro 1977; Bakken 2000) depends on these moral exemplars for the transmission of cultural values. In contemporary China, the social environment in which the 1989 student protesters grew up, textbooks of history and state rituals helped to strengthen the collective memory of historical heroes alongside communist martyrs (Wasserstrom 1990). In extraordinary times that call forth heroic acts, people do not have to consciously recall the great heroes of the past to guide their present action,[6] though some people will. This happened in 1989. Shen (1990) recalls that Tan Sitong was a heroic inspiration for him and his friend on the night of 20 May, the first day of martial law. Faced with imminent repression on the Square, Shen and his friend had told each other that they were not afraid of death and were ready to face it. Then Shen writes,

> we continued walking, then we brought up the name of Tan Sitong, an intellectual who led a campaign for reform during the Qing dynasty. Before he was executed for leading the dissident movement, Tan Sitong had said, 'If not I, who?' Pointing out that reform movements in every country had historically taken the blood of reformers, he had said, 'If it is necessary in China, then let it start with me.' We are both looking to him for inspiration.
>
> (Shen 1990: 300)

About the same time when Shen and his friend expressed their determination to face death, a poster on the Tiananmen Square, dated 20 May, 1989, 1:30 AM, expresses similar sentiments:

> If you think about it, you might say that I am totally incomprehensible. You may think that I'm a lunatic, or at least a rash bloke whose brains are not quite developed yet. No, comrades, I'm not what you think I am. In truth I'm a descendent of Wen Tianxiang, the honest official who lived at the end of the Song dynasty. His famous saying, 'Since antiquity no man has escaped death; let me but leave a loyal

heart to shine in the pages of history,' is etched into my mind and blended with my blood.

(Han 1990: 294)

These words and thoughts manifest a heroic mode in Chinese culture. In the spring of 1989, this heroic mode functioned as a central part of the emotional schemas that shaped the emotional inclinations of student protesters, making possible the three powerful emotional events that changed the course of the movement.

Conclusion and implications

The student movement in 1989 was an unprecedented historical event. Even more than ten years later, its far-reaching impact on Chinese politics and society cannot be fully grasped, because it is still being felt, albeit often in invisible ways. Despite a short period of political repression in the wake of the movement, the Chinese government soon moved to open up China further and accelerate the economic reform. Social and political spaces expanded in the 1990s (Harding 1998; Yang 2002). Although often unacknowledged, the increased political and economic opening must be considered against the historical background of the student movement in 1989. The movement was a deadly call for social and political change. While the movement itself was suppressed, its message had such power that the political regime can only ignore it at its own peril.

Numerous studies have attempted to explain the extraordinary rise and development of the movement. This article contributes to these efforts by offering an analysis of the emotional dynamics of the movement. Adding a dramaturgical twist to Sewell's theory of historical events, I have focused on emotional events and analyzed three critical cases in the course of the Chinese student movement. The analysis shows that critical emotional events can transform the dynamics of social movements and collective action. In all three cases, the events brought challengers, opponents, and audience into heightened relationships. Challengers used 'dramatic techniques' and emotional narratives to shame and challenge opponents and move audiences. Opponents' responses or lack thereof incurred emotional responses and actions from challengers. Proximal and distal audiences contributed to the emotional drama in their own ways. The symbolic spaces where these events took place and the latent, underlying emotional schemas in Chinese culture added meaning and intensity to the dramatic events. These emotional events each decidedly shaped the course of the movement by leading to a higher level of mobilization.

The empirical analysis of this chapter illustrates some of the ways of incorporating critical emotional events into social movement studies. It shows that a historical sociology of dramaturgy that analyzes in temporal order the interactions of the various 'characters' in the emotional drama, as well as the underlying emotional schemas, can reveal how critical emotional events happen and how they may transform the dynamics of collective action. The focus on critical emotional events as unfolding in sequences of interactions allows the analysis to reveal the micro-dynamics of collective action.

One theoretical implication of this study is that the analysis of social movements and collective action must not stop at structural explanations. Even the most thorough-going analysis of structural conditions will fail to explain the dynamics of collective action. By their very nature, the *dynamics* of action do not follow such pre-determined trajectories as may be predicted from underlying structural conditions, although there is no doubt that these conditions matter at the macro-level. Emotional events, like all historical events, are almost always fraught with uncertainties and contingencies (Abrams 1982). In the morning of 27 April, 1989, when groups of students began to gather for a demonstration in Beijing, nobody knew what was going to happen. The public show of support was completely unexpected. The street theater of participant-bystander interactions was an impromptu drama that took on its own life *as* the event unfolded. To understand the causes and consequences of the event therefore requires an intimate analysis of the interactions then and there, of the gestures made, slogans shouted, applauses given, and many more. It is these little things that changed the emotional milieu of the event from fear to solidarity and made the event a final triumph for the movement. Here, historical sociologists face a challenge. The texture of emotional events consists of fleeting and ephemeral details such as gestures, voices, and smiles, yet these details do not often leave concrete records. This is where the ethnographer and the visual sociologist might make unique contributions, for they are uniquely positioned to capture the texture of emotional events.

A second theoretical implication is that the study of collective action might well start with critical emotional events. An emotional event is the expression of heightened emotional interactions among different parties. It may change the course of collective action. A focus on critical emotional events therefore provides an effective entry point into the fluid dynamics of collective action.

A third theoretical implication of this study is that the analysis of critical emotional events in collective action should pay attention to the emotions of audiences, opponents, as well as the movement participants. It is the interactions among these various parties that shape the dynamics of these events. The emotions of movement participants often undulate in response to audiences and opponents, and vice versa. This is almost a truism in symbolic interactionism, yet it has not earned the attention it deserves in the study of social movement emotions. Attention to the emotions of audiences and opponents also entails the analysis of dramatic techniques used by movement organizers and activists to produce or provoke certain emotions from the audiences and opponents. It entails, in other words, an analysis of emotion work that movement organizers perform on themselves as well as on audiences and opponents. Because such emotion work is performed with a tacit or explicit understanding of the latent emotional schemas in specific cultures, the analysis should give due attention to these emotional schemas.

Notes

1 I thank Helena Flam and Debra King for inviting me to contribute to this volume and for providing invaluable comments on the chapter.
2 The English-language publication *The Tiananmen Papers* (Nathan and Link 2001) is a much more condensed version of these two volumes.
3 Interestingly, Chinese translations of Sienkiewicz's works were popular in China and comprised part of the 'revolutionary literary canon' promoted by the Chinese party-state in the decades before the reform era.
4 This is not to argue that challengers cannot build hope and confidence in the absence of public support. For a complementary view, see Tova Benski's contribution in this volume.
5 Cf. Flam (1998) on the influence of the heroic mode of Polish literature on pre-1989 Polish opposition.
6 As Gladney (2004) aptly puts it, their bodily positions of protest follow social dispositions.

References

Abrams, P. (1982) *Historical Sociology*, Ithaca, NY: Cornell University Press.
Aminzade, R. and McAdam, D. (2002) 'Introduction: emotions and contentious politics,' *Mobilization*, 7(2): 107–9.
Bakken, B. (2000) *The Exemplary Society: human improvement, social control, and the dangers of modernity in China*, Oxford: Oxford University Press.
Benford, R.D. and Hunt, S.A. (1995) 'Dramaturgy and social movements: the social construction and communication of power,' in S.M. Lyman (ed.) *Social Movements: critiques, concepts, case-studies*, Washington Square, NY: New York University Press.
Bourdieu, P. (1990) *The Logic of Practice*, Stanford, CA: Stanford University Press.
Calhoun, C. (1989) 'Tiananmen, television and the public sphere: internationalization of culture and the Beijing spring of 1989,' *Public Culture*, 2(1): 54–71.
—— (1994) *Neither Gods Nor Emperors: students and the struggle for democracy in China*, Berkeley: University of California Press.
Cancian, F.M. (1987) *Love in America: gender and self-development*, Cambridge: Cambridge University Press.
Clark, C. (1997) *Misery and Company: sympathy in everyday life*, Chicago: University of Chicago Press.
Deng, F. (1997) 'Information gaps and unintended outcomes of social movements: the 1989 Chinese student movement,' *American Journal of Sociology*, 102(4): 1085–112.
Denzin, N.K. (1984) *On Understanding Emotion*, San Francisco: Jossey-Bass.
Duke, M.S. (1977) *Lu You*, New York: Twayne Publishers, Inc.

Esherick, J.W. and Wasserstrom, J.N. (1990) 'Acting out democracy: political theater in modern China,' *Journal of Asian Studies*, 49: 835–65.

Flam, H. (1998) *Mosaic of Fear: Poland and East Germany before 1989*, Boulder: East European Monographs.

—— (2004) 'Anger in Repressive Regimes: a footnote to domination and the arts of resistance by James Scott,' *European Journal of Social Theory*, Special Issue on Anger in Political Life, (ed.) Mary Holmes, 7(2): 171–88.

Gamson, W. (1990) *The Strategy of Social Protest*, 2nd edn, Belmont, Calif.: Wadsworth.

Gladney, D. (2004) 'Bodily positions/social dispositions,' in *Dislocating China: Muslims, Minorities, and Other Subaltern Subjects*, Chicago: The University of Chicago Press.

Goodwin, J. (2001) *No Other Way Out: states and revolutionary movements, 1945–1991*, Cambridge: Cambridge University Press.

Goodwin, J. and Pfaff, S. (2001) 'Emotion work in high-risk social movements: managing fear in the U.S. and Eastern German civil rights movements,' in J. Goodwin, J.M. Jasper and F. Polletta (eds), *Passionate Politics*, Chicago: Chicago University Press.

Goodwin, J., Jasper, J.M. and Polletta, F. (2000) 'The return of the repressed: the fall and rise of emotions in social movement theory,' *Mobilization*, 5(1): 65–84.

—— (eds) (2001) *Passionate Politics*, Chicago: Chicago University Press.

Gordon, R.M. (1987) *The Structure of Emotions*, New York: Cambridge University Press.

Gude, E.W. (1971) 'Violence as ends, means and catharsis: political violence in Venezuela: 1958–1964,' in J.C. Davies (ed.) *When Men Revolt and Why*, New York: The Free Press.

Guthrie, D. (1995) 'Political theater and student organizations in the 1989 Chinese movement: a multivariate analysis of Tiananmen,' *Sociological Forum*, 10(3): 419–54.

Han, M. (pseudonym), (ed.) (1990) *Cries for Democracy: writings and speeches from the 1989 Chinese democracy movement*, Princeton: Princeton University Press.

Harding, H. (1998) 'The halting advance of pluralism,' *Journal of Democracy*, 9(1): 11–17.

Heider, K.G. (1991) *Landscapes of Emotion: mapping three cultures of emotion in Indonesia*, Cambridge: Cambridge University Press.

Hochschild, A.R. (1979) 'Emotion work, feeling rules and social structure,' *American Journal of Sociology*, 85: 551–75.

—— (1983) *The Managed Heart: the commercialization of human feeling*, Berkeley: University of California Press.

Jasper, J.M. (1997) *The Art of Moral Protest: culture, biography, and creativity in social movements*, Chicago: University of Chicago Press.

—— (1998) 'The emotions of protest: reactive and affective emotions in and around social movements,' *Sociological Forum*, 13: 397–424.

Jiang D. (pseudonym), (1997) 'Yinhong de liuyue.' (Blood-red June). Online. Available at: http://www.cnd.org/HXWZ/ZK97/zk124-1.hz8.htm (Accessed 8 October 1998.

Kemper, T.D. (1990) 'Social relations and emotions: a structural approach,' in T.D. Kemper (ed.) *Research Agendas in the Sociology of Emotions*, New York: SUNY Press.

Landsberger, S.R. (1990) 'Chronology of the 1989 student demonstrations,' in T. Saich (ed.) *The Chinese People's Movement: perspectives on spring 1989*, Armonk, NY: M.E. Sharpe.

Lin, N. (1992) *The Struggle for Tiananmen: anatomy of the 1989 mass movement*, Westport, Conn: Praeger.

Lo, I.Y. (1971) *Hsin Ch'i-chi*, New York: Twayne Publishers, Inc.

Lofland, J. (1995) 'Charting degrees of movement culture: tasks of the cultural cartographer,' in H. Johnston and B. Klandermas (eds) *Social Movements and Culture*, Minneapolis: University of Minnesota Press.

Lutz, C.A. (1988) *Unnatural Emotions: everyday sentiments on a Micronesian atoll and their challenge to western theory*, Chicago: University of Chicago Press.

McAdam, D. (1982) *Political Process and the Development of Black Insurgency, 1930–1970*, Chicago: University of Chicago Press.

McAdam, D., McCarthy J.D. and Zald, M.N. (1988) 'Social movements,' in N.J. Smelser (ed.) *Handbook of Sociology*, Newbury Park, CA: Sage.

McCarthy, E.D. (1989) 'Emotions are social things: an essay in the sociology of emotions,' in D. Franks and E.D. McCarthy (eds) *The Sociology of Emotions*, Greenwich, CT: JAI Press.

Mattley, C. (2002) 'The temporality of emotion: constructing past emotions,' *Symbolic Interaction*, 25(3): 363–78.

Melucci, A. (1988) 'Getting involved: identity and mobilization in social movements,' *International Social Movement Research*, 1: 329–48.

Munro, D.J. (1977) *The Concept of Man in Contemporary China*, Ann Arbor: University of Michigan Press.

Nathan, A.J. and Link, P. (eds) (2001) *The Tiananmen Papers*, compiled by Zhang Liang. London: Little, Brown.

Niming, F. [pseudonym] (1990) 'Learning how to protest,' in T. Saich (ed.) *The Chinese People's Movement: perspectives on spring 1989*, Armonk, NY: M.E. Sharpe.

Ogden, S., Hartford, K., Sullivan, L. and Zweig, D. (eds) (1992) *China's Search for Democracy: the student and the mass movement of 1989*, New York: M.E. Sharpe.

Perry, E.J. (2002) 'Moving the masses: emotion work in the Chinese Revolution,' *Mobilization*, 7(2): 111–28.

Scheff, T. (1997) *Emotions, the Social Bond, and Human Reality*, Cambridge: Cambridge University Press.

Sewell, W.H. Jr. (1992) 'A theory of structure: duality, agency, and transformation,' *American Journal of Sociology*, 98(1): 1–29.

—— (1996) 'Historical events as transformations of structures: inventing revolution at the Bastille,' *Theory and Society*, 25: 841–81.

Shen, T., with Yen, M. (1990) *Almost A Revolution*, New York: Houghton Mifflin.

Shott, S. (1979) 'Emotion and social life: a symbolic interactionist analysis,' *American Journal of Sociology*, 84: 1317–34.

Snow, D.A., Zurcher, L.A. and Peters, R. (1981) 'Victory celebrations as theater: a dramaturgical approach to crowd behavior,' *Symbolic Interaction*, 4(1): 21–42.

Stearns, C.Z. and Stearns, P. (1986) *Anger: the struggle for emotional control in America's history*, Chicago: University of Chicago Press.

Tianhua (pseudonym), (1994) 'Bajiu xueyun de riri yeye-yiwei Qinghua xuezi de jingli, jianwen' (The Days and Nights of the 89 Student Movement, as experienced and seen by a Qinghua University Student), Online. Available at: http://www.cnd.org/HXWZ/ZK94/zk39–1.hz8.htm (Accessed 2 June 1998).

Turner, V. (1969) *The Ritual Process: structure and anti-structure*, New York: Aldine Publishing Co.

Wasserstrom, J.N. (1990) 'Student protests and the Chinese tradition, 1919–1989,' in T. Saich (ed.) *The Chinese People's Movement: perspectives on spring 1989*, Armonk, NY: M.E. Sharpe.

Yang, G. (2000a) 'The liminal effects of social movements: Red Guards and the transformation of identity,' *Sociological Forum*, 15(2): 379–406.

—— (2000b) 'Achieving emotions in collective action: emotional processes and movement mobilization in the 1989 Chinese student movement,' *The Sociological Quarterly*, 41(4): 593–614.

—— (2002) 'Civil society in China: a dynamic field of study,' *China Review International*, 9(2): 1–16.

Yang, L. (1957) 'The concept of "pao" as a basis for social relations in China,' in J.K. Fairbank (ed.) *Chinese Thought and Institutions*, Chicago: University of Chicago Press.

Yu, M.C. and Harrison, J.F. (eds) (1990) *Voices from Tiananmen Square: Beijing spring and the democracy movement*, Montreal: Black Rose Books.

Zhang L. compiled (2001) *Zhongguo liusi zhenxiang* (June Fourth: The True Story), 2 vols. Hong Kong: Mingjing chubanshe.

Zhao, D. (2001) *The Power of Tiananmen*, Chicago: The University of Chicago Press.

Zolberg, A.R. (1972) 'Moments of madness,' *Politics and Society*, 3(Winter): 183–207.

Zurcher, L.A. (1982) 'The staging of emotion: a dramaturgical analysis,' *Symbolic Interaction*, 5(1): 1–22.

Zweig, D. (1992) 'Introduction to part IV: May 12–May 19,' in S. Ogden, K. Hartford, L. Sullivan and D. Zweig (eds) *China's Search for Democracy: The Student and the Mass Movement of 1989*, New York: M.E. Sharpe.

6 Mobilization and the moral shock

Adbusters Media Foundation

Åsa Wettergren

Introduction

Emotions structure and drive social action. This might be a banal insight but nevertheless emotions are still considered suspect in contemporary social science, let alone in the study of social movements. While rational calculation and cognitive aspects of meaning and identity have long occupied the research focus, interest is increasingly turning to the role of emotions (See e.g. Jasper 1998; Calhoun 2001; Goodwin *et al.* 2001).

This development opens up a world of new ways to understand social movements, both regarding the old questions of how and why social movements come into existence and fade away, their relative success or failure, as well as regarding seemingly less important details that surround them such as social movement posters and visuals. Looking at emotions in social movement mobilization further seem to be fruitful in dealing with movements that do not quite fit the traditional pattern of either resource mobilization and redistribution or identity politics (Melucci 1985, 1996; Tarrow 1994; Fraser 1995).

My interest in 'the culture jamming movement' promoted by the Adbusters Media Foundation (AMF) was triggered by their production of sophisticated 'spoof-ads' and 'uncommercials'. Their unusual employment of marketing techniques as a mobilizing strategy could be easily discarded as dubious, but merits a closer look. The question addressed in this chapter is therefore: how can emotion theory enhance the understanding of the AMF visuals as tools for mobilization? In the analysis I will draw on the idea of the 'moral shock' (Jasper 1998; Goodwin *et al.* 2001) and 'sacred objects' (Collins 1990; Durkheim 1994) in combination with the concept of 'symptom' in Lacanian psychoanalysis (Zizek 1989; Evans 1996). The empirical material consists of a sample of spoof-ads and uncommercials[1] as well as Kalle Lasn's book *Culture Jam – the uncooling of America* (1999).

The AMF and the field of culture jamming

Social movements are primarily social constructions and constructions of analysis (Melucci 1985, 1996; Castells 1997; Thörn 1997a). The empirical presence of a potential social movement can be observed because of the *space of interaction around specific contested issues* that it creates between social actors such as groups, organizations and institutions (Eyerman and Jamison 1991; Tarrow 1994). This space of interaction is a discursive space, one that allows for repressed or new discourses[2] to compete with the dominating discourses in society at large thus threatening the hegemonic status of the latter. This space is, however, also a space of inner tensions and identity conflicts.

Founded in 1989 by ex-marketing man Kalle Lasn, the AMF is one of many organizations and groups engaged in culture jamming. Culture jamming is symbolic contentious politics, largely contingent on affluent consumer culture. The contested issue that unites culture jammers is the question of democracy and public space in the context of late capitalism and information society. The control of public space by corporate interests and the commercial mass media is seen to threaten freedom of expression. As an integral part of the protest, jammers question the way the media work, in particular, how they allocate voices to powerful economic interests in society while excluding the majority of the people from serious public debate (Wettergren 2003a, 2003b). Culture jamming is a protest strategy that targets central symbols of dominant discourses, deconstructs them and reintroduces them in alternative contexts, the aim being to reveal their contingency and political/ideological content. Often – as in the AMF case – the targeted symbols are symbols of consumer society and late capitalism, such as corporate logos and advertisement.

The AMF – commonly called the Adbusters – is among the most well-known organizations associated with the concept of culture jamming. Based in Vancouver, Canada, it produces and distributes the Adbusters Magazine, which is non-profit, reader-supported and said to have a circulation of 120,000 copies worldwide (http://adbusters.org/information/foundation/10/02/2004). The organization apparently involves just a handful of active people, with Lasn as the official front figure (and editor of the Adbusters Magazine).

The www.adbusters.org website contains information about AMF, the main projects, goals and means. It also offers various products, including the magazine (recent articles can be downloaded from the website for free), for sale. It is possible to sign up to 'the culture jammers network' and receive information about ongoing activities and calls for participation through the organizing of parallel local events. Culture jamming, we are told here: 'can be to our era what civil rights was to '60s, what feminism was to the '70s, what environmental activism was to the '80s. It will alter the way we live and think.' (http://adbusters.org/information/network/ 10/02/2004).

The visitor is also informed about the organization's 'Powershift advocacy advertising agency', which produces and distributes posters, spoof-ads, post-cards, and uncommercials. Powershift also runs annual campaigns such as 'Buy Nothing Day' and 'Turn off TV Week'.

The representative position taken by the AMF in the field[3] of culture jamming is self-appointed. In this way it stands apart from most of the other groups related to culture jamming which keep away from the articulation of a movement discourse and instead prefer to embrace ambiguity on this point.[4] The following analysis of the construction and use of emotions in culture jamming pertains exclusively to the AMF discourse. However, the analysis illustrates the basic principles of culture jamming in the sense that many groups work with visuals in ways similar to the AMF and all groups use *détourned* (altered, see below) consumer objects as symbols of resistance.

Spoof-ads and uncommercials in context

Spoof-ads and uncommercials are the products of a strategic idea – *détournement* – inherited from the Situationists.[5] In Lasn's vocabulary *détournement* is a general strategy that involves reframing of interaction between 'human beings' and 'corporate machines'.[6] When *détournement* is used in its literal meaning of 'turning around' and applied to corporate symbols such as advertisements, it is also called 'subvertising' – a technique to use the corporations' own means and messages against them. This technique is said to be liberating in two senses: first, it damages 'the brand recognition' of the company and second this subversion brings pleasure and satisfaction to the culture jammer because it is 'fun' and 'exhilarating' (Lasn 1999: 130). Examples of spoof-ads and uncommercials can be seen on the website, and they are available for sale as postcards, posters and videocassettes. The spoof-ads are reproduced in the Adbusters Magazine, but they can also be seen in ordinary fashion/hype magazines and other conventional contexts, as the AMF buys space for their spoof-ads just like any commercial company. The uncommercials are occasionally broadcasted on CNN.[7] The money required buying space for the spoof-ads and uncommercials are collected from supporters' gifts and purchases.

These spoof-ads and uncommercials are best understood in the context of the general movement discourse constructed by Lasn in his book *Culture Jam – the uncooling of America* (Lasn 1999). The book locates the main grievances, such as the alienation of postmodern culture for which Lasn uses other words such as 'mental pollution', the main opponents (the large corporations or the corporate machine), descriptions of the action needed to change this (culture jamming), and fragments of a utopian vision (post-consumer society, sustainable growth, 'authentic' culture). It offers the reader a subject position as 'a culture jammer', and jammers are in turn described as a front-troop whose main achievement is to raise public consciousness about the movements' issues. Once the critical mass is attained, the people will carry the revolution against the tyranny of the corporations and the commercial culture.

The spoof-ads and uncommercials are examples of such consciousness-raising techniques – they are expected to force the viewer out of her/his everyday routine. In *Culture Jam* Lasn explains that an uncommercial works as '. . . a "mindbomb" because of how it explodes in the collective psyche, sending out shock waves of cognitive dissonance' (Lasn 1999: 133). Uncommercials and spoof-ads are therefore viewed as being an effective means of consciousness-raising. Lasn certainly emphasizes the *cognitive* effect of the visuals, but large parts of *Culture Jam* are dedicated to the problem of 'suppressed emotions' in consumer culture and Lasn repeatedly asserts that we may or should feel shame, guilt, disgust, anger/rage, joy, hope and pride at different occasions. Though this may not prove a conscious insight into the emotive aspect of cognition, I will argue that the AMF visuals are loaded with emotions and that it is this that makes them effective.

The centrality of the AMF visuals

Social movement studies usually focus upon *people* – the movement adherents and their internal relationships as well as their relations to bystanders and opponents. As far as the concrete products of social movements are concerned – though texts may also be studied (e.g. Thörn 1997a, 1997b) – the use of *visuals*, such as political posters, in social movement mobilization has had remarkably little attention. As Haunss argues: 'Political posters usually are the fleeting companions of social movements. They serve as means for communication, propaganda, self-representation, information and mobilization. Political posters are messages in the public space' (Haunss 2003).[8]

In the case of the AMF, the visuals are more than just odd political posters. My choice to focus on them was first of all motivated by the fact that the movement promoted by the AMF is largely mediated. It consists of a network of disparate groups in various places, scattered all over the world. Characteristic for culture jammers is that they do *not* organize demonstrations and other large collective gatherings as per traditional movement organizations. The visuals displayed globally in the mass media and on the internet are therefore often the only visible sign of the movement.

Second, the visuals were interesting from the perspective of social relationships, status and power. The visuals then function like consumer objects, connoting certain lifestyles or habitus (Bourdieu 1999; Featherstone 1998). I have argued elsewhere that the culture jammers seem to be located in the social stratum of cultural intermediaries or 'new-media culture intellectuals' of the 'live and wild zones' of information society (Lash 2002), which renders them a certain aura of avant-garde among contemporary social movement activists and non-activists alike (Wettergren 2003a; 2003b). The AMF visuals are generally admired in the world of design and marketing (Klein 1999) as they are professional products, requiring a certain level of aesthetic and cultural knowledge in both production and consumption. Representing a certain social status then, the visuals function as watersheds, dividing those that 'get it' from those that do not. This in turn gives rise to positive or negative emotions.

The AMF visuals communicate emotions in yet another more obvious way. As subverted ads and commercials, they take a free ride on the construction of pleasurable fantasies created by the contemporary consumer culture (Featherstone 1998). Like the ads, the AMF visuals communicate directly to the viewer's emotions and the pleasure of immersion into the fantasy and desire of consumer objects. But the AMF visuals disturb the fantasy; where the viewer expects to find pleasure s/he is instead urged to question the meaning of this 'normal' consumer practice. Instead of pleasure the viewer may experience shame and guilt. As a consequence the strength of the spoof-ads and uncommercials may be that they upset the taken-for-granted relationship between subjects and objects in consumer culture. There is a discrepancy between what they seem to be and what they really are. This discrepancy can give rise to emotions that demand an active reconstruction of meaning.

Emotions in spoof-ads and uncommercials

In this section I will first discuss the ironic mode of the AMF visuals around the example of a 'funny' spoof-ad and then proceed to show how the AMF shapes the emotional response of the viewer by withdrawing humour from irony, introducing guilt and shame. Finally I will discuss the construction of guilt, shame and disgust in two examples that are almost free from the ironic mode.

The construction of pleasure through humour and irony

Irony is a mode of communication that produces emotions – and cognition. Irony can be recognized in three ways: first, there is 'the figure of verbal irony as meaning the opposite of what is said'; second, there is 'dramatic irony as the discrepancy between expectation and result, or the discrepancy between the appearance of a situation and its underlying reality'; and third, irony denotes 'a dominant dialectic mode of thought that permeates the text and thus makes it contradictory, or ambiguous' (Wennö 1993: 8). The Benetton spoof-ad in Figure 6.1 is ironic primarily in a dramatic way – in its fusion between *the form* of conventional advertising with the AMF's *message* of moral condemnation. The message is not

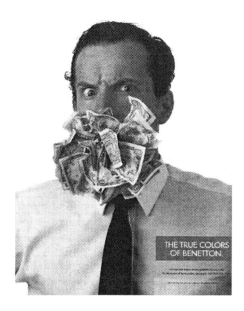

Figure 6.1 'The True Colors Of Benetton' (www.adbusters.org).

hidden but quite clear, so it is advertising against advertising that is ironic. Cognitively, the viewer will understand the act of using the Benetton ad to convey a message about the ruthless exploitation by Benetton as interesting.

Well-fed as most Westerners are with the connotations of the original Benetton campaign that this image reverses (an open-minded, tolerant, multicultural and multiethnic society of young mixed couples, etc), s/he may recognize that the spoof-ad reveals the double nature of the Benetton campaign. Emotionally, irony as a mode of communication has a humorous effect due to the reversal of perspectives. It produces (pleasant) laughter. This use of irony and humour is common to most culture jams.[9] Studying the role of humour in culture jamming Woodside suggests that it generally serves as 'an escape route' if a message runs the risk of breaching a taboo (Woodside 2001: 17). Revealing the double nature of the Benetton campaign indeed points toward *the irony of the Benetton campaign* whose underlying reality is white, male and greedy. This underlying reality is not unfamiliar to any western consumer, it is rather the irony of all commercial campaigns, perhaps the irony of consumer culture. The taboo then is about facing this problem, rather than ignoring it, and humour thus breaches the defence against 'moral lectures'. Humour generates positive emotions that pave the way for a positive reception of the message.

However, when used as means to convey messages, irony and humour entail two problems: the message about the true colours of Benetton in itself is not ironic but because of the ironic mode it runs the risk of being read as such. *Détournement* applied to ads is an ironic strategy and, as Wennö notices, the effect of the ironic demonstration is inherently self-critical and therefore runs the risk of subverting its own position. 'Irony, then, by pretending to say one thing while meaning something else, *remains sceptical to the truth of both* since it invites dubiety of both' (emphasis added, Wennö, 1993: 8). The Benetton spoof-ad may be seen as merely a joke, at the utmost conveying the message that reality is multifaceted and depends on which position you take. The 'truth' is therefore nothing more than a matter of effective marketing strategies. This would undermine the truth claim held by the AMF.

Second, the understanding of irony between sender and receiver presumes shared knowledge and experience (Hochschild 1983: 79–80; Wahl *et al.* 1998). Provided that the images speak *from* a certain social and cultural position *to* the same position, the message will be recognized, detected and result in laughter. Pleasure and satisfaction will be derived as the viewer 'gets it' and, in this moment, identifies with the apparently cool people who produced this playful comment upon Benetton. In general, and depending on how difficult the decoding of it may be, understanding a spoof-ad may confirm social group-belonging along with the status and power associated with its position[10] (Collins 1990, 2001; Kemper 2001).

Following the above, the image may also produce a slight sense of guilt. Perhaps one reason why people are uncomfortable with 'moral lectures', guilt signals that the message implies an *Other* who is being exploited by Benetton. Exploitation does not concern *us* who 'know' that the Benetton campaign is not about celebrating multiculturalism but about money-making. However, *we* can play along with a multicultural fantasy without obligations by buying Benetton branded clothes. Again, such an accusation may be resolved by the ambiguity of irony and the laughter it produces.

Though many spoof-ads follow the same pattern, the AMF seems to distinguish themselves from other producers of spoof-ads by a tendency to move from the construction of pleasure toward guilt or shame. The following examples illustrate how the ironic mode may be used in spoof-ads and uncommercials to produce this effect.

Construction of shame and guilt through the ironic mode

Irony, in its juxtaposition of incompatible stances, will appear humorous but may produce an opposite effect. Irony thus deceives the viewer, because, like a joke, it may incite laughter, but the laughter of irony may lead to feelings of shame and guilt. One example of this is represented by the Smirkoff spoof-ad in Figure 6.2.

The original campaign for Smirnoff vodka offered various imaginative fantasies of what happens to reality when seen through the Smirnoff

Figure 6.2 'Wipe that Smirkoff' (www.adbusters.org).

bottle. In the spoof-ad, Smirnoff is changed into Smirkoff. To smirk is to smile or laugh scornfully. We see ordinary apparently happy kids, but through the vodka bottle we are invited to see the *truth* of vodka: child-abuse and violence in families with alcoholic parents. The spoof-ad suggests that the producers of vodka smirk at the abused child. They make profit out of the little girl's tragedy.

But the image also suggests that *the viewer* smirks at the abused child. Indeed, together with the smaller prints above the subverted logo the text of this spoof-ad tells the viewer to: 'wipe that Smirkoff'. The viewer is being trapped between incompatible emotions of pleasure deriving from the funny ironic composition and shame or guilt because of the tragic content. S/he is urged to make a (uneasy?) choice. If s/he laughs, s/he identifies with a reckless and abusive consumer culture in which alcohol is glorified and its consequences ignored. If s/he takes the image seriously s/he must at least question the use of alcohol, alcohol advertising and her/his own position towards alcohol. As most people are not total abstainers, such a questioning could lead to more general reflections upon exploitation and manipulation of consumer needs and demands.

My next example, *Obsession Fetish* (see spoof-ad version in Figure 6.3), is a 30 second reversed Calvin Klein commercial. It is meant to protest the beauty industry, embodied in Lasn's writings by the Calvin Klein Company.

Following the original, *Obsession Fetish* appears to play on sex and beauty. The actors are a well-built man in underwear and a thin naked

Figure 6.3 Spoof-ad version of *Obsession Fetish* (www.adbusters.org).

woman seen from behind. Isolated words like 'obsession', 'fascination', 'preoccupation', 'fetish' and 'fragmentation' come up on screen and are pronounced by a voice-over. The man peeks into his underpants when the word 'obsession' comes up. Switching into the image of the naked woman's 'undulating' back, the music is accompanied by heavy sighs. Then she leans over a toilet and throws up. The *truth* is suddenly clear and the perspective of the viewer changes: she's not beautifully thin, she's emaciated, and she's not enjoying sex, she's throwing up a meal. The voice-over comments: 'why are 9 out of 10 women dissatisfied with some aspect of their own bodies?' The woman lies down naked on a sofa looking right into the camera, eyes dark. The sentence 'The Beauty Industry is the Beast' emerges on screen.

Obsession Fetish may deceive the inattentive viewer at first even if it almost directly appears to have something 'wrong' with it. The bodies have warts and beauty spots and seem clumsy; there is a slight dissonance between their movements and the music beat that accompanies the picture. The man's anxiety about his penis appears ridiculous. When the woman starts puking it is clear to everyone that this is not an ordinary commercial. In the end the viewer is positioned as part of the 'sadistic gaze' of the camera.

Similar to the Smirkoff spoof-ad, the ironic mode of *Obsession Fetish* gives rise to confusing emotions. It is possible to laugh at the ironic reversal of the CK commercial but laughing at a bulimic or a poor guy with penis obsession would give rise to guilt and shame. Kemper (2001) suggests that guilt is a feeling of power abuse. Guilt would here derive from the fact that the viewer represents the cynical laughter or the sadistic gaze of ruthless consumer culture. Shame on the other hand, though closely related to guilt, arises from the returned gaze. Shame is the self-reflective emotion in which the subject evaluates her/his own behaviour from the standpoint of others (Scheff 1990) and is evoked here by the silent accusation in the gaze of the battered child or the bulimic. *Obsession Fetish* finally evokes disgust – 'a revulsion at certain organic substances' (Gordon 1990: 157) due to the painful impression of the imperfect bodies and the puking woman. Disgust is an emotion that dominates in the AMF uncommercial that I will proceed to analyse next.

Shame, guilt, disgust and fear – minus the ironic mode

The following two examples show how unpleasant emotions are evoked without using the ironic mode of subverting well-known ad campaigns. The uncommercial *Buy Nothing Day* promotes an annual event. It opens with the image of an enormous, obese pig, covering the whole of North America. It grunts and burps and licks its lips, insatiably greedy. The voice-over declares that 'the average North American consumes five times more than a Mexican, ten times more than a Chinese person, and thirty times more than a person from India'. The pig burps loud and long and the picture is cut to enormous waste mountains. The voice explains that American over consumption threatens to kill this planet. Finally we see planet Earth with a sick yellowish aura around it, sinking back into space. The voice advices 'give it a rest. November 28 is Buy Nothing Day'.

The pig is a cultural symbol of voraciousness that may be used in exclamations of disgust and repulsion of other's behaviour, suggesting, for example, that the person we call a pig should be ashamed. There is no victim to shame the viewer in *Buy Nothing Day*, but as a western consumer the film suggests that s/he identifies with the pig and is ashamed. Fear is evoked by the image of uncontrollable waste growth together with the perspective of a *yellow* planet in the universe. A sense of powerlessness may be kept under control and our self-confidence restored however by taking part in *Buy Nothing Day*.

In my final example, *The Product is You*, the viewer is the victim. Here, we meet a man in his late 30's catatonically stuck in front of the TV, zapping. The room is dark, the only light source is the TV-screen. From the TV a voice shouts cheerfully 'there's never been a better time to buy!' then gunshots and police sirens from another channel. The background music is low-key and threatening. The camera moves from the front, facing the man, in a half circle to stop behind him, close up on his neck, which is marked with a barcode. The voice-over follows this camera move declaring, 'your living room is the factory. The product being manufactured ... is *you*'. The picture of the bar-coded man switches into a black screen with the sentence: 'cast off the chains of market structured consciousness!'

The man evokes disgust because he is reduced to a piece of meat or raw material in the production of consumers for sale in the advertising and mass media industry. The lurking dooms-day scenario is frightening. There is a surprising change in perspective from identification to objectification when we see the barcode on the man's neck and hear the voice-over claim that 'the product is *you*'. The viewer who may already be struggling not to identify with passive TV watching, is now urged to look at her/himself from this shame-inducing perspective.

The examples analysed here show a tendency to move from a humorous approach that allows for ambiguous tension to be resolved in laughter, toward an approach that evokes unpleasant emotions and directly accuses or shames the viewer. The pig in *Buy Nothing Day* is funny only until the viewer realizes that *s/he* is the pig. Further, the visuals do not all make use of the ironic mode of reversing well-known ad campaigns, but the fact that they are part of a marketing campaign against consumption and may appear in an advertising space, still makes them ironic and therefore ambiguous. My point is that the remaining ambiguity, while leaving the truth claim of the AMF intact, accentuates the unpleasant emotions evoked because when ambiguity is not resolved in laughter it becomes unsettling. There is no doubt that the AMF visuals aim to affect the audience, to 'move' them in some way. This form of mobilization relates to the notion of 'moral shock'.

The meaning of shock in mobilization

Everyone who has taken part in social movement mobilization will know that identity in terms of readiness to *adopt and act* upon ideas – no matter how convincingly argued – is peculiarly inert. People remain in a state of 'cynical reason' in which 'they know that, in their activity, they are following an illusion, but still, they are doing it' (Zizek 1989: 33).

Kalle Lasn and the AMF are also aware of the problem. 'Postmodern cynicism is rage that can no longer get it up. It is powerlessness, disconnection and *shame*' (emphasis added, Lasn 1999: 141). We have seen that the AMF visuals repeatedly shame the viewer for her/his role in consumer culture. Not surprisingly shame is also central in Lasn's book. On the one hand trying to understand the lack of engagement against consumer culture, Lasn resorts to a theory of manipulation. The commercial mass media are likened to a 'hypodermic needle' that gradually poisons unaware people, 'manipulating our emotions, making powerful new connections between deep immaterial needs and material products' (Lasn 1999: 12). On the other hand, being a victim of manipulation is a shameful condition. Before we return to this point however, we need to take a closer look at what kind of obstacle cynicism really poses to social movement actors.

Giddens (1995) writes about cynicism as being 'a mode of dampening the emotional impact of anxieties through either a humorous or world-weary response to them' (Giddens 1995: 136). In Giddens' typology of adaptive reactions to the awareness of risk (1995: 134–7), 'cynical pessimism' implies a stance where the cynicism makes pessimism bearable 'because of its emotionally neutralizing nature and because of its potential for humour' (1995: 137). Mainly because of its pessimism, cynical pessimism is not a formula for action or radical engagement, but a practical adaptation to the emotional strains of risk awareness.

But cynicism need not only be the result of unbearable pessimism or powerlessness. It could be a normal everyday arrangement to human beings. Zizek explains cynical reason in terms of the *ideological fantasy*, 'the overlooked unconscious illusion that structures reality', i.e. not our *thoughts* about reality, but our interaction with it. This statement pertains to the impossible 'fullness' of the subject. Put simply, humans live the illusion that *the real* (me) is possible to capture within the parameters of the symbolic. However, no matter how many discourses produced (and the real is the *raison d'être* of discourse), the real remains an evasive dimension that like a black hole of nothingness threatens the social construction of meaning. *Identity* is a discursive construction that permits us to live the illusion. Identity requires the construction of the *Other* who is perceived as perfect, a projection of our desire for a whole subject. In the relation to the (perfect) Other, we create our own identity through processes of identification and differentiation (Jörgensen and Phillips 1999; Zizek 1989). In this context moreover there is no difference between ideology and discourse – they both offer subject positions that makes the construction of illusionary wholeness and identity possible.

While identity provides 'enjoyment-in-sense' (Zizek 1989: 75), a loss of meaning altogether would of course be a terrifying anxiety-ridden condition. Thus, as Hochschild puts it from the perspective of emotion theory 'individuals *hold* ideology' (1990: 127) and they hold it with 'emotional anchors' (1990: 128). Goodwin, Jasper and Polletta also emphasize that 'the "strength" of an identity . . . comes from its emotional side' (Goodwin *et al.* 2001: 9). Berezin's (2001) study of Italian fascism further emphasizes the importance of emotions in the construction of political identities.

This connection between emotions and identity shows the necessity of employing emotion theory in the study of social movement mobilization. Lacanian psychoanalysis is fruitful because it provides us with a complementary theory of *how* identity is so strongly emotionally laden. While the inertia of identity appears to rest upon a banal cynicism or laziness connected to the comfortably organized routine of everyday life, the structure of everyday life is a fragile construction that covers up a terrifying void. Hence the feelings of outrage when routine is disturbed, questioned or devastated (Calhoun 2001: 54; Collins 1990; Schütz 1976).[11]

The inertia of identity requires that movement actors literally *move* people. At the base of politically contentious action lies a strong sense of injustice together with moral anger or outrage at the social causes of the injustice (Moore, Jr 1978). Gamson (1992) writes that the collective action frame offered by a social movement has to contain an 'injustice component' that triggers moral indignation. The injustice frame 'is not merely a cognitive or intellectual judgment about what is equitable but also ... a *hot cognition* – one that is laden with emotion' (Gamson 1992: 7). Arguing for a stronger emphasis on emotions in the study of social movements, Jasper (1998) takes this point further in asserting that the 'moral shock' is an important first step in mobilization. A moral shock 'occurs when an unexpected event or piece of information raises such a sense of outrage in a person that she becomes inclined toward political action ...' (Jasper 1998: 409). The concept of moral shock differs from that of an injustice frame in that the former does not require the presence of a movement discourse. The moral shock may take place outside, and irrespective of, a social movement but it needs to lead to engagement in order to render the shocking experience meaningful. Whether an individual or a collective experience, the moral shock may give rise to 'an identity crisis resolved through political commitment' (Moore, Jr 1978: 114). In discourse theory terms, the dislocation of identity (Torfing 1999) that results from a moral shock detaches people from taken-for-granted everyday life and forces them to *renegotiate* identity. The movement discourse then offers reconstructed subject positions/identity.

It follows that movement actors also may try to construct moral shocks in order to make people adopt an injustice frame. In this effort visuals are effective tools because they address emotions directly, they can speak for themselves and circulate in the mass media disconnected from context. Such is the logic behind the AMF visuals and their 'mind bomb' effect. Their goal is to shock the viewer by tapping the fantasy that structures the cynical attachment to postmodern living. The emotional confusion that results can force the viewer to reconstruct meaning through questioning the message and her/his own position in relation to it.

Cognitive framing and the lack of it

Human beings are not inclined to act upon injustices and suffering unless they perceive them as *socially* caused (Moore, Jr 1978; Gamson 1992). Hence, the cognitive framing of a social movement and the construction of a collective identity is about changing people's perspective and definitions of the social world so that it is possible to see these social causes and to question the moral authority of those responsible. The construction of a collective identity and of collective action frames is a well-studied subject in social movement research, from various theoretical angles (Gamson 1992; Melucci 1985, 1996; Tarrow 1994; Thörn 1997a, 1997b).

From the perspective of emotion theory the cognitive frame not only constructs identity but helps perform the emotion work that will turn emotions of powerlessness like fear, anxiety and shame into emotions that inspire action, e.g. anger, hope and pride (Britt and Heise 2000; Gould 2001; Hochschild 1979, 1990; Kemper 2001; Stein 2001). As a consequence the emotional culture of a movement is likely to run against the dominant emotional culture (Hercus 1999; Thoits 1990). Lasn's repeated claims that consumer culture *manipulates our real emotions* indicate that the culture jamming movement is, indeed, partly about breaking dominant emotion rules (Stearns 1994).

While shame is not an emotion that directly inspires action, it may give rise to anger, which is potentially action-oriented (Scheff 1990). Like the AMF visuals, Lasn's book *Culture Jam* offers numerous attempts at shaming the audience. Especially in his version of the American history (Lasn 1999: 65–72), Lasn juxtaposes pride (that used to characterize the once free American people) with shame (that characterize present slavery under the corporate machine). He argues that common social and psychological problems such as burn out, chronic fatigue, depression and other mental disorders are the results of repressed emotions. The way out is the liberation of repressed emotions, the acknowledgement of shame and then rage against the corporate machine. 'Rage is a signal like pain or lust. If you learn to trust it and ride shot-gun on it, watching it without suppressing it, you gain power and *loose cynicism*' (Lasn 1999: 143). 'There's an anger, a rage-driven defiance, that is healthy, ethical and empowering. It contains the conviction that *change is possible . . .*' (1999: 143). What can be observed here is a frame transformation in three steps: first, people must see that they live in shame and that the shame-agent is the corporate machine, second, this should make them angry, and third, anger will lead to revolt. To Lasn, the essence of human nature is 'the desire to be free and unfettered', so the reconnection to real selves and real lives through the free flow of emotions would mean accepting 'the revolutionary impulse' (Lasn 1999).

The visuals and the book *Culture Jam* target the same kind of emotions but unlike the book – which is most likely purchased by people already interested in culture jamming – the visuals appear disconnected from the movement discourse. Apart from the name 'The Media Foundation' or 'The Adbusters Media Foundation' and a telephone number, there is no further information about the organization. Directed at a mass audience unfamiliar with the AMF, the visuals appear as messages from an unknown Other who poses the very unpleasant question: *Who are you?* Questioning the subject threatens to expose the void of identity (Zizek 1989), withdrawing status from the subject and inducing shame and self-disgust. This can be resolved by identification with any of the subject positions offered. 'The process of interpellation-subjectivation is precisely an attempt to elude, to avoid this traumatic kernel through identification: in assuming a symbolic mandate, *in recognizing himself in the interpellation*, the subject evades the dimension of the Thing' (emphasis added, Zizek, 1989: 181).

In the humorous and ironic Benetton spoof-ad any western middle-class person with a reasonable cultural capital and familiar with the original Benetton campaign may understand the image as an ironic joke and leave it at that. As we have seen irony may be double-edged and this spoof-ad allows for cynicism to prevail. But visuals like the Smirkoff spoof-ad and the *Obsession Fetish* uncommercial offer the unpleasant subject position of a perpetrator (who laughs) if the viewer does not reject ambiguity and identifies with the protest against alcohol and the beauty industry. There is a third possibility, however: the viewer may restore her/his self-esteem by reversing the accusation and turn shame and guilt into righteous anger at *the producers* of the message, seeing *them* as cynical since they (ab)use innocent victims for their cause. While such a reaction seems to undermine mobilization to the movement (Kemper 2001: 71), it may still serve the purpose of the AMF because it is an emotional response that upsets the cynical arrangements of everyday life.

In the uncommercials *Buy Nothing Day* and *The Product is You* the viewer is also offered unpleasant subject positions such as perpetrator or victim, and the lack of the ironic mode makes it hard for her/him to turn the accusation around. The unpleasant emotions of shame and disgust are likely to linger on even if s/he tries to shake them off. Again, it may be this negative emotional memory that fulfils the goal by disturbing a taken for granted relationship to consumption. It is also possible that repeated exposure to such visuals would eventually push the viewer to find out more about the AMF.

The AMF discourse and the reasoning about repressed emotions in Lasn's book suggests that *the lack* of cognitive framing is not accidental. All the visuals, whether they are composed in the ironic mode or not, display a surprising change in moods and perspectives. Surprise is 'a frequent tool in rituals of teasing and challenging other people, and is also a tactic for detecting someone's spontaneous feelings by catching them off guard' (Gordon 1990: 156–7). According to Lasn, the real and authentic (spontaneous) emotions about postmodern living are first shame, then anger or rage. The moral shock, then, ought to make the viewer reconnect with these emotions and *people will naturally revolt*. The cognitive frame is superfluous if truth is taken to be obvious when we see it.

We should remember that while emotions are explicitly focused upon in Lasn's discourse, he talks about the *cognitive* effect of the visuals (see quote p. 102). They are conceived to have a consciousness-raising function and the idea of consciousness-raising denotes primarily a cognitive process in which 'issues of conscience objectively exist and persons only need to have their consciousness expanded to focus on them' (Collins 2001: 32). I suggest that the AMF holds a truth claim both regarding true emotions and true cognition, but not necessarily in that order. Analysis shows that emotional impulses are needed to achieve cognitive rearrangements (and that the AMF visuals are constructed this way), but from the AMF standpoint it may rather be the cognitive rearrangements that will free the emotions.

Besides the consciousness raising function of moral shocks vis-à-vis bystanders, the AMF visuals also serve the purpose of reinforcing and confirming protest identity for the already mobilized culture jammers. In my last section I will turn to the dimension of the visuals as sacred objects/symptoms.

The AMF visuals as sacred objects/symptoms

In Durkheim's classic study of religious life, the totem symbolizes the divine principle and the clan. The totem as a symbol inscribed in certain objects renders these objects sacred and central in collective rituals (Durkheim 1994). Collins elaborates on the emotional dimension of Durkheim's ritual interaction, arguing that in its constitution of group belonging, shared values and solidarity, it generates 'emotional energy', which is both invested in and derived from the collective focus upon sacred objects (Collins 1990, 2001). When away from ritual encounters, individuals can be energized and motivated by the emotionally charged sacred objects of the group (Collins 1990).

I suggest that the Lacanian concept of *symptom* parallels and deepens the understanding of the sacred object. The sacred object appears as a symptom – 'the substance of enjoyment, the *real* kernel around which [the] signifying interplay is structured' (Zizek 1989: 72). It contains the dimension of the overlooked unconscious illusion that structures the subject's enjoyment-in-sense (Evans 1996: 189).[12] The sacred object then is the real manifestation of illusory identity and meaning (the totem). It not only embodies and confirms group identity, but like the symptom it is also a ciphered message directed toward the Other who is assumed to know its meaning (Evans 1996: 204; Zizek 1989).

This reasoning puts the AMF visuals at the centre of the movement discourse constructed by Lasn, embodying the kernel of movement identity while organizing the enjoyment of being a culture jammer. Directed towards adherents, the emotionally charged visuals hold and confirm the jammer's identity as a protester against the fantasy that structures postmodern living. The jammer is able to immediately frame the message and relate to it with positive emotions. Hence, as the culture jamming movement is made up of disparate groups as well as individuals, and, as they do not so far make use of manifestations and other large collective gatherings to confirm a collective identity, the visuals may serve as a substitute for other interaction rituals producing emotional contagion (Collins 1990). The adherent escapes the subject positions offered to non-adherents, i.e. perpetrator (guilt/shame) or victim (shame/anger/disgust). Instead s/he will feel energized and strengthened and the emotions s/he experiences will be pleasure and satisfaction due to her/his identification with the group behind the visuals, and relief because this puts her/him beyond blame.

Finally, the visuals contain a message to the advertising industry and 'the corporate machine' that can be read, 'we know how you do it, and we can do it better'. Thus projecting the fantasy of perfection onto the corporate machine confirms the identity of the AMF and their choice of subvertising as a technique for consciousness-raising. It is ultimately the power of the Other that renders power and meaning to culture jamming as contentious politics.

Summary and concluding reflections

This chapter started out by considering how emotion theory can enhance the understanding of the AMF visuals as tools for mobilization. The examples analysed suggest that the AMF visuals are designed to produce a moral shock in the viewer. The intention is to *expand* consciousness and make her/him reconnect with her/his *true* emotions about consumer culture and slavery under the corporate machine: shame, disgust and anger. The visuals also function as emotionally charged sacred objects/symptoms that epitomize the protest identity and group belonging of the culture jammer. In this case the visuals may evoke emotions like pleasure, pride and joy. In the same move the identity of the Other, and its power and status, is confirmed.

The analysis suggests that visuals may play an important role in the mobilizing and consciousness-raising strategies of a movement, especially when it comes to stirring up emotions. It further suggests that emotions hold identity at a depth that makes it hard to mobilize bystanders only with rational arguments. The moral shock may be a first step toward mobilization, and it may be the effect of a movement's mobilizing strategies as well as a single or a series of events taking place outside of the movement discourse. People join social movements when they feel insecure and face a loss of meaning and identity. If this is true, it could explain why mobilization may occur when political opportunity structures (Tarrow 1994) are manifestly *not* open (Gould 2001). One could argue that is the case also with the culture jammers as they try to mobilize in spite of the very stable and secure power alliance between large corporations and American politics. On the other hand, if people tend to mobilize in times of open opportunity structures, this is not because the opportunity to influence power has a strange attraction to people but, more likely, because such times are times of general dislocation and social insecurity.

Notes

1 The spoof-ads come from the www.adbusters.org website and the uncommercials can be seen in the '6 TV uncommercials and the Culture Jammer's video', producer Kalle Lasn/The Media Foundation (acquired in 1999).
2 I use the concept of *discourse* all through the chapter in the meaning defined by Laclau and Mouffe. (Laclau and Mouffe 1985: 105; Jörgensen and Phillips 1999: 34)
3 With the concept of *discursive field* I mean 'the reservoir of allocated meanings that signs have or have had in other discourses, but which are ignored in the specific discourse in order to remove ambiguity'(Jörgensen and Phillips 1999: 37).
4 In the discursive field of 'culture jamming' there are groups who vividly associate themselves with the concept and others who claim to be more peripheral and prefer distinguishing themselves by using other labels on what they do. Even those who claim to be culture jammers may further be ambivalent in their relation to the AMF.
5 The Situationist International was constituted in Paris 1957 by a group of European avant-garde artists, influenced by Dadaism and Surrealism, Anarchism and Marxism. See further (Best and Kellner 1997) and (Thörn 1997b).
6 The concept of 'the corporate machine', which is also used by other culture jamming groups, denotes not only the corporations but also the advertising industry and the mass media.
7 CNN is the only large American broadcasting network that sells airtime to the AMF (www.adbusters.org).
8 See also Ron Eyerman's contribution to this book, in which he writes about the importance of images in moving individuals and groups to protest (pp. 49–50, 52).
9 The general importance of joy and fun as emotional rewards in culture jamming is clearly articulated both by Lasn (1999) and in my interviews with culture jammers conducted in 2002. See also Woodside (2001).
10 'Group belonging' here bears upon the broad social group such as Western middle class, but also one that may appreciate and understand the ingenuity of the way the image is composed, i.e. designers and marketing people, artists etc.
11 See also the discussion about Garfinkel's breaching experiments in Tova Benski's contribution to this book.
12 Lacan in his later works replaces the concept symptom with the concept *sinthome* (Evans 1996; Zizek 1989).

References

Berezin, M. (2001) 'Emotions and political identity: mobilizing affection for the polity', in J. Goodwin, J.M. Jasper and F. Polletta (eds) *Passionate Politics: emotions and social movements*, Chicago: University of Chicago Press.
Best, S. and Kellner, D. (1997) *The Postmodern Turn*, New York: The Guilford Press.
Bourdieu, P. (1999) *Distinction: a social critique of the judgement of taste*, London: Routledge.
Britt, L. and Heise, D. (2000) 'From shame to pride in identity politics', in S. Stryker, T.J. Owens and R.W. White (eds) *Self, Identity, and Social Movements*, Minneapolis: University of Minnesota.
Calhoun, C. (2001) 'Putting emotions in their place', in J. Goodwin, J.M. Jasper

and F. Polletta (eds) *Passionate Politics: emotions and social movements*, Chicago: University of Chicago Press.

Castells, M. (1997) *The Power of Identity*, London: Blackwell.

Collins, R. (1990) 'Stratification, emotional energy, and the transient emotions', in T.D. Kemper (ed.) *Research Agendas in the Sociology of Emotions*, New York: State University of New York.

—— (2001) 'Social movements and the focus of emotional attention', in J. Goodwin, J.M. Jasper and F. Polletta (eds) *Passionate Politics: emotions and social movements*, Chicago: University of Chicago Press.

Durkheim, E. (1994) *Les formes élémentaires de la vie réligieuse*, Paris: Quadrige/Presses Universitaires de France.

Ernesto, L. and Chantal, M. (1985) *Hegemony and Social Strategy – Towards a Radical Democratic Politics*, Thetford, Norfolk: The Thetford Press Ltd.

Evans, D. (1996) *An Introductory Dictionary of Lacanian Psychoanalysis*, London: Routledge.

Eyerman, R. and Jamison, A. (1991) *Social Movements: a cognitive approach*, Cambridge: Polity Press.

Featherstone, M. (1998) *Consumer Culture & Postmodernism*, London: SAGE Publications.

Fraser, N. (1995) 'From redistribution to recognition? Dilemmas of justice in a "post-socialist" age', *New Left Review*, 212: 68–93.

Gamson, W.A. (1992) *Talking Politics*, Cambridge: Cambridge University Press.

Giddens, A. (1995) *The Consequences of Modernity*, Cambridge: Polity Press.

Goodwin, J., Jasper, J.M. and Polletta, F. (2001) 'Why emotions matter', in J. Goodwin, J.M. Jasper and F. Polletta (eds) *Passionate Politics: emotions and social movements*, Chicago: University of Chicago Press.

Gordon, S.L. (1990) 'Social structural effects on emotions', in T.D. Kemper (ed.) *Research Agendas in the Sociology of Emotions*, New York: State University of New York.

Gould, D. (2001) 'Rock the boat, don't rock the boat, baby: ambivalence and the emergence of militant AIDS activism', in J. Goodwin, J.M. Jasper and F. Polletta (eds) *Passionate Politics: emotions and social movements*, Chicago: University of Chicago Press.

Haunss, S. (2003) 'Political posters: tools for mobilization and historical sources', paper presented at Ageing Societies, New Sociology, the 6th Conference of the European Sociological Association, Murcia, Spain.

Hercus, C. (1999) 'Identity, emotion and feminist collective action', *Gender & Society*, 13: 34–56.

Hochschild, A.R. (1979) 'Emotion work, feeling rules, and social structure', *American Journal of Sociology*, 85: 551–76.

—— (1983) *The Managed Heart: the commercialization of human feeling*, Los Angeles: University of California Press.

—— (1990) 'Ideology and emotion management: a perspective and path for future research', in T.D. Kemper (ed.) *Research Agendas in the Sociology of Emotions*, New York: State University of New York Press.

Jasper, J.M. (1998) 'The emotions of protest: affective and reactive emotions in and around social movements', *Sociological Forum*, 13: 397–424.

Jörgensen, M.W. and Phillips, L. (1999) *Diskursanalyse som teori og metode*, Roskilde: Roskilde Universitetsforlag.

Kemper, T.D. (2001) 'A structural approach to social movement emotions', in J. Goodwin, J.M. Jasper and F. Polletta (eds) *Passionate Politics: emotions and social movements*, Chicago: University of Chicago Press.

Klein, N. (1999) *No Logo: taking aim at the brand bullies*, New York: Picador.

Lash, S. (2002) *Critique of Information*, London: SAGE Publications.

Lasn, K. (1999) *Culture Jam: the uncooling of America*, New York: Eagle Brook.

Melucci, A. (1985) 'The symbolic challenge of contemporary movements', *Social Research*, 52: 789–816.

—— (1996) *Challenging Codes: collective action in the information age*, Cambridge: Cambridge University Press.

Moore, B., Jr (1978) *Injustice: the social bases of obedience and revolt*, London: MacMillan Press Ltd.

Scheff, T.J. (1990) 'Socialization of emotions: pride and shame as causal agents', in T.D. Kemper (ed.) *Research Agendas in the Sociology of Emotions*, New York: State New York University.

Schütz, A. (1976) 'The problem of rationality in the social world', in A. Brodersen (ed.) *Collected Papers II Studies in Social Theory*, The Hague: Martinus Nijhoff.

Stearns, P.N. (1994) *American Cool: constructing a twentieth-century emotional style*, New York: New York University.

Stein, A. (2001) 'Revenge of the shamed: the Christian right's emotional culture war', in J. Goodwin, J.M. Jasper and F. Polletta (eds) *Passionate Politics: emotions and social movements*, Chicago: University of Chicago Press.

Tarrow, S. (1994) *Power in Movement: social movements, collective action and politics*, Cambridge: Cambridge University Press.

Thoits, P.A. (1990) 'Emotional deviance: research agendas', in T.D. Kemper (ed.) *Research Agendas in the Sociology of Emotions*, New York: State University of New York Press.

Thörn, H. (1997a) 'Modernitet, sociologi och sociala rörelser', unpublished monograph, Göteborg University.

—— (1997b) *Rörelser i det moderna – politik, modernitet och kollektiv identitet i Europa 1789–1989*, Stockholm: Tiden Athena.

Torfing, J. (1999) *New Theories of Discourse*, Oxford: Blackwell.

Wahl, A., Holgersson, C. and Höök, P. (1998) *Ironi & sexualitet – om ledarskap och kön*, Stockholm: Carlsson.

Wennö, E. (1993) 'Ironic Formula in the Novels of Beryl Bainbridge', unpublished thesis, University of Gothenburg.

Wettergren, Å. (2003a) 'Kulturjam – nya vägar till politiskt motstånd i informationssamhället', in H. Egeland and J. Johannisson (eds) *Kultur, plats, identitet – det lokalas betydelse i en globaliserad värld*, Stockholm: Nya Doxa.

—— (2003b) 'Like moths to a flame: culture jamming and the global spectacle', in A. Opel and D. Pompper (eds) *Representing Resistance: the media, civil disobedience, and the global justice movement*, Westport: Praeger Publishers.

Woodside, S. (2001) 'Every Joke is a Tiny Revolution: culture jamming and the role of humour', unpublished thesis, University of Amsterdam.

Zizek, S. (1989) *The Sublime Object of Ideology*, London: Verso.

7 The problem of emotion in care

Contested meanings from the Disabled People's Movement and the Feminist Movement[1]

Debra Hopkins, Linda McKie, Nick Watson and Bill Hughes

Introduction

The Community Care Act in Britain came into force in 1997. As a result of this disabled people can purchase care services in such a way as to achieve their goals of independence, respect and dignity by choosing their care services, and controlling how they receive them. For the Disabled People's Movement this represents the conquering of a major hurdle, and the key to their liberation from the legacies of the past.

The Disabled People's Movement has successfully campaigned against the institutionalizing forces of the altruistic religious and benevolent organizations of the late nineteenth and early twentieth centuries. The colonizing and demeaning impulses of this legacy continue today, according to the Disabled People's Movement, through professional and welfare discourses, and through representations of disabled people as pitiable, passive and helpless. It is easy to see how such experiences can leave disabled people feeling inferiorized, infantalized and shamed. For the Disabled People's Movement the emotional connotations underpinning these discourses and representations are so deeply hurtful and harmful that the purchase of Direct Payments and revised terminology of care to contractual support and help, along with the movement's adoption of a corporate model, is seen as a necessary, pragmatic response to their problem. In so doing, care is divested of emotion.

Feminists meanwhile are very concerned that this response represents the Disabled People's Movement further buying into the 'malestream' (Fraser 1989) ethos underpinning neo-liberal social policy discourse that has effectively marginalized both disabled people and women. Various feminist theorists propose diversity in approaches and interpretations of care. They more than any other disciplinary constituency have theorized care, and the political construction of care remains their pivotal concern. Despite the theoretical diversity in feminism, the emotional component of care as an integral part of interdependency is generally valorized by feminists. Not surprisingly feminists are concerned about the denial and problematization of emotion in care. They argue that to deny and resist emotion in the giving and receiving of care leaves care workers, overwhelmingly women, commodified and exploited. The imposition of feeling rules associated with the provision of personal assistance through Direct Payments and the social model of disability involves subverting the recognition of the emotional support given to disabled people by their personal assistants. This may have the effect of leaving the disabled person and/or the personal assistant feeling empty and false, but to date this important observation has not been flagged up by feminists. In addition feminists argue that buying into malestream individualistic discourses fails to recognize care and interdependency as fundamental resources necessary for the survival of any society. To dismiss emotion, care and interdependency, warn feminists, is both perilous and unable to stand up to critical scrutiny.

Meanwhile emotion in social life has re-emerged as a central concern for sociologists over the past decade or so. In particular this has found some purchase in debates about social movements (Hercus 1999) and in application to the human service sector, especially in health and social care (Lupton 1996), and associated caring professions.

This chapter will critically examine the ways in which emotion, through contested political constructions of care, have been theorized by both disability and feminist theorists. The tensions between the two perspectives and the centrality of emotion in the polemic is considered. The lack of empirical accounts in 'support' relationships, and consequences thereof will be discussed. We suggest that within the tensions between and within these two social movements reside important lessons about the 'microprocesses of emotion power' in social movements and beyond. Finally we urge the necessity for an empirical research agenda to this end.

The Disabled People's Movement and emotion

The Disabled People's Movement has no organizational locus. It is a term used to describe all those groups, organizations and activists supporting disabled rights and the emancipation of disabled people. It is a way of making sense of the diversity of organizations of disabled people from the Union of Physically Impaired Against Segregation, the Independent Living Movement, Disabled People International and the British Council of Disabled People, for example. The exact number of groups affiliated to, and identifying as a part of the Disabled People's Movement is not known. Clearly there is some uncertainty and lack of clarity about the organization of collective action around rights-based issues for disabled people. Despite this, a typology of rights-based disability groups has been attempted by Charlton (1998: 136), who has identified ten broad categories of organizations ranging from local self-help groups, national coalitions, single impairment groups to international organizations, to name just four.

It is possible to locate the arrival of what is now termed the DPM with the first meeting of the Disabled People's International in the early 1980s. It was at this inaugural meeting that Disabled People's International agreed upon a working definition of disability to include all impairment groups, rather than what had previously recognized purely physically impaired people. Following on from this development, Shakespeare and Watson (2001) have proposed a three-stage emergent disability politics, based on needs:

1   The struggle over the political status of a given need.
2   The debate over the interpretation and definition of the need.
3   The struggle for the satisfaction of the need.

The authors argue that this corresponds to the social location of disabled people through the imposition of the following statements:

1   Disabled people are a disadvantaged, or marginalized constituency.
2   Disabled people comprise a distinct minority, and disabled people should themselves initiate and lead social change for this group.
3   At the heart of the social model of disability is the stance that disability is about discrimination and prejudice, not physical or mental incapacity or limitations.

The DPM has considered it necessary to extricate itself and its members from care, precisely because of the way in which care and emotion are conflated. It has therefore chosen a pragmatic solution to their dilemma: in order for disabled people to live independently, thereby fulfilling their physical needs and their emotional and identity requirements, they have chosen 'personal assistance' and in so doing have claimed to have taken the emotion out of caring. Put like this it is clear that the DPM does not shun emotion per se, rather that the receipt of care frustrates and threatens the emotional self-determination and integrity of disabled people. Restated in another way, the DPM is attempting to fight for personal and collective pride. Given the historical experiences of disabled people in the name of care this is both understandable and commendable.

For the Independent Living Movement in the US and the Disabled People's Movement in the UK 'care' is regarded as a byword for dependency and as a means to colonize and control the lives of disabled people. 'Care' and the emotional connotations that go with it are said in no way to empower, nurture or serve the interests of disabled people. Rather power is located with the caregiver, and images of heroic carers as 'self-sacrificing martyrs' (Rock 1998) and disabled people as 'victims of personal tragedy' (Oliver 1990) are perpetuated. These cultural representations of disabled people are indeed emotionally evocative, and not surprisingly, are images that the DPM is keen to abandon and resist. The DPM has launched its political stance on the basis of rights and interests, a position that denies and resists emotion: '"care" is a word which is value-laden, contested and confused, particularly in the way that it combines an emotional component and a description of basic human services' (Shakespeare 2000: ix).

Shakespeare's summation of care comes to the heart of the problem besetting the two social movements in question here. For the DPM the combination of 'an emotional component and a description of basic human services' presents a confusion, something that is undesirable and erroneous. Meanwhile personal assistance aims to transform care into a contractual arrangement, whereby the disabled person employs the assistant to carry out tasks in an impersonal way, without the expectation of expression of thanks or gratitude. Effectively disability activists have established the 'feeling rules' of the relationship and reframed the relationship as a contractual one. A simple equation is thereby suggested: care minus emotion equals help/personal assistance, and the presupposition is that contractual relationships, even those requiring tasks of an often intimate nature, are devoid of emotion.

The valorization of personal assistance rather than care as expressed by disability activists has evolved from the social model of disability. The social model of disability focuses on the objective social barriers that inhibit participation of disabled people in social life, but does so at the expense of the personal, embodied experience of both disability and impairment. It is a model that has drawn a sharp distinction between the private and the public and marginalized the former. In so doing 'whole areas of disability experience, and thus of disablism, are eclipsed because they are located in the private domain of life' (Thomas 2001: 55). Thomas argues elsewhere (1999: 70) that disability should be redefined to include ways in which the psycho-emotional well-being of disabled people is undermined.

Clearly then there is a call from within disability studies, and most forcefully from disabled feminist theorists (Morris 1993; Corker and French 1999; Lloyd 2001; Thomas 1999, 2001) for greater complexity within readings of the social model of disability and to move towards a theoretical position that recognizes emotion in the experience of both disability and impairment, and the authors of this chapter would add the relationships that take place in the context of disability and impairment. Not surprisingly there is already some evidence that disabled people do not experience personal assistance in purely contractual terms. In Sweden, where disabled people under 65 have a right to personal assistance, research with children with mobility impairments suggests that relationships with assistants are varied and dynamic and may include quite instrumental perspectives as well as notions of assistants as 'parents or friends' (Skar and Tham 2001). There is nevertheless a dearth of empirical research that focuses on this domain of disablism. This certainly hinders both the procurement of a richer understanding of disability and impairment, thereby hindering the emancipatory project of both movements, and the preconditions in which the disenfranchized may flourish.

Feminism and emotion

> care: to be anxious, have regard or liking for; to look after and be disposed to.
>
> Collins (1985: 31)

The difficulty in encapsulating the complex combination of feelings and activities or tasks that constitute care has been articulated by feminists. Researchers (Parker 1981; Ungerson 1983; Sevenhuijsen 1998) have tended to theorize caring in these terms – 'caring about' as the feeling part of caring and 'caring for' as the practical part of tending to others. Much of the tending work of caring relies and builds on particular knowledge of the other, knowledge that is built in tandem with the forging and sustaining of relationships. Finch and Mason (1983) argue that the act of providing care, especially over a long period of time, creates the relationship. Feminists point also to the anticipatory nature of care work, and note that care work often involves planning. This is invisible but nonetheless crucially informs the conflation of the emotional and task related caring actions. These complexities suggest that 'caring expresses ethically significant ways in which we matter to each other' (Bowden 1997: 111).

Another cornerstone of the feminist theories of care relates to the way in which care is associated with gender identity. All feminists concur that caring and gender are inextricably linked: 'caring is "given" to women: it becomes the defining characteristic of their self-identity and their lifework. At the same time, caring is taken away from men: not caring becomes a defining characteristic of manhood' (Graham 1983). Bartky (1990: 65) asserts that 'femininity is an artifice, an achievement'. She goes on to say that the emotion work associated with femininity is disempowering as far as those providing emotional service must suppress their own feelings and emotions to achieve an outward display that offers comfort and support while addressing the emotional needs of others. This emotional giving and yet subterfuge can leave the woman feeling empty, drained and false (1990: 104). The facial smiling associated with caregiving (in prominent images and everyday practice) can conceal feelings of being used yet needed, of being powerful at the point of care but disempowered in the intersection of the reflective politics of gender, care and employment: 'We (women) need to locate our subordination not only in the hidden recesses of the psyche but in the duties we are happy to perform and in what we thought were the innocent pleasures of everyday life' (Bartky 1990: 119).

To deconstruct gender and caring within patriarchy requires radical solutions but to de-couple caring in either employment or the home and family contexts is likely to be a call resisted by many women. Might it be that women should consider the potential for emancipation from the very emotion work that so infuses their sense of identity and well-being? With regard to personal and intimate relationships Bartky comments: 'It may be the case that women's nurturance is not [*sic*] a zero-sum game, i.e. that, in many circumstances women may disempower themselves more in the giving of emotional support than men are empowered in the getting of it' (1990: 105).

The maintenance of society depends on the feminine, silenced provision of care work and emotional support, and assumes that women will largely take up these demands as they constitute their gendered identity. Over the past two decades or so feminist academics (Thomas 1997; Ungerson 2000; Sevenhuijsen 1998; McKie *et al.* 2002) have given more attention to the gendered nature of domestic labour, the provision of care work and emotional support in the family and to friends, and how this has increasingly been taken up, as discourse and in practice, in social policy.

Feminists have taken issue with the provision of personal assistance to disabled people as low paid providers of instrumental help largely on the basis that it exploits women (PAs are overwhelmingly women) and that it underplays the complexity of the care relationship (Graham 1983; Bowden 1997; Adam 1998). The counter-argument is that it is women's choice to do this sort of work. This echoes another thread in the caring literature 'why do women care?' (Ungerson 1983). Feminists have argued that women do caring work, despite the low remuneration and low status, because it is important for the formation of gendered identity, of femininity. Put another way, what women lack in economic capital they make up for in emotional capital. But their capital is not valued by society.

Emotional investment in care work is a silent assumption, but in some contexts it is simultaneously explicitly and negatively sanctioned. Therefore certain professional discourses associate emotionality with subjectivity and see subjectivity as a confounding factor in one's ability to make soundly based and reasoned judgements and assessments and reach unclouded conclusions based solely on the basis of objective facts. From this point of view emotionality is something that can and must be controlled and contrived, a rampaging force to be managed and monitored. Care and caring as activities and emotions and as expressions of femininity are conflated with women's 'natural' propensities, needs and desires as stemming from the realm of instincts. There is growing concern that care services and notions of care in society do not adequately address the stresses and the strains associated with care giving. This further devalues the emotional and material concerns and implications of care and gender (Bowden 1997; Sevenhuijsen 1998). As a result the considerable sense of contradiction, contention and confusion besetting the artifice of emotion and care in late modern welfare states is amplified. In summary, it is the manipulation of emotion in care work that causes feminists great anxiety.

Hochschild's pioneering work with hostesses produced the term 'emotional labour' (1983). Emotional labour remains the dominant feminist account of women and emotion in the work setting, although this account has been critiqued as too generalized and as presenting a rather negative and partial account of the relationship in which emotional labour takes place (see for example Tolich 1993; Wharton 1993). Hochschild proposed that women's emotional skills and capacities are exploited as economic commodities in the market place. Central to her argument is that the value of these skills is not recognized in economic remuneration. Furthermore individual workers must contrive their emotional presentation with clients in such a way as to maintain emotional composure in the workplace, in order to satisfy organizational goals. This work inevitably strips individuals of their emotional autonomy and integrity, and is ultimately estranging and harmful.

Feminists generally value the emotional component of caring, and argue that it is an important and inevitable part of the caring for, itself an essential aspect of every society. However, like disability theorists, feminist theorists and activists argue that the gendered nature of caring work colonizes women, constructing them as 'natural' subjects and vulnerable to exploitation.

To recapitulate, in recent years 'care' has increasingly attracted policy attention, largely fuelled by the 'burden of care' discourse underwriting successive governments' concerns with chronic illness, disability and an ageing population. At the same time the concept of care has been passionately contested by two social movements. For disability theorists care colonizes disabled people, stripping them of their dignity and pride. Crucially emotion in care is the enemy of disabled people, reminding them as it does of the very recent past and the actual or metaphorical confinement of disabled people within institutions. Feminists valorize emotion in care work, and resist the exploitation of women through their care work. For feminists, personal assistance amounts to one group of marginalized people fighting for their liberation on the backs of another group of marginalized people, through the manipulation of emotion. This is perceived by feminists as inevitably counter to the interests of both disabled people and women.

Clearly then both disability and feminist activists are concerned about emotion and care, and are motivated to collective political action and social change. Both resist their respective constitutions as marginalized groups as emergent through care, but their respective responses and calls for change set them, the conceptualization of care and of emotions, very far apart.

The next section will discuss in more detail this clash of perspectives and how emotion is the pivotal factor propelling both of these movements, albeit in polarized directions. Central to this discussion is the juxtaposition of power, inequalities and gender with emotion and subjectivity.

Emotion, power and care

The experiences of disabled people from the nineteenth century on have been informed by various forms of institutionalization and medicalization. Goffman's work on 'total institutions' (1961) paints a chilling and bleak picture of sterile, closed places devoid of human affection, regard and expression. Ostensibly we have moved on from what this image of barbarity and cruelty portrayed, both in the ways in which the rights and interests of disabled people are debated and fought out, and in our appreciations of the emotional complexity of contemporary social and health care settings.

Emotion work has been identified as one way in which power and care in health and social care settings meet (see for example Treweek 1996: Curtis 1991). The work of these authors and the insights procured are important because they identify ways in which emotion can empower health and care workers, providing some degree of counter-argument to the picture of powerlessness, passivity and exploitation that Hochschild identified through her work with air hostesses. In the residential, health and social care settings, what for the nurse attending to the personal needs of a disabled person is a source of personal and professional satisfaction may be for the disabled person a source of their powerlessness. Indeed, in many cases the mechanisms of power may lie not with the provision and carrying out of tasks, but more with the determination of what, when and how tasks are to be *done to* the disabled person. This control over the provision of basic human services, which non-disabled people take for granted, is exemplified by contemporary social work practice, itself mainstreamed by the language of rationality, monitoring and target meeting: the highly dubious 'needs assessment'.

Foucault's (1977) concepts of surveillance and the gaze as a basis for examining power relationships in care settings would not be out of place here. However, it is perhaps his notion of pastoral care (1988) that is particularly fruitful in this analysis. For Foucault 'pastoral care' represents a technique of surveillance based on forms of individualized and nurturant knowledge of the members of a constituent flock by their leader. The shepherd/flock metaphor implies a kindly shepherd who is in the business of controlling the activities of the flock, taking care of, and keeping every individual member and the flock safe. Foucault (1988) noted that many forms of modern social relationships were based on this modality of power. Treweek's research considered emotion work in residential homes for elderly people and noted how formal care discourse of 'total individualized care' eclipsed the social and emotional control agendas operating through routine activities and relationships between staff and residents.

Treweek summises that;

> Foucault's notion of surveillance is compatible with a pastoral conceptualisation of care. Self-surveillance by residents is still very important

for the maintenance of social control in the residential home ... residents were controlled via the emotion work of staff. Through this, and
the emotion incentives provided by those who exhibited the correct
behaviour, residents were encouraged to regulate their own emotions
and behaviour.

(1996: 121)

This analysis clearly demonstrates how attentive benevolent care and nurturance can reside alongside control and manipulation. Bauman warns
that; 'the impulse to care for another, when it's taken to its extreme, leads
to the annihilation of the autonomy of the other, to domination and
oppression' (1993: 11).

It is clear that the disabled people's experiences of institutionalized care
resonate with those of the residents in the care homes for older people.
The DPM's claims that such experiences constitute people as dependent
and helpless and strip them of their self-determination and autonomy are
given amplified plausibility. This pastoral, altruistic imagination and the
institutions it spawns, such as charities *for* rather than organizations *of*
disabled people (Oliver 1990) are an integral part of the apparatuses of
oppression that disfigure the lives of disabled people, according to the
DPM. There is a silent assumption underpinning this and amplified
through the charitable mindset that they need emotional support more
than non-disabled people in order to compensate for their impairment, and
a priori, their emotional fragility. Disabled People's Movement slogans
such as 'piss on pity' eloquently express the degree to which the movement
associates care with emotions that are experienced by disabled people as
threatening and harmful.

Importantly the oppression of institutionalization is still 'felt' by disabled people today, despite the fact that many disabled people have never
experienced actual incarceration. So it appears that the *modus operandi* of
the DPM with respect to emotion, apart from a contingency of disabled
feminists, is to manage emotion as a transmissible and permeable oppressive force which in this reading at least has a lifeforce quite separate from
the particular embodied relationship in the particular political and social
context in which it takes place. But this reading partly frustrates a reading
that gives primacy in interpretation and in analytic potential, to the legitimacy of 'felt emotions' in response to a particular relationship. Denzin
(1990: 86) in imploring an interpretative framework for the study of emotions, claims that 'emotions must be studied as lived experience, ...
emotion must be studied as a process that turns in on itself, elaborates
itself, and has its own trajectory'.

According to the growing body of literature in the sociology of emotions not to scrutinize the transmission of *by proxy* to *felt* emotion would
be foolhardy. Indeed the surveillance and oppression of disabled people
continues today, not only in the traces of contemporary health and social

care practices illustrated above, and in unequal access to services and opportunities to grow and flourish that the more privileged take for granted, but in wider symbols and discourses about who are the truly worthy and therefore deserving (of reward, recognition and superiority) in society – the contributors rather than the burdens. There are indeed other more subtle forms of incarceration, much the more effective because of their pervasiveness and difficult-to-localize nature. It is arguably this to which disabled people are responding today, when they *feel* the legacy of the recent past.

Meanwhile the feminist riposte to outright vilification of care has been intrepid. The manipulation of the emotional economy of care and the resultant exploitation of women's care work are of great concern for feminists, and Direct Payments and personal assistance are exemplary of this manipulation. It is fair to say that the above can be encapsulated by the following: from the feminist perspective the focus must be on the needs and interests of carers. From the standpoint of the DPM the rights and interests must be located with disabled people. Notwithstanding this a number of feminist scholars in arguing for a universalist paradigm of care have gone on to propose an ethics of care as an important element of citizenship in order to 'involve the relatively disenfranchised in the political world' (Tronto 1993: 21).

The macro- and the micro-processes of emotion power

Hochschild's pioneering work with hostesses and the concept of 'emotion work' demonstrated a conceptual link between emotion and gender. In so doing she not only put emotion firmly back in the sociological landscape, but also paved the way for a sociological analysis of emotion and inequalities. More recent work on shame and pride (Scheff 1990) and inferiority and inequalities (Neckel 1996) has consolidated this theoretical nexus. Neckel claims that 'the social history of inferiority paints a mental panorama of social inequality'. He elaborates an example of the sociology of recent German history, and notes how feelings of inferiority are experienced by former GDR citizens since reunification: 'in direct contact with Western lifestyles and suddenly confronted with a fundamental transformation of the frame of reference of their own self-evaluation, inferior perceptions of their biography arose' (1996: 17).

Using this example it is clear to see how the 'frame of reference' of the former GDR citizens may have been severely challenged and disrupted by their sudden and dramatic juxtaposition with western lifestyles, values and symbols. The west with its strong individualist ideology at the same time represents a potent symbol of superiority and status achievement, and the idea that those who aspire can 'have it all'. Indeed Neckel (1996) proposes a genealogy of inferiority in modernity, and claims that a defining feature of this is that feelings of inferiority fundamentally involve a transition from collective status to deficient individuality. We reiterate an earlier point that one of the central presumptions underpinning the currently predominant practice of 'needs assessment' in the UK as the central component of provision of health and social care services for disabled people is that needs assessments identify and compensate for deficiencies in individual's bodily functioning, and *a priori* emotional vulnerabilities. Crucially, although disabled people have been liberated from the *practice* of incarceration the 'frame of reference of their own self-evaluation' (Neckel 1996) for disabled people is that which remains hostile and oppressive to them, at the same time that it is celebrated as a superior form of relationship to the world, and as a superior from of self-consciousness and 'other orientation'. Freedom from incarceration is absolutely not the same as freedom to flourish. In the 'war of equals', where the rule is 'everyone for oneself', feeling oneself still incarcerated thereby becomes an expression of false consciousness, and a sure sign of inferiority indeed!

Closer to home in the context of the social movements in discussion in this chapter, it is clear that some insights from the dramatic example of the spectacular collapse of an oppressive political regime and socialist experiment nonetheless has some analytic potential for this discussion. Both disabled people and women are assigned inferior positions in relation to those of the 'modern normative subject' – that is white, able-bodied male wage earner in the marketplace. Both women and disabled people are assigned inferior positions in relation to the moral, economic and political economies of neo-liberalist societies. But it is not only through their relative positioning and status that women and disabled people are inferiorized and devalued, rather also through the nexus of 'position and experience, as situation and feeling' (Neckel 1996: 18). Neckel goes on to say that it is a defining characteristic of this nexus of inferiority that the situation and the feeling are inextricably linked. The normative and desirable 'frame of reference' set against the experience of powerlessness gives rise to feelings of shame and inferiority, and its *modus operandi* relies on the presence of a recognition of a defect, a negative deviation from a norm, which is personalized and individualized, set against the acceptance of an attribution of superiority. Echoing somewhat Bourdieu's sociology of inequalities and his claim that the most fertile analysis of the perpetuation of inequalities must have as its linchpin the way in which individuals come to accept their inequalities through their very struggles to recognize the game, play the game and win, Neckel's take on the social construction of emotions provides an important dimension to the macro-micro analysis of difference and social stratification.

The reframing of care, with its complexity of emotional and instrumental components, into a contractual relationship represents for the Disabled People's Movement an appeal to the strength within every disabled individual, an appeal to them to refute their situation and feelings of inferiority and shame, and instead to mobilize their collective pride and strength into a mighty counter-force. Crucially it aims to mobilize through the mechanism of reconstituting feelings of inferiority into feelings of self-worth, a strategy used by all social movements. According to Neckel 'inferiority is a social relationship which only exists to the extent that it is felt' (1996: 21).

However, there is a searing contradiction in the pragmatic solution of the DPM, and it relates to an imposition of 'feeling rules' (Hochschild 1983), themselves not innocuous but performing as a very potent mechanism of surveillance deployed by the superior on the inferior. In other words, in this case the feeling rules associated with the giving and the receiving of care, help and support as contracted, we argue may perpetuate inequalities. Here, the rules set a normative agenda, a right and a wrong way, in which disabled people should relate to their personal assistants. It is very easy to see why pity, arguably above all other emotional responses, is most feared, resented, reviled and loathed by disabled people. It is easy to see why these responses go beyond the loathing of the emotion itself, but extend to the vector, the person who displays it. But pity is not always the underlying motivational force behind help and care, and gratitude and giving of thanks does not necessarily have to go hand in hand with bowing to pity, although of course, tragically it often is and does. But this reflexive emotional equation is problematic, and deeply damaging to disabled people. It represents a bowing to the plausibility of a relationship between the giving of thanks and gratitude and the assumption of pity. It represents an expectation or at least its plausibility, that pity will be the motivation for someone's kindness, someone else's regard, because they, unlike the other, are not able bodied, rather than because they are worthy of regard and appraisal for their own sake. This itself sails dangerously close to accepting oneself as inferior to the other, and therefore accepting the inequalities that are so pervasive in the lives of both disabled people and women as marginalized groups. Indeed Simmel (1999) has identified 'Dankbarkeit' or 'gratitude', rather than being a perpetuator of inequality and inferiority, as an important feeling action in social cementing.

The relationship between a disabled person and their personal assistant often requires tasks of a very intimate and repetitive nature. Having knowledge of what is to be done, and the preference for the way in which it is done comes as a result of a relationship sustained over time. It embodies the thinking about and the anticipation of needs and preferences, and this continuity and fluidity is clearly in the interests of both players in the relationship. In the case of disabled people and their personal assistants, this may be what gives rise to a sense of loyalty, trust and mutual regard in the relationship, ensuring not only the perpetuation of the relationship, but the reciprocal giving of a bit more, such as the personal assistant staying five or ten minutes longer, remembering the other's birthday, a disabled person allowing more flexible work arrangements around exam time, for instance (many personal assistants are students).

Additionally, as elaborated elsewhere by the authors (Watson *et al.* 2004), caution is urged about the adoption of a corporate representation of the provision of support and help to those who are particularly seen to be 'in need'. The DPM, through Direct Payments, seeks to give disabled people employer status, and therefore power in the relationship to determine the conditions of their support and help. This is quite understandable. But there is a concerning dimension to this reframing, and it has to do with the presumptions underpinning the transition of position from welfare recipient to that of employer. Neckel (1996) claims that among a range of responses to the painful feelings associated with inferiority and shame, exists that of conformity. We have attempted to illustrate how disability activists may be unwittingly being drawn into a mode of conformity by adopting positions and feeling states vis-à-vis the normative subject: male, able-bodied, white, employed in the marketplace. The particular constitution of independency refutes and ignores the inescapable and inevitable interdependency in all of our lives, and turns those 'in need' into problems. We argue that the 'rise' from welfare beneficiary to employer will not alone elevate the inferior status of disabled people, and therefore not their feelings of inferiority, because what they are purchasing is not a valued social resource. Instead there may be unanticipated costs for the DPM, disabled people and the predominantly women who are their personal assistants.

Towards an emancipatory model of care

We know staggering little about how disabled people form relationships with their carers, and personal assistants. This dearth of empirical work surely represents a stumbling block for interested academics and activists. Certainly it is reasonable to assume that such relationships are characterized by fluidity and change, and a range of intertangled and fluctuating emotions. It is also certainly reasonable to argue that the lived experience of the relationship and the emotional ambiguities therein become eclipsed in 'the contract', as a pragmatic solution. Although the social model of disability has undoubtedly progressed the rights and interests of disabled people, there are some theorists, themselves living with disability, who have drawn cautionary notes around some of the presumptions of this model. These generally relate to the drawing of sharp, binary distinctions between impairment and disability. Pinder draws attention to the tensions inherent in: 'the search for clear-cut, univocal messages crucial for the success of any political movement, and the necessarily more complex and subtle reality of people's lived experience' (Pinder 1997: 304).

Pinder goes on to argue for an approach to understanding disability that draws out the 'ambiguities of lived experience ... to come to grips with the many interlocking webs of significance in which impairment and disability are embedded' (1997: 302). We have previously indicated that disabled feminists have urged disability activists not to discount the reality of disabled people's experiences of impairment, in favour of promoting the social model of disability and the emphasis on the politics of disablism. Although feminist theorists have pointed out the negative consequences of 'feeling rules' imposed on women through the manipulation of emotion in their caring work, there is clearly a parallel to be drawn here in relation to the imposition of feeling rules on disabled people in their relationships with their personal assistants. As a central part of the quest for self-determination, disabled people must be given the opportunity to determine their own feeling rules and modes of engagement as a part of their quest for dignity and pride.

We have already indicated that there is a lack of empirical research looking at the relationships between disabled people and those who provide their help and support, in the context of paid personal assistance. This is clearly a problem. However, our theoretical work contributes to the literature on social movements because of its examination of two social movements opposing one another, a departure from the dominant theme in the literature that focuses on one social movement and its resistance to the dominant discourse. Looking at two social movements concurrently has great theoretical potential. It focuses the critical gaze on the inextricability of emotion from social life and action, and its political potential. It places care at the centre stage of social life, and reminds us of its significance, not because it is a 'policy problem' to be handled and dealt with, but because of its fundamental and enduring ethical and moral character. We all need care. It is the primary social relation that sustains human life, although actual care practices vary throughout the life course, and are experienced differently by different individuals according to stage in life course, and other life conditions. Current policy discourse, however, constitutes certain individuals and groups as problematic, through the scripting of care in relation to need and dependency, rather than through the recognition and appraisal of interdependency in social relations.

The critical examination of what happens when two social groups come to loggerheads over care and emotion can tell us something about the morphology and perpetuation of inequalities. Perhaps most profoundly the struggle over care and the problem with emotion therein has highlighted the urgency of the need for opening up 'discourse bridges' (Fraser 1989) that will urge us to imagine, and fight for a society based on trust, respect and interdependency.

Note

1 We would like to thank Jochen Kleres, University of Leipzig, for his reading of the drafts, his helpful comments and his thoughtful and critical discussion around the literature and the preparation of this chapter.

References

Adam, B. (1998) *Timescapes of Modernity: the environment and invisible hazards*, London: Routledge.

Bartky, S.L. (1990) *Femininity and Domination: studies in the phenomonology of oppression*, London: Routledge.

Bauman, Z. (1993) *Postmodern Ethics*, Oxford: Blackwell.

Bowden, P. (1997) *Caring: gender sensitive ethics*, London: Routledge.

Charlton, J.I. (1998) *Nothing About Us Without Us: disability, oppression and empowerment*, Berkeley: University of California Press.

Collins Dictionary (1985) London: Collins.

Corker, M. and French, S. (1999) 'Reclaiming discourse in disability studies', in M. Corker (ed.) *Disability Discourse*, Buckingham: Open University Press.

Curtis, P. (1991) 'Midwives in Hospital: work, emotion and the labour process', Unpublished thesis, University of Manchester.

Denzin, N. (1990) 'On understanding emotion: the interpretive-cultural agenda', in T. Kemper (ed.) *Research Agendas in the Sociology of Emotions*, Albany: State University of New York Press.

Finch, J. and Mason, J. (1983) *Negotiating Family Responsibilities*, London: Routledge.

Foucault, M. (1977) *Power/Knowledge*, New York: Pantheon Books.

—— (1988) 'Politics and reason', in L. Kritzman (ed.) *Politics, Philosophy, Culture*, London, Routledge.

Fraser, N. (1989) *Unruly Practices: power, discourses and gender in contemporary social theory*, Cambridge: Polity.

Goffman, E. (1961) *Asylums*, Harmondsworth: Penguin.

Graham, H. (1983) 'Caring: a labour of love', in J. Finch and D. Groves (eds) *A Labour of Love: women, work and caring*, London: Routledge and Kegan Paul.

Hercus, C. (1999) 'Identity, emotion and feminist collective action', *Gender & Society*, 13: 34–55.

Hochschild, A.R. (1983) *The Managed Heart: the commercialization of human feeling*, Berkeley, CA: University of California Press.

Lloyd, M. (2001) 'The politics of disability and feminism: discord or synthesis?', *Sociology*, 35(4): 714–28.

Lupton, D. (1996) '"Your life in their hands": trust in the medical encounter', in V. James and J. Gabe (eds) *Health and the Sociology of Emotions*, Oxford: Blackwell Publishers Ltd.

McKie, L., Gregory, S. and Bowlby, S. (2002) 'Gender, caring and employment in Britain', *Journal of Social Policy*, 30(2): 233–58.

Morris, J. (1993) *Independent Lives? Community care and disabled people*, London: Macmillan.

Neckel, S. (1996) 'Inferiority: from collective status to deficient individuality', *Sociological Review*, 41(17): 17–34.

Oliver, M. (1990) *The Politics of Disablement*, Basingstoke: Macmillan.

Parker, R. (1981) 'Tending and social policy', in E. Goldberg and S. Hatch (eds) *New Look at the Personal Social Services*, London: Policy Studies Institute.

Pinder, R. (1997) 'A reply to Tom Shakespeare and Nicholas Watson', *Disability and Society*, 12(2): 301–5.

Rock, P. (1998) *Food for Thought, The Carer's Movement: dangers ahead?*, available at: http://www.leeds.ac.uk/disability-studies/archiveuk/archframe.htm (Accessed 30 June 2002).

Scheff, T.J. (1990) 'Socialization of emotions: pride and shame as causal agents', in T. Kemper (ed.) *Research Agendas in the Sociology of Emotions*, Albany: State University of New York Press.

Sevenhuijsen, S. (1998) *Citizenship and the Ethics of Care: feminist consideration on justice, morality and politics*, London: Routledge.

Shakespeare, T. (2000) *Help: imaging welfare*, Birmingham: Venture.

Shakespeare, T. and Watson, N. (2001) 'Making the difference: disability, politics and recognition', in G. Albrecht, M. Bury and K. Seelman (eds) *Handbook of Disability Studies*, London: Sage.

Simmel, G. (1999) *Soziologie. Untersuchungen über die Formen der Vergesellschaftung*, Gesamtausgabe Band 11. Hrsg von O. Rammstedt. Frankfurt a. M. Suhrkamp.

Skar, I. and Tham, M. (2001) 'My assistant and I: disabled children's and adolescents' roles and relationships to their assistants', *Disability and Society*, 16(7): 917–91.

Thomas, C. (1997) The baby and the bathwater: disabled women and motherhood in social context, *Sociology of Health and Illness*, 19(5): 622–43.

—— (1999) *Female Forms: experiencing and understanding disability*, Birmingham: Open University Press.

—— (2001) 'Feminism and disability: the theoretical and political significance of the personal and the experiential', in L. Barton (ed.) *Disability Politics and the Struggle for Change*, London: David Fulton Publishers.

Tolich, M. (1993) 'Alienating and liberating emotions at work', *Journal of Contemporary Ethnography*, October: 361–81.

Treweek, L.G. (1996) 'Emotion work, order and emotional power in care assistant work', in V. James and J. Gabe (eds) *Health and the Sociology of Emotions*, Oxford: Blackwell Publishers Ltd.

Tronto, J. (1993) *Moral Boundaries: a political argument for an ethic of care*, London: Sage.

Ungerson, C. (1983) 'Why do women care?', in J. Finch and D. Groves (eds) *A Labour of Love: women, work and caring*. London: Routledge and Kegan Paul.

—— (2000) 'Thinking about the production and consumption of long-term care in Britain: does gender still matter?', *Journal of Social Policy*, 29(4): 623–43.

Watson, N., McKie, L., Hughes, B., Hopkins, D. and Gregory, S. (2004) '(Inter)dependence, needs and care. The potential for disability and feminist theorists to develop an emancipatory model', *Sociology*, 38(2): 331–50.

Wharton, A. (1993) 'The affective consequences of service work, managing emotions on the job', *Work and Occupations*, 20 (May): 205–32.

8 The emotional significance of solidarity for social movement communities

Sustaining Catholic worker community and service

Erika Summers-Effler

Structural and social constructionist positions on emotions

The question of sustaining community in a Catholic worker house highlights the role of emotion, but what sorts of analytic leverage can the concept of emotion provide for understanding the processes that sustain the community? The answer to this question depends on how we understand emotion. There has been an assumption in the sociology of emotions literature that emotions are either structurally determined or culturally constructed (Kemper 1981; Hochschild 1983). If emotions are entirely culturally constructed, they are grounded in cognitive assessments based in particular cultural lenses (DiMaggio 1997), and therefore emotions would not provide analytic leverage beyond a rich understanding of the implications of culture for interaction. While there is certainly a cultural component in the experience and meaning of emotion, by treating emotion as a subset or product of culture (Goodwin *et al.* 2001: 9; Jasper 1998), those who take a completely cultural constructive approach neglect the role of the social structure of interaction in generating emotions.

Structural determinist perspectives suggest that social structure produces particular patterns of emotions. For Kemper (1990) the concept of social structure stands for differences in power and status, which is how macro-sociologists conceive of structure. Collins (1990) and Scheff (1990) also promote a structural perspective, but their understanding of structure is more similar to Goffman's micro-perspective (1967). Their work is based in a conception of a micro-structure comprised of patterns of face-to-face interaction – patterns of inclusion/exclusion and power on the level of interaction. A micro-conception of structure is only indirectly related to the more macro-conceptions of structure through diffuse patterns of power and status (Collins 2001b).

If emotions are structurally determined they provide analytic leverage in helping us to explain the sorts of configurations of interaction behind particular emotions. Thus a structural approach to emotions enables us to consider less directly the patterns of interaction that are sustained by particular group and/or individual emotions. This is particularly useful when considering the case of altruism or other sorts of behavior that are better understood in emotional rather than narrow rational terms. However, if the structural position overrides the relevance of culture and the patterns of cognition that comprise culture (DiMaggio 1997), then we only gain analytic leverage for understanding how group processes sustain emotion and particular types of activity at the expense of the insights that an understanding of culture and cognition can provide.

The contrasting claims raised by the cultural and structural perspectives on emotion also pervades research on emotion in social movements. While Kemper has called for a structural approach to emotions in social movements (2001: 59), which would specify the social structural conditions that generate particular emotions or groupings of emotions, research on emotions in social movements has primarily been from a cultural constructivist position that emphasizes expectations and cultural meanings (Goodwin *et al.* 2001: 12). I argue that this either/or perspective on emotion is a false dichotomy, reminiscent of the rational/emotional dichotomy that plagued sociology until recently (Ferree 1992, Damasio 1994).

The structural and cultural perspectives on emotion need not be mutually exclusive (Goodwin *et al.* 2001: 13, 15). In fact, a combination of structural generation and cultural construction makes for a powerful theory of emotions. If we grant that micro-structural positions generate basic emotions, for example Scheff's assertion that pride results from social inclusion and that shame results from social exclusion (1990), or Collins's assertion that positioning relative to micro-patterns of power, status, inclusion, and exclusion will result in high or low emotional energy (1990), we can still allow that expectations and norms, as Hochschild (1983) and Jasper (1998) suggest, play the significant role in our understanding of the meaning of these experiences and how we behave in response to them. For example, Barker (2001: 188) points out that 'rituals possess sensuous, aesthetic qualities, drawing people into collective performances where bodies are meaningfully active together. But these emotion-laden qualities do not exist apart from content, meanings, reasons, perceptions, memories, aspirations.' Including a structural perspective within a cultural framework will allow us to ask a number of questions. What kinds of social relational conditions favor emotions that enable social movements communities to sustain themselves (Kemper 2001: 59)? How do group cultures that support continued opportunities for building positive emotions emerge from patterns of interaction within the groups? These questions are not exclusively about structure, culture, ideology, or framing. They encourage students of social movements to consider micro-structural conditions that help participants to repeatedly identify and connect emotionally with others.

In this research the emotion of solidarity is primary in sustaining the Catholic workers social movement activity. Cognition, symbols, and culture set the stage and provide the opportunity for interactions that create solidarity; in turn solidarity-producing interactions have significant cognitive, symbolic, and cultural implications. Other work in collective identity and framing has addressed the more cultural and cognitive aspects of social movement activity (Snow *et al.* 1986; Snow and Benford 1988; Taylor and Whittier 1992; Jasper 1998; Polletta and Jasper 2001). Building on this body of work, I focus primarily on the structure of interactions that underlie the creation of solidarity, and then I bring culture back in the conclusion.

There are different conditions necessary for creating solidarity across various structural positions. I consider conditions that produce two major types of solidarity in a Catholic worker community. First, I examine emotions which flow between activists and the community members whom they aim to help. Since the Catholic workers primarily come from a different social class than the people in the Catholic worker neighborhood, solidarity is a necessary bridge reducing otherwise existing social distance and discomfort. Second, I consider what Jasper refers to as reciprocal emotions (1998) or participants' day-to-day feelings for each other (Taylor and Whittier 1992; Taylor 1995; Taylor and Rupp 2002). As Kemper points out, 'social movements are not always in the "firing line"' (2001: 61); much of the time the emotions most relevant to social movements are those associated with internal group dynamics. Social movement emotion work also happens between activists who must negotiate working together, and sometimes living together, often without pay and the support/confines of traditional organizational structures.

Emotion, solidarity, and agape

Drawing on Durkheim (1995 [1912]) and Goffman (1967), Collins argues that individuals gain emotional energy, which feels like confidence, enthusiasm, and willingness to initiate interaction, from participating in face-to-face interaction or group level rituals that produce solidarity (Collins 1990). Emotional energy is the individual spin-off of the creation of solidarity on the group level (Collins 1990). Aron and Aron argue from a slightly different perspective, but with similar theoretical consequences, that people find experiences of self-expansion, enlarging one's self to include another or others, deeply emotionally rewarding (Aron and Aron 2000). I combine these theories to suggest that people are drawn towards experiences of solidarity, and that these experiences of solidarity produce emotional energy because they are experiences of self-expansion, where our sense of self, not only our cognitive identity but also our feeling of our self, grows to include others.

This proposition points towards a phenomenon that the pragmatist philosopher, Peirce, described as agape. Agape is a cherishing and nurturing love where one sacrifices one's own perfection to the perfectionment of one's neighbor (Peirce cited in Anderson 1995: 105). In moments of agape we experience the needs and feelings of the other as our own; the other not distant from us, but one of our beloved own (Anderson 1995: 105). If ritual produces emotional energy through self-expansion, we could describe this emotional experience and the resulting cognitive consequences as agape. Catholic workers actively produce the emotional capacity to sustain their work and their community through ritual and the self-expansion that bring about experiences of agape.

In order for self-expansion and the resulting solidarity and emotional energy to occur, the self must become permeable. Within this Catholic worker community, the boundaries of the self become permeable primarily in three ways: material vulnerability, ritual, and laughter. The first is central for maintaining solidarity with the neighborhood; the second two are central to maintaining solidarity within the community. All three processes can undermine the presentation of an autonomous self (Goffman 1959) that can prevent the experience of self-expansion.

The research

The original Catholic worker community has grown into a loose association of independent houses that range from formal, non-profit, hierarchical structures at one end, to informal personalist houses of hospitality, which are closer to the original Catholic worker ideal, at the other. I have conducted participant observation in a more traditional Catholic worker community from fall 2000 through to spring 2003. This particular house is located in an impoverished, predominantly Latino and African-American, urban neighborhood in a large east coast city in the US. On average there have been three Catholic workers living in the house, plus three to five 'guests', people who would otherwise be homeless. Another ten to 15 extended community members are deeply involved in the work of the house, so that there were often five to seven 'staff' in the house at any given time. Besides hosting guests, the community gives food at the door during lunch and dinner, has after school tutoring for the kids in the neighborhood, maintains what they refer to as a clothing room that is open to the people of the neighborhood, and goes to regular peace protests.

I spent my time with the Catholic workers helping with all of the activities of the house (from feeding people to making signs for protests) and participating in community activities (from house liturgies to casual discussions over coffee). During my time there I saw people come and go from the community, both Catholic workers and guests, and I got to know the core community members, the extended support community, and the people from the neighborhood. Based on this participant observation, I argue that solidarity is the backbone of a lifestyle and movement that requires long-term altruistic efforts.

Vulnerability, agape, and the day-to-day work of Catholic workers

If people are usually wrapped up in their performance of themselves (Goffman 1959), the performance wears thinnest at moments of pain, grief, embarrassment, or open need or dependence. The intensity of the moment pulls us into the moment, leaving little room for the perspective and distance required for a seamless performance. Moments of vulnerability represent opportunity for social failure, but they also offer the potential for self-expansion as the presentation upholding the self as a discrete individual becomes less secure. A route to extend one's self to include another, to get that jolt of emotional energy from self-expansion, is to be willing to share one's pain or take another's pain on as one's own in a moment of communion. Pain and vulnerability are some of the best moments for self-expansion because pain is universal. It cuts across culture, meaning, and symbols, and the path to helping is relatively obvious, especially if the pain or vulnerability is material rather than emotional. The Catholic workers in this community regularly work to open themselves to the pain of others to create solidarity with their neighborhood and extended community.

The Catholic workers live in solidarity with the poor. They give away most of their possessions and move into houses in poor neighborhoods. This initial purposeful impoverishment is a great initial equalizer between the Catholic workers and the people of the neighborhood. Solidarity is facilitated through the Catholic workers' own experience of vulnerability and uncertainty. By living in the same neighborhood and in similar conditions, the Catholic workers create routine face-to-face encounters and the potential to politicize the everyday experiences they share with their neighbors (Taylor and Rupp 2002: 141). They too know what it is like to have nothing in the bank and no idea how they will pay their bills. They rely on the generosity of friends and strangers to make ends meet. Events such as big community dinners, Christmas parties, and spontaneous community gatherings for the neighborhood affect the Catholic workers beyond just feeling good about having served the poor for a holiday dinner (the typical feel-good charity effort). They do not leave and go home; these are *their* holiday dinners and parties as well. The Catholic workers' ability to identify, not just cognitively but emotionally, helps to prevent the demeaning power dynamic that can be associated with charity. Their ability to connect enables both the helper and the person being helped to feel more like 'we're all in the same boat.'

I can best explain the emotional experiences associated with self-expansion and agape through field notes I have taken about my own experiences interacting with people in the neighborhood. The following section is based on an interaction I had with a neighborhood woman who is crack addicted and regularly engages in prostitution. One afternoon she came to the Catholic worker house for a shower and change of clothes. I helped her pick out clothes. While I do not share the Catholic workers' emotional experience of having to beg for my sustenance, I was vulnerable in this interaction because I was trying to gain intimate access to the organization to do my participant observation. At this point, this woman was better connected to the community than I was. If I had come to the Catholic worker house with the sole intent to help people, I might have felt that I was in a position of power, but since my goal was to fit in, and I perceived that she could help or hurt this process, we were vulnerable to each other. She was materially vulnerable and I was socially vulnerable.

We had a great time picking out an outfit for her in the clothing room, as if we were shopping together. 'Oh, that's cute!' 'That won't work at all.' 'That would look great on you!' By the time we were done picking out the clothes, I had a heightened awareness that if circumstances in our lives had been slightly different, I could have been her and she could have been me. She left to shower and came back to show off her new outfit.

> While we were in the room and she was getting ready to leave, it became clear that she wanted a hug, and I wanted to hug her too. I hesitated for a second and then reached out and hugged her. She was so vulnerable, thankful, easily made happy, and she felt like a reed when I hugged her. It filled me with a strange combination of joy, pride, relief, humility, and power.
>
> (field notes)

The evidence for self-expansion is in the combination of emotions that I experienced: pride and humility, relief and power, and the overarching emotion of joy. The experience is pleasurable and contains apparently contradictory emotions that reflect our different positions in the interaction. It was not apparent where my humility ended and hers began, nor where my relief ended and hers began. It is important to note, however, that there was hesitation on both of our parts. For my part I recognized the risk in extending myself and had to choose to make the deeper connection with this woman. We can assume that her reservation represented the assessment of some risk as well. When the connection is made in these moments of informal interaction rituals, the selves of the helper and the person being helped expand to include the self of the other; the distinction between the helper and the one being helped seems to break down. Helping feels more like being on the same team rather than giving charity.

Delving into the pain of the world may look like a masochistic activity, but it is a central part of how the Catholic workers derive emotional energy from their lifestyle. It opens the Catholic workers up to connections that are deeply satisfying, and allows them to do work that may appear to be self-sacrificing while minimizing the threat of 'burnout' associated with helping professions. These agapic connections entail more than identifying with someone for whom one is sacrificing; it is a risky strategy for gaining positive emotions. When the connection is made, there is self-expansion and positive emotional energy for all involved; when the workers or guests extend themselves and are rejected, those who take the risk lose emotional energy. Understanding the process of self-expansion and the resulting gain in emotional energy goes beyond theories of altruism that still situate motives solely within individual actors, such as nested interest (Frank 1990) or expressions of individualism (Wuthnow 1991). Instead, it situates the goal that motivates action between rather than within individuals. The emotional current that pulls those participating in the interaction towards self-expansion, despite risk and hesitation, grows out of the interaction itself.

Creating and maintaining solidarity within the community

Ritual

Ritual is the foundation of solidarity and ultimately meaning (Durkheim 1995 [1912]). In a time when loose and overlapping networks heighten the importance of individuals in social life (Carrithers *et al.* 1985; Wuthnow 1991), the Catholic workers use ritual – laughter in particular – to create a sub-universe of shared meaning (Flam 1996: 103) where the individual is de-emphasized in order to achieve their most basic goal of living in community. Religious order communities have structures that foster the consideration of the group before the self, but as an anarchist community, the Catholic workers have no formal structures that help to accomplish their most fundamental goal of community solidarity. Instead, the Catholic workers create opportunities for group ritual to build and maintain solidarity (Goffman 1967; Durkheim 1995). Almost all movements use ritual to support the emotional life of the community (Taylor and Rupp 2002: 145). Ritual transforms the emotions that brought about the ritual – anger, sadness, friendship, frustration, fear, etc. (Taylor 1995; Goodwin *et al.* 2001) – into solidarity, enthusiasm, and morality (Collins 2001b: 29; Roscigno *et al.* 2002). Being entrained within a collective focus of attention, the process of acting together, and sharing an awareness of this focus generates emotional energy; it is the emotion that makes up solidarity and allows the participant to feel stronger as a member of the group (Collins 2001b: 29).

The tradition of a weekly community gathering is an example of the type of routine rituals that the Catholic workers create. Once a week the extended community, mostly white middle class supporters but also some guests and people from the neighborhood, participate in a community dinner at the Catholic worker house. It might seem like an extra strain on the community to host people from the outside when they are already busy and taxed working on the needs of the people of the neighborhood, but during this weekly ritual, which often involves the formal ritual of liturgy, the extended group reaffirms the Catholic workers as the sacred symbols of the community (Durkheim 1995 [1912]). Because the Catholic workers are the center of attention and praise, these weekly dinners are an emotional boost to the Catholic workers from their extended community.

The Catholic workers also routinely engage in informal rituals of telling stories about divine intervention. This is another type of important routine ritual that I observed:

> Lynne went on to tell the story of how their car needed a new transmission and that it cost too much money to fix. She said that she had prayed to St. Francis, saying that there would be lots of work that she wouldn't be able to do without a car, but that she would leave it up to God. A month later, they got a new car by way of a donation from a professor. Next, she told the story of coming home to find that the house had been broken into, and that all of their possessions worth anything had been stolen. Moments after walking into the house and finding it in this state, they received a phone call from a priest who was going to come by to drop off a $1,000 check. I had heard both of these stories before, and I could see that telling them was an important community ritual. Most of the other people in the room had heard the stories before as well, but the stories were not to inform, they were to inspire, and they did.
>
> (field notes)

The stories and the ritual of telling the stories parallel each other; as the content of the stories begins with despair and ends with joy, so too does the ritual. In this case the ritual began during a down time in the group, when the group's connection to the local food bank had been severed. The negative feelings of despair were transformed into 'miraculous' positive emotion and group feelings. Negative emotions are excellent for staging rituals because they strongly focus attention. Initial negative emotions also draw people into the ritual by creating a need for their counterparts, for the solidarity and emotional energy that produce positive emotions. Evoking negative emotions on the individual level would likely lead to further feelings of hopelessness and helplessness, but on the group level it creates emotional intensity and focus that helps to bring off a successful ritual.[1]

Laughter

One might anticipate that a group whose moral standards include lack of ownership, income, and security would be serious and either self-congratulatory or self-critical, but peals of laughter regularly echo through the community's house:

Today one of the guests commented that when they were staying upstairs they would hear the Catholic workers howling in laughter downstairs. She said her husband wondered at how much they laughed, and had suggested jokingly that they were smoking something. Both Lynn and guest laughed hard as she relayed this story.

(field notes)

This group laughter appears to be a release valve from the multiple stresses and sources of shame the Catholic workers routinely encounter: inability to effectively help a neighbor, the instability and chaos of the neighborhood, financial stress, and the stress of living in a community with people who have vastly different personalities, and sometimes vastly different expectations for what living in a community should be like.

Shame is the emotional consequence of a threatened social bond; conflict, for example, can be a recurrent source of shame (Scheff 1990). If shame is not diffused, it will lead to internal shame spirals, where one becomes ashamed of being ashamed, which may lead to more shame or rage, which would lead to another level of shame, and so on (Scheff 1990). Undiffused shame may also lead to interpersonal shame spirals, where others in the interaction are ashamed of the failure of the interaction, which leads to rage or shame and another layer of shame for being ashamed (Scheff 1990). Both internal and interpersonal shame spirals have potential negative consequences for the social bonds of all of those involved in the interaction (Scheff 1990). Undiffused shame can lead to self-consciousness and negative self-feelings that may ultimately threaten the cohesion of a group (Scheff 1990). For example, sometimes the guests of the Catholic worker community disappoint the Catholic workers by stealing from them or lying to them, and the Catholic workers talk about feeling like 'suckers' or 'fools.' During these times the Catholic workers sometimes blame each other, saying things such as, 'I knew that Brent and Terry were lying to us, but you insisted that we let them stay,' thereby assigning personal blame for having been taken advantage of by a guest. When this happens anger builds within the community, seeming to ricochet off of the individual Catholic workers. Scheff points out that laughter is the most effective way of diffusing shame (1990: 173). By diffusing shame, laughter helps to diffuse the tension around conflict in the group (Scheff 1990), which ultimately helps to maintain solidarity within the group.

Specifically, self-deprecating humor is central to maintaining solidarity and a sense of cohesion within the group. It acts almost as a sort of confession – it wipes the individual clean of shame, so that they can quickly heal any rift in group solidarity and rejoin the group without self-consciousness.

Lynn said that the ice cream was in the basement because the refrigerator upstairs was broken. I asked, half seriously, if they were waiting for God to get them a new refrigerator. Everyone thought this was really funny; most were doubled over in laugher. The laughter was irresistible, contagious, I found myself laughing as well. I'm not sure what we were laughing at; it wasn't my question, but my question definitely triggered it. Finally, Lynn stopped laughing long enough to say that she was debating whether to call the repair man or not, and that she had had a few discussions with St. Francis about it. After saying this, she was immediately consumed with laughter again.

(field notes)

This sort of laughter helps to maintain connections with the larger sympathetic supporters of the community. There is an inherent conflict based in divergent beliefs. It is crucial that the more religious community members are able to mediate between their own religious views and those of the people surrounding them, as they continually interact with those who do not share their faith. While their mysticism helps to sustain the Catholic workers, even their closest supporters are not necessarily likely to believe that God could or would help with broken refrigerators. The Catholic workers ability to laugh about their religious beliefs and mysticism allows them to dispel any shame that might result from interacting with those who do not have such intense or mystical religious views.

Differences in level of commitment also produce shame that must be diffused to maintain an extended support community for the Catholic workers. When a movement is high risk and altruistic, appealing to potential supporters is a complicated matter. The whole movement is the conscience constituency, so core members are not people who have more personal interest at stake, but rather they are the participants who are the most committed. They could easily take the moral high ground (See Flam 1996 for a discussion of honor in the Committee for the Defense of the Workers (KOR) movement), but this is not necessarily useful for attracting new members or maintaining a less involved support community. While presenting themselves as moral authorities may provide a temporary gain, it undermines their main strategy for gaining and sustaining emotional energy. The Catholic workers are distinctive in that they strive to build solidarity not only between the central participants, but also their extended community and the people they serve, and a 'holier than thou' attitude is stratifying. Organizers in altruistic movements must walk a line between maintaining solidarity and pride within the group by stressing the moral righteousness of the group, and attempting to maintain needed but less committed supporters. An implicit moral deficiency that brings about shame for those less involved and committed must be defused in order to maintain the extended support community. Laughter is particularly effective in bridging this apparent moral gap.

Conclusion: bringing culture back into the picture

Social structural conditions may generate predictable emotions, however the significance of these emotional responses is in large part cultural (Taylor 1995: 228). The emotional and the symbolic are thoroughly integrated in the process of creating meaning (Damasio 1994). Symbols without emotional value have little meaning, just as emotions without symbolic information have little meaning. For example, above I emphasize the interactional structure of ritual in my analysis of the Catholic workers' ritualized storytelling, but their storytelling rituals have important cognitive framing components as well. These storytelling rituals are not just about energizing the group, but also the symbols associated with their work and their style of approaching their work.

In Flam's work (1996), we see that a social movement community will build a self-contained sub-universe of meaning to manage the anxiety associated with the high-risk of participation. We can see this with the Catholic workers as they tell stories of taking great risks, 'putting themselves in God's hands,' only to be rewarded through apparently divine intervention. In these stories, they reaffirm culturally based cognitive tools for framing their demanding, chaotic, and financially insecure lifestyle as work that is 'closely guided by God.' The end effect is that rather than feeling anxious, they feel that they may not even be 'worthy' of the lifestyle that they are trying live. These culturally constructed symbolic tools help to lead the Catholic workers to future interactions where there are opportunities to enjoy satisfying solidarity building and self-expanding interactions with people in their social movement community and in their larger neighborhood. There is a cyclical process between culture and micro-structure. Patterns of interaction generate emotions that give weight and meaning to symbols. These symbols are the bases for a shared group culture that help to support continued opportunities for solidarity building and self-expansion. This process of creating emotionally generated symbols and using symbols to guide future interactions, enables the Catholic workers not only to continue, but also largely to enjoy their work.

The limit of the Catholic workers' ability to build solidarity with the neighborhood illustrates both the connection between group culture and its cognitive implications, as well as how patterns of interaction have emotional consequences. Bridging power differences to create and maintain solidarity is challenging. The Catholic workers' commitment to living in poverty provides a structural opportunity that makes this sort of connection possible, but it far from guarantees it. Although there is micro-structural opportunity for building solidarity and agape, sometimes culture in the form of expectations, previously established meanings, and stereotyped interactions can prevent the connection from happening. In order to identify with the Catholic workers, people from the neighborhood need to recognize the Catholic workers' material vulnerability and see themselves in a shared struggle with the Catholic workers. Some people from the neighborhood see the Catholic workers as the Catholic workers wish to be seen; they see that they are poor as well and that they live the way that they do because they believe that the lifestyle is just. Others, however, see the Catholic workers as 'suckers,' 'strange white people' (although not all of the Catholic workers are white) who do not seem to notice that people are taking advantage of them. With these people solidarity and agape are nearly impossible to achieve.

The Catholic workers sometimes lose their ability to identify with their neighbors as well. They sometimes see themselves as a community in poverty that makes 'good' choices, while some of the people from the neighborhood make 'bad' choices. In such moments, the workers involved in such discussions often point out that the grandmothers from the community (who are raising most of the children) are doing everything that they can to survive, and that they can only think 'one day to the next'. The implication is that longer-term strategies might bear better fruit, but no one can hold the neighbors responsible for only seeing the short-term.

At other times the Catholic workers have discussions where they point to much more obvious 'bad' choices. However, those involved in these conversations usually imply again that even these questionable choices are not ultimately the fault of the individuals making them, suggesting they are the product of a lack of hope, education, and opportunity. These discussions and the shared interpretative schemas that grow out of them enable the Catholic workers to maintain solidarity with each other and compassion for the people of the neighborhood, but they can also distance the Catholic workers from potential interactions that would enable them to achieve solidarity with their neighbors as peers in the struggle for the radical transformation of society. Thus the affect of culture in the form of readily available scripts and frames for interpreting behavior can affect the potential for taking advantage of the opportunity for solidarity and self-expansion that the structure of interaction affords.

While I have focused primarily on a micro-structural approach to understanding solidarity, clearly culture in the forms of ideology, norms, cognition, and expectations plays a role in the process of creating and maintaining solidarity. Social movement communities develop emotion cultures that help to frame the emotional experiences of members (Taylor and Whittier 1992; Taylor and Rupp 2002: 142). We can see this with the Catholic workers in that their beliefs play a crucial role in promoting interactions that will allow for self-expansion, solidarity, and agape. The Catholic workers' beliefs also give them tools for understanding these connections, which sometimes support their work and other times undermine their ability to identify with the people of the neighborhood. Understanding that culture plays an important role in this process adds a piece to a structural solidarity/self-expansion model of motivation (Collins 1990;

Aron and Aron 2000; Summers-Effler 2002) by suggesting that culture and ideology can put one in the right place and help one to interpret the structurally based potential for self-expansion and solidarity.

By considering how mutual vulnerability, ritual, and laughter create micro-structural opportunities for solidarity building and self-expansion, we are able to answer our original question and see how continuing opportunities for intense and satisfying interactions sustain the Catholic worker community in the face of little apparent progress towards their stated goal of the radical transformation of society.

Note

1 There is no doubt that these narratives are part of symbolic as well as emotional work. These rituals serve to create solidarity and emotional energy around the ritual itself, but also to reconnect positive group emotions to their ideology and to the physical, emotional, economic risks they take. We can also analyze these storytelling interactions as narratives central to the framing process and the social construction of the community's meaning (Snow and Benford 1988; Snow *et al.* 1986), but for the purposes of this chapter I highlight ritual, emotional, and patterns of interaction. In the conclusion of the chapter, I point towards connections between the two perspectives.

References

Allahyari, R.A. (2000) *Visions of Charity: volunteer workers and moral community*, Berkley: University of California Press.
—— (2001) 'The felt politics of charity: serving "the ambassadors of God" and saving "the Sinking Classes",' in J. Goodwin, J.M. Jasper, and F. Polletta (eds) *Passionate Politics*, Chicago: University of Chicago Press.
Anderson, D.R. (1995) 'Peirce's agape and the generality of concern,' *International Journal for Philosophy of Religion*, 37: 103–12.
Aron, A. and Aron, E.N. (2000) 'Self-expansion motivation and including Other in the self,' in W. Ickes and S. Duck (eds) *The Social Psychology of Personal Relationships*, New York: Wiley.
Barker, C. (2001) 'Fear, laughter, and collective power: the making of solidarity at the Lenin Shipyard in Gdnask, Poland, August 1980,' in J. Goodwin, J. Jasper and F. Polletta (eds) *Passionate Politics*, Chicago: University of Chicago Press.
Carrithers, M., Collins, S., and Lukes, S. (1985) *The Category of the Person: anthropology, philosophy, history*, New York: Cambridge University Press.
Collins, R. (1990) 'Stratification, emotional energy, and the transient emotions,' in T. Kemper (ed.) *Research Agendas in the Sociology of Emotions*, New York: State University of New York Press.
—— (2001a) 'Social movements and the focus of emotional attention,' in J. Goodwin, J.M. Jasper, and F. Polletta (eds) *Passionate Politics*, Chicago: University of Chicago Press.
—— (2001b) 'Situational stratification: a micro-macro theory of inequality,' *Sociological Theory*, 18: 17–43.
Damasio, A.R. (1994) *Descartes' Error*, New York: HarperCollins.

DiMaggio, P.J. (1997) 'Culture and cognition,' *Annual Review of Sociology*, 23: 263–87.

Durkheim, E. (1995 [1912]) *The Elementary Forms of Religious Life*, New York: Free Press.

Ferree, M.M. (1992) 'The political context of rationality: rational choice theory and resource mobilization,' in A. Morris and C. McClurg (eds) *Frontiers in Social Movement Theory*, New Haven: Yale University Press.

Flam, H. (1996) 'Anxiety and the successful oppositional construction of societal reality: the case of KOR,' *Mobilization*, 1: 103–21.

Frank, R.H. (1990) 'A theory of moral sentiments,' in J.J. Mansbridge (ed.) *Beyond Self-Interest*, Chicago: University of Chicago Press.

Goffman, E. (1959) *The Presentation of Self in Everyday Life*, Garden City: Doubleday.

—— (1967) *Interaction Ritual: essays on face-to-face behavior*, Chicago: Aldine.

Goodwin, J., Jasper, J.M. and Polletta, F. (eds) (2001) *Passionate Politics: emotions and social movements*, Chicago: University of Chicago Press.

Hochschild, A.R. (1983) *The Managed Heart: commercialization of human feeling*, Berkeley: University of California Press.

Jasper, J. (1998) 'The emotions of protest: affective and reactive emotions in and around social movements,' *Sociological Forum*, 13: 397–424.

Kemper, T.D. (1981) 'Social constructionist and positivist approaches to the sociology of emotions,' *American Journal of Sociology*, 87: 336–62.

—— (1990) 'Social relations and emotions: a structural approach,' in T.D. Kemper (ed.) *Research Agendas in the Sociology of Emotions*, Albany: State University of New York Press.

—— (2001) 'A structural approach to social movement emotions,' in J. Goodwin, J.M. Jasper, and F. Polletta (eds) *Passionate Politics*, Chicago: University of Chicago Press.

Nepstad, S.E. and Smith, C. (2001) 'The social structure of moral outrage in recruitment to the U.S. Central America peace movement,' in J. Goodwin, J.M. Jasper, and F. Polletta (eds) *Passionate Politics*, Chicago: University of Chicago Press.

Polletta, F. and Jasper, J.M. (2001) 'Collective identity and social movements,' *Annual Review of Sociology*, 27: 283–305.

Roscigno, V.J., Danaher, W., and Summers-Effler, E. (2002) 'Music, culture, and social movements: the case of song and southern textile worker mobilization,' *International Journal for Sociology and Social Policy*, 3: 141–74.

Scheff, T.J. (1990) *Microsociology: discourse, emotion, and social structure*, Chicago: University of Chicago Press.

Snow, D.A. and Benford. R.D. (1988) 'Ideology, frame resonance, and participant mobilization,' *International Social Movement Research*, 1: 197–217.

Snow, D.A., Rochford, E.B., Worden, S.K., and Benford, R.D. (1986) 'Frame alignment processes, micromobilization, and movement participation,' *American Sociological Review*, 51: 464–81.

Summers-Effler, E. (2002) 'The micro potential for social change: emotion, consciousness, and social movement formation,' *Sociological Theory*, 20: 41–60.

Taylor, V. (1995) 'Watching for vibes: bringing emotions into the study of feminist organizations,' in M.M. Ferree and P.Y. Martin (eds) *Feminist Organizations*, Philadelphia: Temple University Press.

Taylor, V. and Rupp, L.J. (2002) 'Loving internationalism: the emotion culture of transnational women's organizations, 1888–1945,' *Mobilization*, 7: 141–58.

Taylor, V. and Whittier, N. (1992) 'Collective identity in social movement communities: lesbian feminist mobilization,' in A. Morris and C. McClurg (eds) *Frontiers in Social Movement Theory*, New Haven: Yale University Press.

Wuthnow, R. (1991) *Acts of Compassion: caring for others and helping ourselves*, Princeton, NJ: Princeton University Press.

9 Sustaining activism through emotional reflexivity

Debra King

When I got sick, working as a unionist, I went and did a course in counselling. And I still do regular counselling. I do a form of co-counselling, and that's really made a difference . . .

(Emma)

Bringing about social change is a mammoth undertaking. It requires both personal and systemic change; it is multi-dimensional and long-term; it involves small wins, many setbacks and few groundbreaking shifts; it is a risky venture. While it is a venture that continually attracts people, it is also one that burns them out, making them 'lose heart' (Kovan and Dirkx 2003; see also, Kleres this volume) or, as with Emma, become sick, apathetic or even cynical. Indeed, it is somewhat surprising that so many activists manage to sustain their activism over long periods, sometimes even lifetimes. The question is *how* do they do this? Finding ways of sustaining activists will be beneficial to individual activists, the longevity of social movements and, ultimately, the success of social change.

For Emma, the key to sustaining her activism was co-counselling.[1] As a feminist unionist she had fought for the recognition of women's rights in male dominated and heavily masculinized organizations. Finding her work rewarding but emotionally exhausting she was brought to the brink of burnout upon the birth of her first child. She became physically ill and discussed that period of her life as one where her identity was fragmented between activist, mother and worker. Instead of giving up on her activism, however, she developed strategies for coping with her emotional exhaustion, physical illness, and fragmentation of the self. One of these strategies was a form of peer counselling known as co-counselling or re-evaluation counselling.

In contrast with other therapeutic discourses, co-counselling has an explicitly political framework (Rosen 1978). At one level, it eliminates the expert-client power relationship found in professional counselling relationships. Instead, the co-counselling relationship is a reciprocal one in which people take turns at being the 'listener' and 'listened to'. At another level, it has a social change agenda whereby people aim to liberate themselves (and each other) of the emotional ties that bind them to the values and ideas of dominant society. It is this goal of emotional liberation that activists found most useful. In addition, they needed strategies to sustain their emotional attachments to oppositional ideological positions. In essence, co-counselling provided a forum within which activists, like Emma, could bring their emotions and politics into line and sustain their participation in social movements.

Emma's was not an isolated story. It was, in effect, part of an emergent theme from a larger research project that examined how passion influenced the relationship between work and identity for activists. After two years of being a member-researcher in three social change organizations, and conducting 20 interviews with key activists involved in a range of social movements, it became clear that many participants were using forms of counselling and meditation as strategies for sustaining themselves as activists. Interestingly, the peace organization I was researching also integrated aspects of counselling practices into their meeting structures and decision-making processes. Members were encouraged to attend to both the emotional and rational aspects of their peace work, with opportunities to develop the skills necessary for this to occur being provided within the organization. The organization's co-ordinating group viewed this strategy as a means of sustaining the necessary levels of emotional energy required for long-term social change or, to put it another way, of avoiding activists leaving the organization due to emotional exhaustion. Only two activists from this peace organization were part of the original interview process (one of whom was involved in co-counselling). However, a further six interviewees discussed using co-counselling as a strategy for sustaining their activism, while two others used a form of active meditation. I reviewed the snowball sampling process for indications of bias, and once satisfied that this appeared minimal (only one co-counsellor referred me to another co-counsellor), I began to investigate co-counselling, focusing on why activists found it so useful as a strategy for sustaining their activism.

In this chapter I examine co-counselling as a form of activist identity work. To do this, I draw upon Touraine's (1995) discussion of non-commitment, aligned to what I call deintegration, in the construction of the Subject as social movement; and Hochschild's (1979, 1983) discussion of dissonance in her theory of emotion work and emotional labour.

Deintegration is a process through which individuals separate out from society's dominant norms and values. They need to do this so that they can develop themselves as a Subject – a reflective, creative, productive actor – rather than merely exist as an ego attached to society (Touraine 1995: 282–4). In demonstrating non-commitment to dominant norms and re-aligning their commitment to oppositional ideologies, activists are exemplars of such individuals. They explicitly exist in the space between integration and de-integration. Existing in this space, however, is likely to create a level of conflict or dissonance at both the emotional and cognitive levels. This is particularly so if there is a time-lag between an activist's shift in their cognitive and their emotional frames. To achieve and sustain an activist identity, this dissonance needs to be overcome. Hochschild argues that emotional reflexivity, the process through which emotional work is conducted, will help to address this issue.

Evidence suggests that activists' experiences of deintegration and dissonance often lead to burnout, withdrawal or cynicism. I therefore argue that if the Subject is to become – and remain – social movement, greater emphasis needs to be placed on the emotions and emotional reflexivity. Such reflexivity however, has to extend beyond Hochschild's focus on the manipulation of emotions to one that also incorporates the problematization of emotions: to an emotional reflexivity that operates not just on emotions, but also through them. Co-counselling is the case study through which these aspects of activists' identity work are explicated.

For activists, co-counselling provided three sources of support for them to become, and remain, a Subject. First it encouraged activists to problematize the 'true self', or what Touraine might call the Ego, in order to deintegrate from society and reframe their emotional and rational responses accordingly. Second, in recognizing the effect of emotive dissonance in this process, co-counselling provided activists with the skills to be emotionally reflexive. There were two aspects to this. Activists learned to both objectify the emotions and reflect upon them to ensure that the appropriate emotion was displayed; and to subjectively reflect through the emotions to re-create the emotional frames required to sustain their identities as activists. Third, the co-counselling community had a supportive, emotional culture through which activists could express non-normative (Taylor 1999, 2000) or deviant emotions (Hercus 1999), and construct and maintain their 'deviant' identities as activists. Importantly, this culture was external to their main activist social movement organizations. This level of independence allowed activists to also work through problems that arose from within their social change work.

Emotive dissonance and the subject as social movement

Dissonance is one reason that burnout occurs in workers (Brotheridge and Grandey 2002; Bolton 2001; Tracy and Tracy 1998) and, more specifically, activists (Hercus 1999; Smith and Erickson 1997). While some workers can separate themselves out from the behaviour required that causes dissonance, for activists it is endemic to their identities *as* activists. Maintaining an oppositional stance on issues requires activists to constantly negate the hegemonic messages and norms that permeate society. Dissonance is an outcome of deintegrating from these social norms and values. Sustaining their identities as activists therefore entails perpetual vigilance and attention to this aspect of their identity work. It is not, however, just the dissonance of ideas that activists need to attend to, but also the dissonance of emotions. This requires emotion work, an aspect of deintegration that Touraine neglects.

For Touraine (1995), the Subject is late modernity's agent of change. While it is possible for any individual to be a Subject, it would seem that activists are Subjects *par excellence*. As such they provide useful insights into the process of subjectivization. Capable of actively producing society, the Subject constructs itself and exists in the space between social integration and deintegration, or commitment and non-commitment (Touraine 1995: 282–6). Thus while it is recognized that the Subject exists within a plethora of discourses and structures which influence the ways in which they become integrated into society, the process of deintegration is seen as essential if the subject is to develop a 'will to act and to be recognized as an actor' (Touraine 1995: 207). Without deintegration, individuals would simply be caught in the web of discourses and social structures that merely reproduce society. It is through striving for deintegration, however, that the Subject becomes social movement.

While self-reflection in the construction of the subject is discussed in Touraine's argument concerning the emergence of the Subject (1995: 227), I feel that it is a somewhat underdeveloped aspect of his theory. His wariness regarding the narcissistic practices of reflexivity, the conservatism of the theories of reflexivity that he reviewed, and his aversion to theories of subjection have led to the marginalization of reflexivity in his theoretical framework. Part of Touraine's inability to recognize the importance of reflexivity is that he focused primarily on the rational, cognitive aspects of subjectivation. As argued in this chapter, however, deintegration requires an engagement with the emotional as well as the cognitive attachments to internalized knowledge.

Hochschild (1979, 1983) highlights the extent to which emotions are associated with the internalization of social norms in her study of emotive dissonance and emotion work. In short, she argues that emotional dissonance is created when a person is expected to feel something other than what they are actually feeling. In order to feel the expected emotion, it is possible to either surface act (pretend) or deep act and subsequently integrate the new emotional expectation into their sense of self. It is necessary, therefore, to do emotion work on the self. Hochschild goes on to identify three techniques associated with this emotion work: cognitive, bodily and expressive (1979: 562). Although separate, all three of these techniques are essentially cognitive as they involve the management or control of different aspects of an emotion: you change your ideas, physical symptoms or the expressive gestures related to a feeling. The emotions are objectified and then 'worked' upon. The feeling itself is not problematized. The urge is to feel the 'correct' feeling, rather than worry about why you felt inclined to feel the 'wrong' feeling in the first place. However, in my research I argue that it is not sufficient to merely manage the emotions, they need to be problematized and reflected through for activists to become Subjects.

Merging Hochschild with Touraine, then, it is evident that deintegration requires the reframing of messages, situations or emotions in ways that are not aligned to the dominant framing rules. Framing rules provide the social guidelines by which individuals ascribe definitions or meanings to situations; they are the 'rules for managing feeling [which] are implicit in any ideological stance' (Hochschild 1979: 566). They, in turn, influence the feeling rules or the social expectations about how people should respond to a situation emotionally, as well as the display rules which govern how these emotions should be expressed (Hochschild 1979). Because frames are socially constructed and because they differ in different social situations there can be a number of ways of framing the same situation. Framing depends on perspective. How you attain this perspective depends on which social norms and values you subscribe to, and whether these are hegemonic or not in your particular culture. Extracting yourself from the emotions related to a dominant frame in order to feel the emotions related to an oppositional frame can be more complex than extracting yourself from oppositional frames. This is because the dominant framing process is constantly being reinforced, reiterated and socially valued. This level of immersion often means that you are often not even aware that you are acquiring the emotions associated with them. It is for this reason that activists can feel that their emotions and politics simply do not line up.

Deintegration, however, allows activists' emotions and politics to line up. Activists therefore need to be constantly engaged in the emotion work that allows this to happen. I argue that for activists to sustain this level of emotion work over long periods of time, they need to become skilled in practices of emotional reflexivity and have a supportive emotional culture within which to explore the emotional and cognitive aspects of the framing process. In this research, activists used co-counselling to meet these needs. In this way the activists could be seen to be engaging in the process of becoming a Subject.

Researching co-counselling

Co-counselling was developed in Seattle (USA) in the 1950s by Harvey Jackins, a blacklisted trade union activist. It spread outside of Seattle in the late 1960s, and reached Australia in the early 1980s. It is currently being practiced in over 75 countries, has its own body of literature (and publishing company), and theory of identity and intelligence (Jackins: 1994b). In contrast to other forms of popular psychology, the theory behind co-counselling has an explicitly political basis (see Rosen 1978 for a comparison). That is, it provides a framework for linking personal and social change through a process of problematizing the relationship between emotions and internalized oppression. This political focus on what it calls 'wide-world change' is evident in its publications such as their international journal, *Present Time*. My analysis of the 3,932 articles[2] published over the period 1977–1992, indicated that articles on Wide-World Change, Class/Classism and Racism featured in the 'top 10' subject matters covered by the journal, with Wide-World Change coming second only to co-counselling practice.[3]

Researching co-counselling as an activist strategy was not easy. Within the organization there were norms and rules about not opening itself up to external scrutiny to the extent that it has a reputation of being secretive and cult-like (Rosen 1978). I was not allowed to be a participant observer, nor was I allowed to interview members of the organization. I was informed that I had to become a co-counsellor and be a member-researcher. My first formal contact was through an invitation from the coordinator of the peace organization that I was researching to attend an 'Introductory Co-counselling' meeting specifically targeting social activists. I then followed this up by doing the ten-week 'Fundamentals Class' and engaging in co-counselling sessions with members of the class. My involvement in the class gave me easier access to the formal literature on co-counselling through their library, journals and newsletters and enabled me to have informal 'conversations with a purpose' (Chenitz 1986: 79) with people in the organization. At the same time I interviewed two activists explicitly on their use of co-counselling. Marny was a practising co-counsellor who had a leadership role within the organization and within her activist organizations. Barbara was an 'ex' co-counsellor who was a feminist-environmentalist before moving into a more 'personalized' form of activism (Lichterman 1996).

My data therefore consisted of the accounts from seven activists in the original research, my research journal of being a co-counsellor, interviews with the two activist co-counsellors, informal conversations within the co-counselling community, and the co-counselling literature. In selecting co-counselling as a case study, I do not wish to imply uncritical support of it. I am aware of (and share) concerns that co-counselling has cult-like qualities, may reproduce 'victim' modes amongst practitioners, and is probably inadequate for dealing with serious mental health problems.[4] In addition, it could be argued that it merely substitutes one form of internalized constraint with another (i.e. co-counselling), although there was little doubt that the activists used co-counselling as a 'liberating' practice in much the same way that Touraine speaks about subjectivation. However, I am not undertaking an analysis of co-counselling per se,[5] rather the aim is to demonstrate how activists saw it as useful in challenging internal obstacles to creative and flexible thinking: in becoming a Subject.

Co-counselling theory

Membership in the co-counselling community is based on the acceptance of a one point programme, which is that co-counselling will be used to 'recover one's occluded intelligence and help others do the same' (Jackins 1994b: 16). Recovering this intelligence is seen as the key to bringing about both personal and social change.[6] The task in co-counselling is to reverse the damage caused by distress experiences, thereby recovering the blocked intelligence and enabling people to integrate thinking, feeling and acting in ways that are more appropriate to the immediate situation. In order to recover this intelligence it is necessary to engage in a reflexive process so that the information can be re-evaluated and re-stored in the brain and then be accessed in creative ways. Emotions are central to this re-evaluation process.

In effect, co-counselling theory argues that the brain reacts differently to good and bad experiences, that is, experiences where a person has or has not received attention to their emotional displays – be that joy, crying, anger, frustration or boredom (Jackins 1994a: 21–66). Sometimes new experiences tap into a 'record of distress', restimulating the original experience and the feelings that went with it. Thus a person's ability to think flexibly and intelligently about the new experience becomes blocked and any new information cannot be evaluated. This results in the cumulation of distresses and mis-stored experience. The cumulative effect of these distresses is that patterns of thinking and behaviour are formed in which feelings and actions have very little logical connection with what is actually happening. In co-counselling theory, this mis-storing of feelings and thinking is believed to lead to irrational and inappropriate action and is claimed to be one of the main reasons why oppressions such as racism, classism or sexism are reproduced. The essence of the recovery process is emotional discharge which, it is argued, facilitates the re-evaluation of mis-stored information (Jackins 1994a: 78–81).

Emotional reflexivity is therefore viewed as central to the processes of personal and social change. Without recognizing the ways in which emotions are inherently associated with particular ways of thinking and acting, and without having the skills to reflect on the relationship between emotions and thinking, it would be difficult to deintegrate from social values and norms.

Co-counselling the subject

I have argued that sustaining an identity as an activist requires constant attention to the process of deintegration, a central aspect of which is emotional reflexivity. Except for the framing, feeling and display rules around emotional suppression and expression, the skills involved in attaining coherence between emotions and politics or ideologies are rarely articulated and, even more rarely, taught. As a practice of emotional reflexivity, co-counselling provides a space within which this can occur. For within co-counselling, both individuals and the organization are encouraged to be reflexive – not just to look at or work on their emotions but to also shift patterns of thinking by incorporating and working through emotions.

In this section, I use the empirical data to focus on three aspects of co-counselling that assisted activists to become a Subject: it provided a forum within which activists could problematize the notion of a 'true self'; its practices of emotional reflexivity, where emotions are both the object and subject of the reflexive process, provided the skills for activists to disrupt internalized knowledges and achieve deeper levels of deintegration; and the processes, practices and structure of the co-counselling community pro-vided a supportive environment, external to particular social movement organizations, where activists could express their emotions and have dif-ferent modes of integrating personal and social change modelled.

Problematizing the 'true' self

Hochschild's claim that emotional dissonance is the discrepancy between one's real emotions and the emotions one is expected to feel (1983: 89–90), assumes a notion of a 'true self'. It is when this true self is alien-ated by the requirement to feel differently that emotive dissonance occurs (Tracy and Tracy 1998). The process of managing or working on the emo-tions associated with particular values and ideologies can either change the sense of self through deep acting, that is, become someone who 'naturally' feels the new emotions (Hochschild 1979, 1983) or engage in surface acting to develop a fragmented sense of self whereby emotional stances are 'adopted' but not incorporated into a way of being. In either case, the new emotional stance is seen to challenge the 'true self', the self that is integ-rated into particular social norms, and be an imposition on that self.

For activists, it is somewhat different. In their case, the challenge to the true self, or what Touraine calls the Ego, is welcomed because it is only through the splitting of the Ego into Subject and Self that activists can deintegrate and become social movement. If they are to fully deintegrate from the dominant norms and construct a (new) self around oppositional ideologies, they have to embrace both the new emotional and cognitive frames. Their problem is that they are often not aware of the extent to which they have emotional attachments to the old ideological frames, which then restrict their deintegration from dominant social norms and values. It is this problematization of the true self and its continued hold over their emotional frames that activists sought to explore through co-counselling.

Interestingly, co-counselling does have its own version of the 'true self'. Indeed the fundamental premise of co-counselling is that all humans are 'naturally' intelligent, good, loving and zestful, and if they do not always act this way then it is because their thinking has been disrupted by oppres-sive social structures and socialization processes (Jackins 1994a: 28). Some of the activists in the research took issue with this essentialist view of human nature. However, they proposed a more pragmatic approach which accepted that, if humans are not naturally anything (i.e. they are socially constructed), then they all have the capacity to be 'intelligent' in the co-counselling sense (Marny):

> I think that our ability to be flexible and to think well and be creative, kind of gets smashed around a bit as we get older. I think we need to reclaim that intelligence, that power.
>
> (Kate)

Getting back to this power involved removing the layers of emotional attachments to the different social norms and values associated with oppressive behaviours.

Activists who did co-counselling recognized the need to constantly deintegrate from the dominant ideological and emotional frames. These activists had been confronted by the fact that social change did not just need to happen 'out there' in society, but also within themselves. For, as long as their Ego or true self existed, they would be implicated in reproducing the social problems for which they were trying to find solutions. In Marny's words, the activists understood that they needed to 'unmake the effects of oppression on our own lives at the same time we try to unmake the oppressive system'.

Itzin's (1985) discussion of using co-counselling to accept Margaret Thatcher as her 'sister' demonstrates the extent to which patriarchal norms are internalized, even by feminists. She argues that unless feminists deintegrate from these norms, they will be implicated in reproducing patriarchy within society (1985: 75). For example, feminists might reproduce patriarchy through their attachment to competitive environments, through their disdain of women who fully embraced patriarchy, through the denial of their own bodies and so on. Recognizing the internalization of oppressive norms is what Marny referred to as the times when her 'emotions and politics just don't line up':

> Where I just feel like I can't do that, and the underlying message is I can't do that because I'm a woman. Sometimes it's not just that you never got taught to do it, but that you just FEEL like you just can't! Or you feel that you can do some things, or perhaps you shouldn't always be the one cleaning up in the kitchen at the end of every event that your organization organizes, and maybe one day it will be a man in the kitchen doing it instead! Feeling the pull to do those things, you know. Like somebody's got to clean up the kitchen and feeling that it HAS to be me. Those kinds of places where your emotions and your politics just don't line up, and you struggle to work out how to bring them together.
>
> (emphasis in original)

One of the difficulties for activists is that they are located within a society that reiterates and values ways of thinking and feeling associated with various oppressions. The need to 'unmake' the effects of oppression on themselves is therefore constant. They have to be vigilant in ensuring that they do not inadvertently lose focus or become reintegrated into these 'old' frames. Co-counselling helped activists to maintain a level of deintegration that allowed them to sustain their activism. It did this by explicitly recognizing oppression/integration as having both emotional and rational dimensions. Furthermore, it encouraged activists to problematize these emotional frames in order to think through the issues associated with various forms of oppression. This, however, required more than just rethinking the emotion, it also involved re-feeling it. As Itzin argues:

> But to imagine the end of THE oppression [patriarchy] and yet the continuance of self and mutual oppression is a way of making ourselves aware of the power of *internalised oppression* in our lives. It also reveals how eliminating internalised oppression is more than a case of mind over emotion. If it were just a matter of *deciding* not to, then feminists at least, with a feminist consciousness, would not allow ourselves to be divided from other women, knowing as we do how very detrimental . . . this is.
>
> (emphasis in original 1985: 76)

Emotional reflexivity therefore needs to move beyond Hochschild's cognitive approach of objectifying the emotions and working on them so that you can *feel* the 'right' way, which has been so pervasive in emotional labour research. For activists it is somewhat different. They require a more subjective, emotional form of reflexivity in which the emotions are felt and discharged so that they can feel *and think* in a more coherent way.

Beyond the cognitive approach to emotional reflexivity

Co-counsellors use both an objective, 'management' approach and a subjective, emotional approach to emotional reflexivity. The objective approach is used when acting 'in the moment', particularly when dealing with their response to their own or other people's emotions. The ability to recognize the possible reasons for people's emotional responses and then work through this with clarity is evident from Marny's description of what happened in some of the meetings she attended:

> When I'm in a meeting and I'm feeling something very intensely, firstly I'm more likely to notice that I am feeling something and identify it as feeling something. Be in a position to decide, does this have anything to do with what's going on around me, or is this to do with the fact that this is reminding me of all the thousands of meetings when people behaved in this appalling way. And to make some decisions about what to do about it: I'm feeling this, but I don't have to act on it, for

example, was something that was never said to me as a child. If you're feeling something, you're feeling something and that's interesting, and it might be useful information, but because you're feeling something it doesn't mean you have to act on the basis of it, you know. Just because the person in the meeting makes you feel angry doesn't mean that you have to thump them or yell at them or attack them in any way, or remove yourself from the situation. You can decide what you want to do and deciding on the basis of how you feel doesn't necessarily help.

Marny's emotion work in this context, was not to feel the 'right emotion' but to ensure that her emotions were not impacting on her ability to reason, her intelligence. She might then take the deviant emotion – her anger – to a co-counselling session and examine the basis for it. Although this approach could have a moderating effect on activists – anger, for example, is a prime motivator for activists (Hercus 1999) – it does not prevent the activist from being angry or expressing anger. They just need to think about whether or not the level of anger is appropriate to the moment. If it is, then it gets expressed; if not, then it gets taken to a co-counselling session. This level of reflexivity requires separating out emotion and reason, both within the self and in the surrounding environment. While often having the skills to address emotions expressed by others, or those that infiltrate an organization's culture, Marny still has difficulty doing so in a public forum where, for example, gender politics might blur the problem:

> When I was more involved in the peace movement than I am now people would say in meetings 'People are being killed in Iraq, blah blah blah, its terrible we must do something', and they'd be shouting and they'd be red in the face. And what's really going on so often in meetings where that kind of stuff is going down and where they vent that intenseness of urgency, is stopping the meeting from doing anything that might be quiet, thoughtful, reflective, effective. What's really going on is that someone is feeling something so intense or painful that they don't know how to recognize or deal with it. ... What would really be good would be for someone to just quietly sidle up next to them and just say 'it must hurt so much to think of all those people dying'. But no man who is being a 'good man' by the 'rule book' of what it means to be a man, especially in a public place, will accept that.

The ability to identify and understand the impact of particular emotions on thinking, and to moderate your own approach to activism on the basis of this is a skill that co-counsellors aimed to develop. Their recognition of, and ability to reflect upon, the inter-relatedness between the different forms of oppression, their emotional context and its effect on thinking was considered a powerful tool in bringing about effective social change.

The personal side of social change, where activists recognized the need to deintegrate, requires a different form of emotional reflexivity, one that is subjective and which problematizes the emotions. Once deviant emotions (where there is dissonance between their emotions and their politics) were recognized the issue was taken to a co-counselling session or workshop. As discussed earlier, these emotions were often viewed as being attached to a particular form of oppression – class, sexism, able-ism, ageism, racism – and that without 'letting go' of the emotion, then they would not be able to let go of the oppressive or oppressed behaviour. In co-counselling, 'letting go' was a mixture of consciousness raising (Itzin 1985: 77) and discharging the emotion. The aim was to get a person to actually feel the emotions that were preventing them from deintegrating from the oppressive behaviours – from thinking more clearly and creatively. This was achieved by contradicting negative oppression-created feelings and replacing them with positive ones. The difficulty of accepting these new feelings raises old emotions – crying, anger, boredom, laughter – which are expressed, and continue to be expressed until the person can accept the new positive 'reality' with confidence and joy. Itzin describes this process as one that allows people to 'step outside her [*sic*] feelings of powerlessness' (1985: 79). As Barbara's story illustrates, only after going through this process could she let go of her old feelings and 'move on':

> She [the co-counsellor instructor] was counselling on class stuff. She was a working class woman, I'm a middle class woman and she was a lot older than me. And she'd been talking about class stuff and what the dominant habitual emotions of each class is, and how that works. And, it was just amazing, because she was so gentle with me and she hardly did anything ... and I was crying so hard, in front of all these other women. And it was like, oh my goodness me! It was just slime, you know, that sort of crying. But it was sort of really liberating in a way too, it was that thing about – yeh it was real and I felt heard about whatever it was. And once you feel heard you can move on, you don't have to do it again.

While not all discharge is this intense, it does illustrate the extent to which unresolved emotions are implicated in the way that we think and act in the world. Barbara's claim that it was a 'liberating' experience alludes to the way that the process allowed her to realign her thinking and emotions and therefore free up her capacity to think and behave creatively in her social change work.

I have argued here that for activists to become deintegrated from dominant values and norms, they also have to be deintegrated from the emotions that accompany them. While a cognitive approach to emotional reflexivity – reflecting on the emotions – was one aspect of this, it certainly was not sufficient. Activists also needed to problematize and reflect through the emotions for deintegration to be effective. Co-counselling provided an environment and tools where this could be performed on an ongoing basis by supporting activists to express deviant emotions and construct deintegrated identities. It also provided a space for activists to replenish their emotional energy for social change, and a model for achieving social change both personally and in their social movement organizations.

An external, supportive, emotional culture

For the most part co-counselling occurs outside of a specific social movement or social movement organization, although some of its practices can be integrated into meeting procedure and decision-making processes. Despite their obvious relevance, little attention has been given to external organizations that support activist activity. Instead, much of the focus in social movement research has been on the role of social movements/ organizations in meeting activists' needs. For example, research indicates that involvement in social change activities will be maintained if social movement organizations provide activists with opportunities for developing a sense of efficacy and satisfaction (Einwohner 2002). Alternatively, mobilization is considered to be more likely if there is an optimal level of correspondence between collective and individual identities (Snow and McAdam 2000; Stryker 2000). Although important, the insights gained from these studies only covers one perspective on sustaining social activism. When viewed from the activists' perspective, different issues become apparent. Not only is activism sustained (or not) through an activist's interaction with social movement organizations, but also through their involvement with other organizations, groups and social formations. For example, religious organizations (Mack 2003), workplaces, the family (Johnson 2003; Klatch 2000; Naples 1992), and activist subcultures (van Dyke 1998) have been found to influence an individual's propensity to continue as an activist. During the latter half of the twentieth century another form of support for activism gained credence, the counselling community (see for example, Taylor 1999, 2000; Itzin 1985). Within these communities the focus has been on the construction and support of activists' deintegrated identities, and the expression of deviant emotions.

To a certain extent activists need to stand 'outside' of society in order to change it. To do this they construct 'deviant' or deintegrated identities as activists – deviant from the perspective of mainstream society. The emotional pressures of being constructed as deviant are evident in Groves' (1995) study of the emotion work that animal liberation activists engage in to both get their message across to hostile audiences and to appease their family, friends and co-workers who find their activism personally confronting. Sometimes, a social movement organization recognizes this and provides support for activists in constructing and maintaining their deviant identity. In Taylor's study of a women's self-help (also a form of peer counselling) movement in the area of postpartum depression, the organization is viewed as important for helping women to 'challenge the ideology of intensive mothering ... [by] defining a new kind of mother who challenges the prevailing gender code' (2000: 291). This is achieved through the collective redefinition of self, and through the cultivation of emotion cultures that are open, empathetic and legitimize women's experiences.

Co-counselling provided a similar function, but did so outside of any particular social movement. Its membership was diverse, incorporating activists from numerous social movements; activists not aligned with any particular social movement; and people who were not activists. Its independence in this way allowed activists to discuss problems that were created through their involvement in social movement organizations. Part of Marny's difficulty in sustaining her activism was that, in her social movement organizations, she was often surrounded by activists that drained, rather than restored, her emotional energy. Co-counselling provided a forum where this issue, as well as her own needs, could be discussed:

> Some of the long-term activists that I know ... have become very rigid, have become very discouraged and very despairing and very tired. Not that I don't relate to any of those things, but ... I want to be able to maintain both my own sense of hopefulness and energy and keenness, and my capacity to think freshly and act freshly and stay flexible. So I see co-counselling as a maintenance tool for those things.

For other activists, however, their more personalized approach to activism meant that they did not have any of the kinds of support provided by involvement in a social movement. These activists sought out support in a similarly 'personalized' way. For Lian, a young activist involved in a wide range of actions – from Aboriginal rights, youth homelessness, violence against women and peace – but who does not 'belong' to any particular organization, co-counselling provided a supportive network for her to continue her activism:

> I have a nice network of people that I talk to and say how pissed off I am and stuff. And they understand that its just feelings, its not what I really think which is that there's hope. .... And I do it with people who are hopeful, who do believe that its possible to change things, I don't do that with people who don't care.

Alternatively, some activists started off as co-counsellors and then moved into social movement organizations. In this context co-counselling was a kind of training ground for activists, providing them with the tools, support and confidence required to operate in other spheres. This is illustrated in a quote from a letter in the publication 'Wide-World Change':

> Many of us in RC [co-counselling] have moved now to the point of wanting to make a real commitment to making changes in the world. It is a logical point to come to, after having moved on our own individual oppressions, our roles as oppressors, and our powerlessness.
>
> (Angella-Dodd 1979: 41)

These quotes indicate that co-counselling provided an emotional culture that is conducive to supporting activism. Despite being 'external' to their spheres of activism, there is, in Snow and McAdam's (2000) terms, a level of identity correspondence between the activists and the co-counselling community. Three aspects of the co-counselling community contributed to this feeling of correspondence. First, the organization's practices reinforced a notion of social change based on equity, justice and continuous improvement. For example, it had a progressive system of payment for courses and workshops, and its policies were always in draft format. Partly a response to the failure of dogmas to bring about effective social change, and partly because they believe that the 'best' or 'right' solution has yet to be developed, the policy process had the effect of instilling a sense of continuous improvement and untapped potential within the organization. It also prevented co-counsellors from becoming totally integrated into the co-counselling community. In effect, it maintains the tension between integration and deintegration, not only in mainstream society, but also within its own organization.

Second, the organization's processes provided public affirmation of the necessity of deintegration, and the emotional context within which it occurs. For example, the counselling process both recognized and provided support for all its members to be leaders in ways that are non-hierarchical and inclusive. Within meetings and workshops, emotional responses (including suppression of emotions) were attended to so that members could be even more effective in articulating their needs or issues. Meetings also had processes that challenged mainstream assumptions about the 'right' way of doing things.

Third, the organizational structure challenged members to recognize and understand the numerous ways in which they participate in the reproduction of oppression and the status quo. One way in which this was most evident is in its 'liberation constituencies'. These constituencies, or groups, consist of people who have been subjected to particular forms of oppression plus others who have chosen to become their allies. People from the working class, for example, are oppressed by the middle class values and emotional attachments to such values that predominate in society. A class-based liberation constituency would therefore consist of working class people who are working through the ways in which they have been oppressed, and their 'allies' – middle class people who are working through ways in which their values and emotional attachment to such values have been oppressive. At the time of interviewing, there were 37 constituencies operating in South Australia and most of the co-counselling activists belonged to at least one of them. Working within the constituency structure was viewed as being useful for tackling both the personal and structural aspects of oppression, and it pushed activists beyond their personal boundaries. Such constituencies therefore provided an environment where social change was being practiced as well as discussed.

Conclusion

As activism becomes more individualized and ties to particular collective identities weaken, it becomes ever more important to understand the processes through which activism is being constructed as a personal identity. While Touraine's theory of the Subject offered an explanation of this process that focused on the tension between commitment and non-commitment, his cognitive-normative approach precluded discussion of the emotional dimensions of becoming a Subject. In addressing this issue, I argued that Hochschild offers a partial answer in her notion of emotional reflexivity that is primarily used when attending to the emotive dissonance created through changing ideological frames. However, as the study into co-counselling demonstrated, it is necessary to go beyond Hochschild's objectification of the emotions in emotional reflexivity. In co-counselling, the practices of emotional reflexivity used by activists to deintegrate from dominant ideological frames also incorporated a subjective component. Activists went through a process of re-feeling and discharging the emotions associated with old ideological frames in order to develop new emotional frames and feeling rules that were more in line with their new ideological frame. This process of emotional reflexivity both affirmed activists' values and identities as a Subject, while simultaneously challenging them to think more clearly by understanding the emotional bases to oppression and oppressive behaviours.

Co-counselling offered a supportive, external environment within which activists could engage in this level of emotional reframing. Their ability to sustain an activist identity over long periods of time was therefore assisted by being part of this kind of supportive group. What is interesting is that the group was external to the social movement organizations to which the activists belonged. This raises questions as to the relationship between co-counselling and social movement organizations.

The central argument of this paper has been that having a practice of emotional reflexivity, which incorporates both objective and subjective dimensions, is integral to activists becoming and remaining a Subject. Using co-counselling as a case study offered insights into how this practice was achieved and its relationship to personal and social change. Co-counselling communities can be found in many liberal democratic countries, as well as in some other areas of the world. The question remains, however, as to whether activists engage in this kind of practice of emotional reflexivity outside of co-counselling communities. Or, alternatively, whether individuals who engage in practices of emotional reflexivity are more likely to become and remain activists. Answering these questions is beyond the scope of this paper. Nevertheless there are indications that such practices are prevalent, although maybe not in such an overtly taught or theorized way as co-counselling. For example, politically oriented self-help groups, such as Taylor's postpartum groups, appear to relate the emotional aspects of personal change to wider social issues. In addition, the concept of 'therapeutic culture', although often critical of the self-absorbed navel-gazing that therapy can sometimes generate, also indicates that individuals are increasingly engaging in counselling practices. At one level, then, people are recognizing the need to become more skilled in using their emotions and linking this to the ways in which they think and behave. What is often lacking here, though, is the political framework. Perhaps what distinguishes co-counselling from forms of 'professional' counselling is the way that it explicitly links emotional reflexivity to personal *and* social change. Without such an explicitly political basis, activists might well have been 'counselled' into compliance with the status quo, with consequences likely to lead to them disengaging from, rather than maintaining their participation in, social movements.

Another question relates more closely to social movement processes. For if practices of emotional reflexivity are not widespread then perhaps there is a need for activists and social movement organizations to consider ways that they can be developed and integrated into personal and social change activities. Attending to emotions in social movements and in social change activities requires more than generating anger or pride, or managing feelings of hopelessness and fear, or developing emotional attachments to people and causes. Attaining and sustaining activist involvement also requires attending to deviant emotions, to developing practices of emotional reflexivity, and to understanding the link between emotions, ideological frames and the potential for individuals to become a Subject.

Notes

1 Co-counselling is also known as Re-evaluation Counselling. Re-evaluation Counselling is primarily the theory behind the practice of co-counselling. For consistency I use the term co-counselling to include both the theory and practice.
2 Letters and poems were not included in this figure or the subject analysis.
3 The relevance of co-counselling to social change is also mentioned in the non co-counselling literature, for example, Roby (1995); Staggenborg, Eder and Sudderth (1993–1994: 38); MacLachlan (1992); Epstein (1991); Lakey (1987: xiv). Hotchkiss (1997) has provided a sociological analysis of co-counselling, but this focuses more on personal rather than social change.

4 These concerns were discussed by some of the interviewees who nonetheless defended co-counselling as a practice and process. Some of these issues are also discussed on websites dedicated to the principles of co-counselling, but not the organization (for example: The Re-evaluation Counseling Resources Site (http://www.cocowebs.com/liberaterc/), which provides information related to The International Re-evaluation Counseling Communities that IRCC has censored and suppressed'.

5 Co-counselling has been discussed in these terms by Scheff (1972), Somers (1972) and Rosen (1978). For the most part co-counselling resists attempts to develop a comprehensive physiological or psychological theory or to incorporate any such theories into their own.

6 For an introduction to, and overview of, co-counselling visit http://www.rc.org.

References

Angella-Dodd, C. (1979) 'Toward a wide world change proposal', *Wide World Changing*, 2: 41–3.

Barbalet, J.M. (1998) *Emotion, Social Theory, and Structure*, Cambridge: Cambridge University Press.

Bolton, S.C. (2001) 'Changing faces: nurses as emotional jugglers', *Sociology of Health and Illness*, 23(1): 85–100.

Brotheridge, C.M. and Grandey, A.A. (2002) 'Emotional labor and burnout: comparing two perspectives of "people work"', *Journal of Vocational Behavior*, 60: 17–39.

Chenitz, W.C. (1986) 'The informal interview', in W.C. Chenitz and J.M. Swanson (eds) *From Practice to Grounded Theory: qualitative research in nursing*, California: Addison-Wesley.

Einwohner, R. (2002) 'Motivational framing and efficacy maintenance: animal rights activists' use of four fortifying strategies', *Sociological Quarterly*, 43(4): 509–26.

Epstein, B. (1991) *Political Protest and Cultural Revolution*, Berkeley: University of California Press.

Groves, J.M. (1995) 'Learning to feel: the neglected sociology of social movements', *The Sociological Review*, 43(3): 435–60.

Hercus, C. (1999) 'Identity, emotion, and feminist collective action', *Gender & Society*, 13(1): 34–55.

Hochschild, A.R. (1979) 'Emotion work, feeling rules and social structure', *American Journal of Sociology*, 85(3): 551–75.

—— (1983) *The Managed Heart: the commercialization of human feeling*, Berkeley: University of California Press.

Hotchkiss, S. (1997) 'Leaping and singing, not rattling: inclusive strategies for transformative change', paper presented at The Australian Sociological Association Conference, Wollongong University, December.

Itzin, C. (1985) 'Margaret Thatcher is my sister: counselling on divisions between women', *Women's Studies International Forum*, 8(1): 73–83.

Jackins, H. (1994a) *How 'Re-evaluation Counseling' Began*, Seattle, Washington: Rational Island Publishers.

—— (1994b) *The Human Side of Human Beings: the theory of re-evaluation counseling*, 3rd edn, Seattle: Rational Island Publishers.

Johnson, J.M. (2003) '"How would I live without Loulie?" Mary and Lousia

Poppenheim, activist sisters in turn-of-the-century South Carolina', *Journal of Family History*, 28(4): 561–78.

Klatch, R.E. (2000) 'The contradictory effects of work and family on political activism', *Qualitative Sociology*, 23(4): 505–19.

Kovan, J.T. and Dirkx, J.M. (2003) '"Being called awake": the role of transformative learning in the lives of environmental activists', *Adult Education Quarterly*, 53(2): 99–118.

Lakey, G. (1987) *Powerful Peacemaking: a strategy for a living revolution*, Philadelphia: New Society Publishers.

Lichterman, P. (1996) *The Search for Political Community: American activists reinventing commitment*, Cambridge: Cambridge University Press.

Mack, P. (2003) 'Religion, feminism, and the problem of agency: reflections on eighteenth-century Quakerism', *Signs*, 29(1): 149–77.

MacLachlan, J. (1992) 'Managing AIDS: a phenomenology of experiment, empowerment and expediency', *Critique of Anthropology*, 12(4): 433–56.

Naples, N.A. (1992) 'Activist mothering: cross-generational continuity in the community work of women from low-income urban neighbourhoods', *Gender & Society*, 6(3): 441–63.

Re-evaluation Counseling (1995–2004) available at: http://www.rc.org (accessed 3 March 2004).

Re-evaluation Counseling Resources Site (n.d.) available at: http://www.cocowebs.com/liberaterc/ (accessed 3 March 2004).

Roby, P. (1995) 'Becoming an active feminist academic: gender, class, race and intelligence', in A. Goetting and S. Fenslemaker (eds) *Individual Voices, Collective Visions: fifty years of women in sociology*, Philadelphia, Temple University Press.

Rosen, R.D. (1978) *Psychobabble: fast talk and quick cure in the era of feeling*, New York: Atheneum.

Scheff, T.J. (1972) 'Reevaluation counseling: social implications', *Journal of Humanistic Psychology*, 12(Spring): 1–14.

Smith, D.A. and Erickson, R.J. (1997) 'For love or money? Work and emotional labor in a social movement organization', in B. Cuthbertson-Johnson and R.J. Erickson (eds) *Social Perspectives on Emotion*, Vol. 4, Greenwich: JAI Press.

Snow, D.A. and McAdam, D. (2000) 'Identity work processes in the context of social movements: clarifying the identity/movement nexus', in S. Stryker, T.J. Owens and R.W. White (eds) *Self, Identity and Social Movements*, Minneapolis: University of Minnesota Press.

Somers, B.J. (1972) 'Reevaluation therapy: theoretical framework', *Journal of Humanistic Psychology*, 12(1): 42–57.

Staggenborg, S., Eder, D. and Sudderth, L. (1993–1994) 'Women's culture and social change: evidence from the National Women's Music Festival', *Berkeley Journal of Sociology*, 38: 31–56.

Stryker, S. (2000) 'Identity competition: key to differential social movement participation', in S. Stryker, T.J. Owens and R.W. White (eds) *Self, Identity and Social Movements*, Minneapolis: University of Minnesota Press.

Taylor, V. (1999) 'Gender and social movements: gender processes in women's self-help movements', *Gender & Society*, 13(1): 8–33.

—— (2000) 'Emotions and identity in women's self-help movements', in S. Stryker, T.J. Owens and R.W. White (eds) *Self, Identity and Social Movements*, Minneapolis: University of Minnesota Press.

Touraine, A. (1995) *Critique of Modernity*, Cambridge Mass.: Basil Blackwell.

Tourish, D. and Irving, P. (1995) 'Group influence and the psychology of cultism within re-evaluation counselling: a critique', *Counselling Psychology Quarterly*, 8(1): 35–50.

Tracy, S.J. and Tracy, K. (1998) 'Emotion labor at 911: a case study and theoretical critique', *Journal of Applied Communication Research*, 26(4): 390–411.

van Dyke, N. (1998) 'Hotbeds of activism: locations of student protest', *Social Problems*, 45(2): 205–20.

10 The entanglements of shame

An emotion perspective on social movement demobilization[1]

Jochen Kleres

Introduction

This chapter explores the role of emotions in the process of social movements' demobilization. Whereas others (Voss 1996; Kamenitsa 1998) have proposed a cognitivist perspective on demobilization, my aim here is to explore the role of emotions. I will demonstrate that analyzing emotion provides a powerful tool which allows for a more comprehensive understanding of demobilization processes.

In general, the issue of social movement decline and demise is neglected within social movement theory (see e.g. Joppke 1991: 44; Kamenitsa 1998: 246; McAdam *et al.* 1988: 728). Nevertheless, there is a limited body of literature on demobilization however narrow, scattered and disparate (for a brief overview see Kamenitsa 1998). One strand of arguments points to dynamics that lie within social movement organizations. In this vein, a number of scholars have explored the unfavorable impact of changes in membership structures. Among the factors thus unearthed are factionalism (McAdam 1999; see Kamenitsa 1998), the influx of new members with diverging backgrounds and orientations (Stoper 1999; Schmitt-Beck and Weins 1997; Rucht 1995) and the insufficient integration of (new) members (Miller 1999; Schmitt-Beck and Weins 1997; Rucht 1995; Polletta 2002).

At this point it is important to bear in mind Benford's (1993) argument who cautions us not to assume that internal frictions necessarily create negative consequences. He shows that decline of one social movement organization (SMO) could in fact also imply the growth of another. Factionalism, he points out, can also increase coherence within the factions. A comprehensive explanation of decline would then have to specify conditions under which internal tensions cause organizational collapse instead of giving birth to alternative organizations or leading to organizational splitting. However, Benford does not provide a theoretical framework to answer this question. My case study suggests, that emotion theory may be of particular use in forging such a framework.

Another strand of demobilization theory focuses on negative experience of various kinds. Hirschman (1982), for instance, studies why people grow disenchanted with public involvement but limits his focus to expectations and time budgets. Rucht (1994) has shown how escalating protest by the French anti-nuclear movement moved public opinion to strongly oppose this movement. The subsequent campaign defeat resulted in the movement becoming deeply apathetic. Analyzing the Swedish anti-nuclear movement, Flam (1994) describes how a referendum campaign ended in political defeat for the movement and affected its demobilization. She also provides arguments why this negative episode kept the movement simmering on a low scale for many years. In doing so, she anticipated an argument that Voss (1996) has developed more explicitly focusing on framing theory. In her analysis of the Knights of Labor, an American labor movement in the late 1890s/early 1900s, Voss makes the point that discouraging events, like defeat, cannot as such provide a full explanation of a movement's demise. Instead we need to ask why such events lead activists to give up their commitment rather than to keep them going or even intensifying their activism. Voss seeks the answer in specific traits of movement frames, which enable activists, at varying degrees, to cognitively ward off potentially frustrating events. Her idea is that of cognitive shields ('fortifying myths') that render possibly discouraging occurrences in a way that activism can continue making sense to the individual. Without these 'fortifying myths,' episodes of lost political struggles, for instance, can strip activism of making sense.

Although enlightening, the language of these sorts of arguments points to another dimension that has thus far been left unexplored. Terms such as disenchantment, disappointment, apathy, discouragement or frustration suggest the necessity of looking beyond the cognitivist analysis to emotional aspects of movement activism.

The overall scant attention to issues of demobilization in social movement theory, however, persists in the burgeoning body of research on emotional dimensions of insurgency. Jasper (1998) addresses demobilization but doesn't go much beyond identifying the gap (see also Goodwin *et al.* 2001b). Analyzing the role of affect and sexuality in a particular movement, Goodwin (1997) does address the issue of demobilization. But his analysis is limited to a very specific aspect only. Apart from these two researchers, most authors writing from an emotion's perspective fail to consider demobilization at all (see for example Goodwin *et al.* 2001a). A number of studies focus on the ongoing dynamics of mobilization as mediated by emotions, but ignores demobilization too. For instance Yang (2001) introduced the concept of emotional achievement to study the development of Chinese student mobilization over a certain period of time. He emphasizes, however, only the positive, creative outcomes of mobilization: 'given that individuals actively seek emotional achievement and that social movements provide unique avenues for such explorations, the dynamics of micro-level movement mobilization may be seen as a function of the emotional process of the movement' (p. 594). As will become clear in this chapter, social movements may come to lack this very feature and therefore threaten participants' sense of identity. Gould (2001) studies emotional ambivalence in gays and lesbians and examines how the balance between contradictory emotions shifts over the course of time. Like Yang, however, she focuses only on movement emergence. Britt and Heise's (2000) study of how shame and fear are turned into anger and pride has a similar focus.

The case study being presented here aims at addressing some of the shortcomings described above. Departing from the work on demobilization, emotion theory is used to analyze the ongoing dynamic of a particular SMO beyond its emergence and the eventual dissolution of this organization in particular.

The gay movement in eastern Germany

My case study will be the main national lesbian and gay organization in Germany, the Lesbian and Gay Association Germany [*Lesben- und Schwulenverband Deutschland, LSVD*]. Successful on a national level, it dissolved in Saxony in 1999 and thus signaled the final demise of the gay movement in eastern Germany. In order to establish the specific social context for my analysis, let me first turn to a descriptive account of the gay movement in eastern Germany.[2]

Looking back

After unsuccessful attempts at organizing lesbian and gay activism in Berlin in the mid-1970s, lasting activism emerged in Leipzig in 1982, when gays and lesbians organized under the auspices of the Protestant Student Community in Leipzig (Working Group Homosexuality; *AKH*), starting a diffusion process which ultimately affected the entire country. This created opportunities for gays and lesbians to organize outside the church. Starting out in Berlin in the mid-1980s secular groups eventually spread throughout the country. These were typically affiliated with state-sanctioned organizations such as the official youth organization *FDJ*. In sum, by the time the German Democratic Republic was dissolved, movement groups were present in all major cities in East Germany (see Kleres 2000).

After the Wende: differentiation and demobilization

The gay movement gained significant momentum from the *Wende*[3] and changed its structure rapidly. This can best be described as differentiation – a process that was most salient during the early 1990s.

Prior to 1989 gay groups pursued a diverse set of social, cultural and more explicitly political activities. Ecclesiastic gay groups had coined the term 'gay adult education college' [*schwule Volkshochschule*] for this. Differentiation entailed departure from this inclusive approach and generated more focused groups. Whereas many new groups disappeared soon after their inception, some groups created after the *Wende* established themselves in the longer term. Together with both old groups they form today's institutional backbone of the movement in Leipzig (see Kleres 2001).

The local HIV/AIDS-Organization *AHL* [*AIDS-Hilfe Leipzig*] is one of them. Rooted in the pre-1989 East German gay movement it was formally founded in 1990. Besides social activities *AHL* has also served as a platform for new groups. These would often start out as part of *AHL* activities with some of them eventually becoming more loosely tied to *AHL*. Examples are a leather/SM-group, a group of deaf gays, a theatre group and a coming-out group. In the same vein, the gay monthly *Queer* was launched in 1993. It soon became independent. Subsequently it expanded its geographical scope and merged in 1998 with a western magazine, thus losing much of its eastern roots. Its high degree of professionalization as well as its privileged financial situation and infrastructure puts into perspective the vibrancy and mobilization capacity of *AHL* (Kleres 2001: 141).

Another notable result of the post-*Wende* developments has been the installation of two (later reduced to one) *Representatives for Same Sex Ways of Life* within the municipal administration. Functioning as a link between city administration and gays and lesbians, their successes (e.g. influencing education policy, gaining police co-operation regarding violence issues), however, do not reflect the strength of the gay movement at all, since they are not based on a broader involvement of movement activists and larger scale mobilizations (Kleres 2001).

Whereas the process of differentiation may have created a promising impression of organizational growth in the early-1990s, in the long-run the movement underwent continuing decline. Most notably this was the case regarding the two pre-1989 groups. Both witnessed steady decline in participation and became increasingly depoliticized. The church-based group *AKH* – once a crystallization point of the movement – decided to disband in 2002 due to severe lack of volunteer support. Despite gaining public funding and thus having good infrastructure, the church-independent group *Rosa- Linde* became marginalized in the long run as well, growing increasingly depoliticized.

The impression of pervading demobilization is further confirmed if one pays attention to how the institutional skeleton has been filled. The local gay pride parade in Leipzig provides a good illustration. Participation kept declining from the outset in 1992. Organizing groups ceased to be interested in it and in mutual co-operation more particularly. In 1996 no such event was organized. Another effort was made in 1997 when FallGay Cravings [*HerbstGayLüste*] was launched as an explicitly apolitical, mainly social and cultural event. But after an initial success co-operation among participating initiatives faded as did the overall attendance. Many other efforts at organizing gay life in Leipzig have similarly failed. A monthly gay cinema evening was abandoned in 1996 due to lack of interest. Many groups were planned but never started or disappeared soon after their inception: self-defense groups, transgender groups, a group to research the history of gays in Leipzig, movie nights at *RosaLinde*, or a local chapter of the organization *Homosexuals and the Church* [*Homosexuelle und Kirche*]. A forum for all gay and lesbian groups is organized by the municipal *Representatives*, but attendance is poor and the status of the forum is precarious. A similar, regional forum failed due to insufficient cooperation among participating groups.

The overall picture testifies to a diversified set of gay institutions in the city. At the same time, especially after a promising phase in the early 1990s, the movement has continually lost momentum and its mobilization capacity has kept declining. Participation in group activities has dropped and theme-focused activities have grown more and more sparse. Cooperation among groups has become increasingly difficult. One of the major gay groups disbanded in 2002.

Westernization: the demise of the Saxon SVD chapter

Today the Lesbian and Gay Association Germany *LSVD* is the primary lesbian and gay organization of interest at the national level. It began still in the German Democratic Republic (GDR) in 1990 as a gay organization – hence *SVD*. Interestingly, it managed to expand from the East into the West (Kleres 2001: 138–9). This is contrary to the overall trend of transferring western institutions to the East. In this process, the *SVD* was joined by activists from the western movement who shared its distinct orientation towards citizen rights. On a national scale the *(L)SVD*[4] was able to win considerable political successes, most notably the legislation (2000/2001) on so-called registered lifetime partnership for lesbian and gay couples which, to some extent, gives them similar legal status and advantages as married, straight couples have.

Starting out as an adaptation of the old movement to new political and societal circumstances, the *SVD* came to pursue merely political goals in terms of citizen rights and divested itself to a great extent of any social or cultural involvements. At the same time it chose not to assume the form of an umbrella organization but to function merely as an organization of interest instead. Still before reunification, the *SVD* expanded to become a pan-German organization. The general programmatic thrust was maintained yet adapted to the new political system. However, as will be demonstrated below, western activists gained organizational power and so could tailor programmatic details, emphasis and strategies according to their own, specific preferences. In 1999 the *SVD* expanded a second time when it turned itself into a lesbian and gay organization (hence *LSVD*).

Despite national successes, the *(L)SVD* in eastern Germany is a failure, since its regional chapters lack the momentum of the federal organization.

The Saxon chapter provides particularly good insights into the eastern dynamic since it displays it in an extreme form. It disbanded in 1999 when the national parent organization decided to include also lesbians. The demobilizing 'illness' affecting all eastern chapters can best be described as westernization. This term points to the most recurring theme in the interview material,[5] namely the ever increasing influence and power of western activists within the organization since it had become a pan-German association. It was in the course of this development, that the *(L)SVD* assumed the form of an association of interest, rather than an umbrella organization, in order to devise effective organizational structures. Internally this had the effect of strengthening hierarchical structures. In addition, the organization limited itself to parliamentary politics thus abandoning social and cultural activities. In effect the *(L)SVD* increasingly distanced itself from the activists, especially those in the East. For instance, easterners by and large disappeared from the national board. In fact only one of the eastern activists has remained as a board member on the federal level.[6] The headquarters were subsequently moved from Leipzig to Cologne, closer to leading western activists. The annual meetings are held there as well. Many interviewees have described this as a 'takeover'. Moreover, the attitude of western activists, board members in particular, has been described as 'arrogant' and 'ignorant'. The board has also been described as being 'out of touch with the base' and even accused of not paying sufficient attention to the needs of individuals in the (eastern) base. This resulted in a general sense of frustration among members in the East. It led many of them to grow increasingly passive or to leave the organization.

These aspects of westernization culminated in the dissolution of the regional Saxon chapter of the *SVD* in 1999. The immediate cause for this was the decision taken on the national level to include lesbians in the organization. Initiative for this change came from the national board. This caused considerable opposition from the Saxon chapter. Prior to 1989 in the GDR the tensions between gays and lesbians led them to part ways. The *SVD* had thus been founded as an exclusively gay organization. As such, it scored successes, in contrast to lesbians and their organizations which were far less fortunate. Given the previous conflict, the prospect of lesbians being given a guaranteed share in the *LSVD* ('lesbians reaping others' accomplishments'), raised critical voices in the East.

What really caused dissent, however, was the undemocratic way this decision was taken. Propositions of the Saxon board to better include the distant Saxon constituency by holding a postal vote were circumvented. Ninety-five percent of the Saxon members were in support of this motion. A considerable number of lesbian guests were granted membership shortly before the vote shortcutting the standard procedure. Interviewees have reported the discussion climate as rather closed without a prior broad opinion-forming process. The prevailing impression was that the decision had been rushed through. After members of the regional board stepped down in reaction to this, new candidates could not be found and the chapter was dissolved.

In a condensed way, this example illustrates westernization as easterners saw it: hierarchical decision structures, a spatially and structurally distant federal board and little connectedness with the issues at stake for people at the local level in the East.

Westernization and emotions

Members of the Saxon chapter reacted to increasing westernization passively, by quitting, and eventually by dissolving the organization. The question can be asked, why eastern members hardly publicly voiced, and much less organized, their protest? Why didn't they take an alternative course of action? How could westerners so easily takeover an originally eastern organization (with only tacit dissent)? This is even more startling when considering that the easterners possessed their own organizational platform, the Saxon chapter. Another option would have been to establish a different organization that better represented the interests of eastern German gays. I will demonstrate here that emotions provide a particularly useful analytical tool to come to grips with these questions. To this end, the following section analyzes emotions that were evoked in easterners during the course of westernization.

Excursus: shame and inferiority

To anticipate my general finding, let me state that the underlying logic here is ultimately determined by conditions of shame disguised as feelings of inferiority. Before I can document this using the interview material, a few theoretical remarks on shame and inferiority are necessary. Simmel (1992 [1901]) characterizes the conditions that are apt to elicit shame as a combination of a total exposure of the self to the other together with its evaluative critical appraisal. Of crucial importance is that the evaluative attention to the self is directed at the entire person rather than only discrete aspects of it. As Neckel (1991) pointed out, from this perspective interpretative schemas become pivotal in determining the outcome of the interaction. Inferiority can be seen as a particular condition that gives rise to feelings of shame. Neckel (1991, 1996) defines it as a combination of the lack of power with an evaluative component: only relative to someone else, that is within a social relationship, one can feel inferior while pursuing the same interest. Inferiority is, then, a state in which the inferior-feeling self suffers from a deficit of resources to realize interests relative to the other. This does not translate automatically into feelings of shame, however. Again, interpretative schemas are crucial. It is only when inferiority is perceived as characteristic of one's entire person that shame will be the outcome. From this perspective, shameful inferiority results from a negative self-evaluation based on an experience of powerlessness.

A methodological problem pertains to the low visibility of shame (Scheff 1988, 1990; cf. also Katz 1999: 144–5). Shame has a recursive dynamic in that it is often seen as shameful to be ashamed. For this reason individuals try to hide this emotion from others but also from themselves. Drawing on Helen Lewis, Scheff (1988, 1990) distinguishes two types of shame: overt, undifferentiated versus bypassed. In the first case the person in question will experience strong emotions which are not identified as shame but rather as feeling inadequate, incompetent, defective, awkward etcetera. In contrast, bypassed shame is indicated by much more subtle indications such as more rapid, repetitive speech. The ashamed person avoids the pain before it is fully felt. With these few theoretical elaborations in mind, let me now turn to my empirical case.

Asserting the SVD *in times of uncertainty*

The *Wende* and the transformations thereafter were a time of uncertainty, skepticism and fear for the eastern German gay movement and the newly founded *SVD* regarding future prospects in a unified Germany. More specifically, this period entailed a general dispossession of experience and political identities for eastern German gays and movement activists as Gehling's (1993) analysis suggests. The *Wende* brought them into much closer contact with the western movement. This movement's sometimes more glaring achievements – think of gay switchboards or a vibrant gay sub-culture – made the eastern movement's accomplishments look somewhat unspectacular. A significant migration of eastern gays to western cities (Kleres 2001: 144–5) magnified this impression for those who remained in the East. The mythical quality of the West (Gehling 1993: 34–53), upon which many desires and fantasies were projected, worked to the same effect. The loss of the old GDR-state as a political opponent further deprived activists of a meaningful context (Kleres 2001, 2002). At this point the specter of impending shame is already discernible. Drawing on Goffman (1967) it can be proposed that shame was prominent among eastern activists as they were exposed to new groups that embodied supposedly more advanced levels of movement achievement. All this was crucial to the perception of western superiority. Fears born out of uncertainty should also be read as fears of losing self-esteem and standing naked in front of superior counterparts. What uncertainty and fear then come down to is fear of shame.

Eastern activists, however, were in a position to counter threatening shame. From Gehling's (1993: 108–9) vantage point, the very founding of the *SVD* in 1990 is to be seen as a pro-active attempt to counter the threat to own self-esteem and to develop a sense of pride instead. As pride is the dialectical counterpart of shame (see Gould 2001: 138), however, feelings of uncertainty and fear were never completely overcome, and shame kept lingering on even after the founding of the *SVD*. One *SVD* activist recalls that he was confronted with many programmatic alternatives and strong criticism when he traveled to the West in order to promote the *SVD*. He then felt unsure and skeptical about the possibilities of asserting the *SVD*.

This emotional constellation of both pride and impending shame helps us to understand eastern activists' subsequent interactions with their western counterparts. On one hand, when western activists attempted to incorporate the eastern movement, easterners came to act with great self-confidence and developed a sense of self-assuredness and pride. They kept their organizational autonomy for a good while. For instance, when the western national gay organization *BVH* (later disbanded in 1997) tried to incorporate the newly founded *SVD*, this was bluntly refused. Church-based groups and *RosaLinde* had similar experiences. The pride of eastern German activists is also expressed in the term 'inverted reunification'[7] that was coined to refer to the *SVD's* westward expansion into a national organization in 1990.

On the other hand, when *SVD*-activists finally gave in to western Germany, as western activist joined in, this was due to their sense of uncertainty and the fear which eastern activists still felt faced with the necessity to assert their organization in an unknown political system. Even critical interviewees still speak of western involvement as a 'necessity.' As they recall, they felt happy about their new colleagues' support, much-needed political knowledge and competence. Skepticism and fear turned into hope and elation when western competence made it seem possible to steer the *SVD* through difficult times and when westerners seemed to endorse the eastern approach. When asked to describe exactly what hopes they attached to that joint venture, interviewees named the hope for togetherness and co-operation on equal terms and spoke with pride and enthusiasm about their own, eastern German approach to gay politics:

> But I sure had ideas of getting to know to each other and of learning from each other and fighting together with double power for our goals. I did hope that the *SVD* would become an all-German association, that wouldn't deny its eastern German decent [. . .]. And in the beginning I felt a little like a competent representative of the eastern Germans who was there from the beginning and who knew a lot.

> That was indeed a great sense of awakening [. . .] to contribute actively to the process of growing together from a socio-political, citizen movement or whatever vantage point.

Implicit in the perceived necessity to include westerners is already the acknowledgment of some kind of eastern inferiority. At this point, however, eastern activists were still taking pride in their activism which balanced the threat of shame. Inferiority could still be seen as pertaining only to parts of the self rather than to the entire person. Under these conditions, uncertainty and fear could turn into hope and enthusiastic expectations for a common future of mutual benefit. Still, as these feelings followed upon or overlaid uncertainty and fear they were based upon the underlying condition of shame, leaving eastern activists vulnerable to future shaming occurrences.

Western endorsement of his approach made one key eastern leader feel a surge of pride – both as a person and as an easterner – about having founded the 'right' kind of gay organization. His happiness mingled with gratitude to western activists for their support. His words reveal a basic ambiguity felt by eastern German activists who agreed in the end to share the organization with western Germans. Happiness mixed with humble gratitude and a sense of inferiority, visible in the peculiar use of the word *Besserwessi*,[8] point to a constellation of emotions that was soon to be at the core of eastern-western interaction in the *SVD*:

> I was *happy*, that some from the West helped us with it [. . .], because I had a hunch at the time, and today I know it for sure, that we wouldn't have been able to do it alone and that we could be *happy*, to have been able to *gratefully* lay the association in the good hands of *Besserwessis* (in the good sense of the word).
>
> (emphasis in original)

Westernization

With westernization setting in, East–West interactions turned out to differ from the harmonious ideals, however. Apart from formal aspects westernization also entailed a new approach to organizing gay politics that easterners had difficulty identifying with. Given the small size of social spaces for gays in eastern Germany, eastern members felt that there was a lack of a strategy for creating and shaping public spaces for gays. Such a strategy would need to aim at closer relationships between movement organizations and individual members and would thus imply creating a tangible organizational culture connecting social, cultural and political aspects as it had been done in pre-1989 groups. Instead, western ideas, goals and strategies prevailed. Specifically eastern or commonly developed ideas ceased to play a role within the *SVD*. Decisions were increasingly seen as dominated by western activists. When it came to core aspects of westernization, a distinctly reproachful mood came to prevail. In a general way, westernization was seen as a tacit but determined 'takeover' of the organization, which ended with open 'occupation.' Eastern ideas and inputs were arrogantly and ignorantly put aside by the national board:

> But gradually I have realized, that the westerners influence the *SVD* more and more and dominate it and take it under their wings. [...] But I had the impression that by means of a 'friendly takeover' (thus gently but with determination), the West first infiltrated us and then occupied us.

> I increasingly got the impression then, and still today I believe that the west-pioneers wanted to conquer the *SVD* from the beginning.

> My impression is, that all nationwide campaigns were planned in the West and then realized without making the slightest effort at taking into account eastern German sensitivities and a different historically conditioned socialization of many gays in this [part of the] country.

> members [don't] come close to feeling involved in the [decision making] process let alone being taken seriously. Other opinions have been listened to but have been overridden without any substantial process of clarification, for only one way (that is to say theirs) is the right one.

For many, westernization frustrated their hopes of growing together and ideals of co-operation among equals. To some degree, this did result in feelings of anger and a reproachful rhetoric. But contrary to Hercus (1999), Gould (2001), and Polletta (2002), as easterners felt increasingly dispossessed of their organization, relative quiescence and growing passivity became dominant rather than efforts at self-assertion.

The facets of inferiority and its micropolitics

From the beginning East–West interactions proved to be somewhat at odds with ideals of harmonious equality, although some of the shared experience was at first impressive:

> In any case, I was sitting there in the beginning and was astonished at how experienced and self-assured those *Wessis* [see note 8] were. For example, leading a big gathering and handling votes and motions; with how much consummate ease and certainly how flawless, in formal-legal respect, they could manage this stuff (or throw it out). They knew always exactly what needed to be done, when and how, and that did impress me a lot [...].

Observing the self-assuredness of westerners in general, the same interviewee felt admiration and envy at the same time, as he felt that he himself lacked those qualities. Feelings of admiration confirmed the perceived necessity of bringing in western skills to insure the survival of the *SVD*.

Envy, and the perceived personal lack of those very qualities, point to the underpinnings of westernization both on western and eastern sides; to the feelings of inferiority that westernization evoked among eastern activists. However, at this early point, inferiority still gave rise to envy rather than shame, envy being an emotion that could entail much different consequences such as spurring ambition.

As westernization spread throughout the organization, a different feeling became dominant. A recurring theme in the interviews was that of feeling superfluous. Western disregard and neglect of ideas and stakes of eastern activists was one reason for the new emotion. Easterners also increasingly ceased to be represented in the organization. The prevailing impression was that the *SVD* had forgotten its eastern base, treating it as irrelevant to the practices of the *SVD* politics: a sense of disappointment and hurt became paramount, making disengagement seem logical:

[...] for one simply forgets the basis, what problems do they have, what worries, what needs are there.

[The easterners on *SVD* gatherings knew] oh, I can't say anything here anyway [...] because I can't know it any better.

they [the national board] are not interested in me anymore. The problems that I have here – those are just some peanuts and those in the West are simply so and so many years advanced with their development also with regards to the gay movement [...] and they simply don't have time for these sorts of things.

and the formerly active easterners gradually withdrew. I think many simply felt superfluous. [...] Now I'm not interested in the *SVD* anymore at all (if it still exists), I don't even feel like doing gay political work. *That is for others now.*

(emphasis added)

But at one point the feeling came up in me, that the *Wessis* [see note 8] knew everything better anyway and didn't listen and didn't make it possible to grow together.

And then they [the easterners] said to themselves: Well, let's leave it to the westerners, they can do it better anyway [...] and besides they look better than we do, more crisp, healthier, more styled.

These excerpts show how easterners experienced the western neglect of their needs and issues as acts of evaluation. They believed that western Germans saw them as insignificant, irrelevant. These words capture inferiority feelings on the part of eastern activists. They also reveal a sense of impotence as easterners failed to counter these evaluations as illegitimate. Feelings of superfluousness and irrelevance were linked to the traits of westerners and their dominant role in the organization. These knew everything better, could do everything better and – with an ironic twist – they even looked better.

A sense of betrayal set in: westernization came to mean dispossession, resonating with a more general theme in eastern Germany.[9] Referring to the inclusion of lesbians in the *SVD* one interviewee states:

> People felt betrayed and cheated for the second time, in the sense: we first fought against conditions in the zone,[10] which were really blatant, we really took personal risks, then they were dominated by the West and now they are deprived of the fruits of their work for the second time as another group [i.e. lesbians] is just taken in.

Once a sense of western superiority became established as the baseline of East–West interactions, it also became the source of subtle, but effective, power that was wielded over eastern activists. In effect, the dichotomy of eastern inferiority and western superiority functioned to dampen eastern dissent and prevent confrontational reactions to westernization. Even when easterners voiced their own opinions, they were not in a position to assert themselves against western arguments:

> It was then at events, at the common, central events that through their experience, through their knowledge, through their expertise, through their different way of acting they [the westerners] were more and more determining what was going on there, in which direction and who has the say, many easterners then simply withdrew, they knew, well I have no say here anyway, what I do say will either be corrected immediately because I can't know it any better and so on or there is that assertion that we have experienced everywhere, well we in the West have done that for 40 years like that and in the West we do this anyway. And then there was no convincing argument left over anymore, that was the most convincing argument, be it good or bad, if it was done some way in the West, it had to be done that way in the East and that was in fact partly a bit hurting too and it led many people to simply say go and do your bullshit yourselves.

> But somehow it revolved more and more around those ideas and goals and methods and strategies that came from the West ('That's how we've always done it in the West'; 'That's the way it goes here in the Federal Republic'; 'That's always been our idea') which were rarely questioned; and the eastern German or new common ideas didn't play a role (anymore).

Shame

Consistent with the assumption of low visibility of shame, interviewees failed to mention the word shame. However, when they talk about East–West-interactions, they employ the language of shame or rather, they use expressions that one knows as shame markers (see Scheff 1988): people felt superfluous, they 'couldn't know it any better,' 'westerners will do it better anyway' etcetera. Ironic twists ('they even look better than we do, more crisp, healthier, more styled') made it possible to keep one's distance from painful perceptions but, in a way, are to be taken in a literal sense as they confirm a distinct feeling of inferiority. Interestingly, even looking back today, interviewees are reluctant to criticise westerners on a fundamental level and try to put things into a perspective – another marker of shame (Scheff 1988: 401, cf. also Katz 1999: 166–7). For example, key aspects are seen as not inherently bad, or westerners may not have had bad intentions:

> that it [the *(L)SVD*] was so dominated and taken into their hands, that they then also gave it a different direction somehow, which may not be wrong, I don't want to say that at all with this, but it was no longer, say, the association, that we had founded in the GDR [. . .]

At the outset I argued that shame was not the only possible outcome of East–West encounters. When eastern and western gays started their co-operation, despite the inequality of skills, eastern activists assumed an ideal of mutual co-operation among complementary equals for the common betterment, seeing their own resources as different rather than inferior. Envy instead of shame prevailed at an early stage. However, in the long run distinct feelings of shameful inferiority surfaced. Crucial for shame to be the outcome of inferiority are interpretative schemas that attribute inferiority to one's identity rather than merely to discrete aspects of it.

Arguably, the hope for co-operation between different, yet equal partners with unique experiences has functioned as a shield against a sense of shameful inferiority. Inferior skills of easterners were thus perceived as an insignificant aspect of the trade off between East and West. Refuting this assumption, however, their political input was regularly discounted and they were decreasingly represented in the organization. This struck easterners at their very self-understanding as political actors, the more so as these causes often pertained specifically to the situation in eastern Germany.

As theorists point out, shame tends to result in avoidance and quiescence. Linking shame with inferiority and power, Neckel (1991: 99–100, 164–6) sheds more light on this. He argues that shaming episodes have consequences for the power distribution among social actors. Through feeling ashamed, one acknowledges the subordination to the standards of the 'shaming other' and these standards become reinforced. This diminishes the power of the shamed person as this person is turned into an object of evaluation rather than an active participant in evaluating others. Future claims of this person are deprived of legitimacy: the power to set and enforce standards in interactions turns into the fear of having to experience shame in future situations again. As individual actions are believed to be manifestations of inferiority (cf. also Katz 1999: 156–7) disparagement is constantly to be feared. It is this fear that prevents the ashamed self to put one's power to test. Shame will then result in avoidance and passivity.

From this perspective, shame provides a compelling explanation for eastern reactions to westernization. Passivity and quiescence were predominant among eastern *SVD* members and pervaded the Saxon chapter up until its dissolution. Significantly, the dissolution itself was not a vigorous act of self-asserting protest. After several Saxon board members stepped down (in itself, an act of protest), the chapter simply faded out as vacant board positions could not be staffed again. Nobody was found to fill in the gap and without a complete board, the organization ceased to exist simply for legal reasons.

Conclusion: the entanglements of shame

As Scheff (1988: 399), drawing on Cooley, has reminded us individuals are virtually always either in a state of shame or pride. In this sense, the underlying logic of the Saxon *SVD* chapter's development can be analyzed in much the same way as a dynamic that is ultimately shaped by shame. To summarize: the threat of shame was prominent in the eastern German gay movement very soon after the *Wende*. In the early stages, however, eastern gay activists succeeded in countering this threat of impending shame. However, shame kept lingering as political prospects remained uncertain. This double-sided setup helps explain different outcomes of early East–West encounters. Eventually it resulted in the *SVD*'s decision to expand into the West in order to benefit from western political skills. The optimistic expectations about the shared harmonious future turned fear into hope. As these hopes and expectations were frustrated by westernization, eastern activists were thrown back to feelings of shame that they wanted to avoid in the first place. Inferiority provided a basis for the micro-politics of shaming.

As this account shows, shame was endemic to the eastern gay movement all the way. The consequences of shame for the movement over time, however, differed greatly. Speaking about shame as a prismatic experience, Katz (1999: 146–7) analyzed shame as refracting 'in so many shades of feeling and [taking] such diverse metaphoric shades [...].' Indeed, as for the *SVD* it gave rise to a whole range of other emotions like uncertainty, fear, hope and enthusiasm. Although transferred into pride, shame kept lingering and could therefore undermine this pride at a later point, once westernization made itself felt in all its demeaning consequences. Whereas in the beginning, the threat of shame induced proactive attempts at re-appropriating the political field, shame eventually worked to cause eastern demobilization. As this shows, the role of shame in social movements is in fact more multifaceted than is suggested in the pertinent literature. Here, shame is conceived of as either a hindering starting condition prior to mobilization that is thus to be overcome (e.g. Gould 2001; Britt and Heise 2000), or as spurring mobilization by shaming bystanders out of their passivity (Yang 2001; Kim 2002). As the analysis of the *SVD* suggests, however, shame can also motivate activism as the threat of impending shame induces countering strategies of prideful re-appropriation.

More importantly, however, the case of the *SVD* arguably demonstrates the pervasive and persistent quality of shame. It reaches beyond the point where shame is being overcome and thus keeps affecting further developments by leaving individuals vulnerable to future shaming experience. It does so by engendering numerous other emotions depending on how activists try to counter and avoid shame, or fail to do so, as well as on the contexts they act in. These strategies in turn may have unexpected consequences, such as reinforcing shame. This highlights the nexus between shame and pride. Elias (1997: 436–7) alluded to the persistence of shame when he wrote about the virtual impossibility of lower class people to adopt the standards of social superiors. Even when successful on the surface, they find it impossible to adopt these standards with the same natural ease, leaving aspiring individuals in an emotionally distorted state. More recently, Gould (2001) has introduced the concept of emotional ambivalence to point to the parallel existence of shame and pride in gays and lesbians. She elaborates how this ambivalence is to be attributed to powerful societal institutions which instill negative feelings about the self, whereas the lesbian and gay movement promotes positive feelings such as pride. She also recognizes, but does not elaborate theoretically, the idea that shame and pride are dialectical counterparts, the latter resting on the denial of the former. In a similar vein, Scheff (1990) points to a common core of both emotions when he describes shame and pride as outcomes of either negative or positive evaluations of the self. What is implicit in both arguments is that such evaluations require a notion of a specific self as distinct in unique ways. It is through the drawing of borders between people and separating them into categories that shame can be kept simmering on a low scale, even when seemingly overcome, and be elicited again at a later point (cf. also Katz 1999: 150–2). Again we are referred to interpretative schemas for shame to arise. The role of such schemas, however, is not limited to attributional processes but pertains on a more fundamental level to the constitution of the self as a distinct, potential object of evaluation.

This adds an ontological aspect to Simmel's (1992 [1901]) argument about the total exposure of the self as one of the pivotal conditions giving rise to shame. After all, the case of the *SVD* is a vivid example of how a new divide – the East–West distinction – has pervaded a social movement and ran across the basic shared identity as gay. This new categorization and the emotions it spurred worked to undermine a collective gay movement identity as a unifying core.

Notes

1 I would like to thank the editors for their helpful support and sound advice. I am indebted to Eron Witzel who carefully corrected my English.
2 I will focus on the gay movement as it is represented in Leipzig, the biggest Eastern German city outside Berlin. Leipzig still has the broadest range of gay movement activities in the east and a longstanding tradition of gay activism.
3 *Wende* [turning point] is a common term to point to the East German revolution of 1989.
4 As the organization has changed its name several times, I will use the acronyms SVD, the inclusive *(L)SVD* or simply *LSVD* depending on which period I refer to.
5 Semi-structured interviews were carried out with ten leading activists, some of which had quit by the time the interview was held. Others were still active in the movement. The interviews took place in the first quarter year 2002. With four of these interview partners additional interviews were done via email in March 2003.
6 Two eastern lesbian board members at this point hardly provide identification points for eastern gays, as the decision to include lesbians was embedded in westernization.
7 Note the sexual innuendo in 'inverted.'
8 Meaning better westerner literally, this derogatory term describes westerners as know-it-all or arrogant. Interestingly it's used here in a literal, positive sense in order to point to higher western competences. Short form: *Wessi.*
9 Re-privatization of property in the course of re-unification had resulted there in a lot of property being transferred back to the (western) initial owners or their heirs. In a similar sense, western companies taking over and closing down eastern business have contributed to this theme.
10 A derogatory term for eastern Germany, used ironically here. It refers to the so-called east-zone of the post-World War II occupation zones.

References

Benford, R.D. (1993). 'Frame disputes within the nuclear disarmament movement,' *Social Forces*, 71: 677–701.
Britt, L. and Heise, D. (2000) 'From shame to pride in identity politics,' in S. Stryker, T.J. Owens and W. White (eds) *Self, Identity, and Social Movements*, Minneapolis: University of Minnesota Press.
Elias, N. (1997) *Über den Prozeß der Zivilisation*, 2nd volume, Frankfurt am Main: Suhrkamp.
Flam, H. (in collaboration with Jamison, A.) (1994) 'The Swedish confrontation over nuclear energy: a case of a timid anti-nuclear opposition,' in H. Flam (ed.) *States and Anti-nuclear Movements*, Edinburgh: Edinburgh University Press.

Gehling, R. (1993) *Fremde im eigenen Land. Soziale Anpassungsprozesse homo-sexueller Männer aus der ehemaligen DDR*, Munich, Vienna: Profil Verlag.

Goffman, E. (1967) *Interaction Ritual: essays in face-to-face behavior*, Chicago: Aldine.

Goodwin, J. (1997) 'The libidinal constitution of a high-risk movement: affectual ties and solidarity in the Huk rebellion 1946 to 1954,' *American Sociological Review*, 62: 53–69.

Goodwin, J., Jasper, J.M. and Polletta, F. (eds) (2001a) *Passionate Politics: emotions and social movements*, Chicago: University of Chicago Press.

—— (2001b) 'Introduction: why emotions matter,' in J. Goodwin, J.M. Jasper and F. Polletta (eds) *Passionate Politics: emotions and social movements*, Chicago: University of Chicago Press.

Gould, D. (2001) 'Rock the boat, don't rock the boat, baby: ambivalence and the emergence of militant AIDS activism,' in J. Goodwin, J.M. Jasper and F. Polletta (eds) *Passionate Politics: emotions and social movements*, Chicago: University of Chicago Press.

Hercus, C. (1999) 'Identity, emotion, and feminist collective action,' *Gender & Society*, 20: 34–56.

Hirschmann, A.O. (1982) *Shifting Involvements*, Princeton, NJ: Princeton University Press.

Jasper, J.M. (1998) 'The emotions of protest: affective and reactive emotions in and around social movements,' *Sociological Forum* 13: 397–424.

Joppke, C. (1991) 'Social movements during cycles of issue attention: the decline of the anti-nuclear energy movements in West Germany and the USA,' *British Journal of Sociology*, 42: 43–60.

Kamenitsa, L. (1998) 'The complexity of decline: explaining the marginalization of the East German women's movement,' *Mobilization*, 3: 245–63.

Katz, J. (1999) *How Emotions Work*, Chicago: Chicago University Press.

Kim, H. (2002) 'Shame, anger, and love in collective action: emotional consequences of suicide protest in South Korea,' *Mobilization*, 7: 159–76.

Kleres, J. (2000) 'Gleiche Rechte im Sozialismus. Die Schwulen- und Lesbenbewegung der DDR,' *Forschungsjournal Neue Soziale Bewegungen*, 13: 52–63.

—— (2001) 'Cherries blossoming in Eastern Germany?,' in H. Flam (ed.) *Pink, Purple, Green: women's, religious, environmental and gay/lesbian movements in central Europe today*, New York: Columbia University Press: East European Monographs.

—— (2002) 'Demobilisierung sozialer Bewegungen,' unpublished diploma-thesis, University of Leipzig.

McAdam, D. (1999) 'The decline of the civil rights movement,' in J. Freeman and V. Johnson (eds) *Waves of Protest: social movements since the sixties*, Lanham, Maryland: Rowman and Littlefield Publishers [reprint from: Freeman, J. (ed.) (1983) *Social Movements of the Sixties and Seventies*, New York: Longman].

McAdam, D., McCarthy, J.D. and Zald, M.N. (1988) 'Social movements,' in N.J. Smelser (ed.) *Handbook of Sociology*, Newbury Park: Sage.

Miller, F.D. (1999) 'The end of SDS and the emergence of Weatherman: demise through success,' in J. Freeman and V. Johnson (eds) *Waves of Protest: social movements since the sixties*, Lanham, Maryland: Rowman and Littlefield Publishers. [reprint from: Freeman, J. (ed.) (1983) *Social Movements of the Sixties and Seventies*, New York: Longman.]

Neckel, S. (1991) *Status und Scham. Zur symbolischen Reproduktion sozialer Ungleichheit*, Frankfurt am Main: Campus Verlag.

—— (1996). 'Inferiority,' *Sociological Review*, 44: 17–34.

Polletta, F. (2002) *Freedom is an Endless Meeting: democracy in American social movements*, Chicago: University of Chicago Press.

Rucht, D. (1994) 'The anti-nuclear power movement and the state in France,' in H. Flam (ed.) *States and Anti-nuclear Movements*, Edinburgh: Edinburgh University Press.

—— (1995) 'Deutsche Vereinigung und Demokratisierung. Zum Scheitern der Bürgerbewegungen,' *Forschungsjournal Neue Soziale Bewegungen*, 8: 12–19.

Scheff, T.J. (1988) 'Shame and conformity: the deference-emotion system,' *American Sociological Review*, 53: 395–406.

—— (1990) 'Socialization of emotions: pride and shame as causal agents,' in T.D. Kemper (ed.) *Research Agendas in the Sociology of Emotions*, Albany: State University of New York Press.

Schmitt-Beck, R. and Weins, C. (1997) 'Gone with the wind (of change). Neue soziale Bewegungen und politischer Protest im Osten Deutschlands,' in O.W. Gabriel (ed.) *Politische Orientierungen und Verhaltensweisen im Vereinigten Deutschland*, Opladen.

Simmel, G. (1992 [1901]) 'Zur Psychologie der Scham,' in his *Schriften zur Soziologie: eine Auswahl*, Frankfurt am Main: Suhrkamp.

Stoper, E. (1999) 'The student nonviolent coordinating committee: rise and fall of a redemptive organization,' in J. Freeman and V. Johnson (eds) *Waves of Protest: social movements since the sixties*, Lanham, Maryland: Rowman and Littlefield Publishers. [reprint of *Journal of Black Studies* 18 (1977): 13–28.]

Voss, K. (1996) 'The collapse of a social movement: the interplay of mobilizing structures, framing, and political opportunities in the Knights of Labor,' in D. McAdam, J.D. McCarthy and M.N. Zald (eds) *Comparative Perspectives on Social Movements*, New York: Cambridge University Press.

Yang, G. (2001) 'Achieving emotions in collective action: emotional processes and movement mobilization in the 1989 Chinese student movement,' *The Sociological Quarterly*, 41: 593–614.

11 Sisterhood and exclusionary solidarity in a labor women's organization

Silke Roth[1]

Emotional bonds and social movement participation

While networks have received considerable attention from social movement scholars, the social movements literature that dealt with emotions has for a long time either been dismissed, as was typical for the classical social movement approaches (for reviews see Snow and Oliver 1995; Snow and Davis 1995), or ignored, as was typical for feminist research (see Ferree 1992; Taylor 1995, 1996; Taylor and Whittier 1998). Lately emotions have re-emerged in social movement research. The crucial role of emotions for social movement emergence, development, and decline is now acknowledged (Goodwin *et al* 2000, 2001; Aminzade and McAdam 2001). From quite early on, Flam (1990) explored how emotions helped to mobilize social movements. Furthermore, she addressed the question of individual identity and 'emotional liberation' as preconditions for joining movements (Flam 1993), and analyzed how activists manage their fears (Flam 1998). As these scholars point out, the role of emotions in social movements affects political opportunity structures (emotion cultures), framing processes, identity formation, repertoires of protest, movement outcomes, and indigenous organizations and social networks. It is the last point that this chapter is concerned with.

Affective bonds and personal loyalty that are related to the pre-existing networks play an important role for the recruitment process (Lofland 1996: 234). I will show in this chapter that such bonds are also crucial for maintaining active membership in a social movement organization. As Lofland (1996: 237) has pointed out, after seven to eight years movement organizations tend to have more former than current members. Since most movement organizations are characterized by a high membership turnover, an important question is how relationships among members affect staying or leaving a movement organization. One important aspect concerns emotions that are created through relationships. Jasper (1997) argues that collective emotions are key sources for identification with a movement and they thus sustain movement identities. He distinguishes two kinds of collective emotions that are created in social movements – reciprocal emotions and shared emotions. Reciprocal emotions 'concern people's ongoing feelings toward each other. These are the close, affective ties of friendship, love, and loyalty, but also their negative counterparts such as rivalry, jealousy, and resentment' (Jasper 1997: 187). Gould (2002) argues with respect to the AIDS activist movement that emotion work is crucial for social movement sustainability: 'ACT UP meetings were more than meetings; although sometimes long, tedious, and contentious, they were also cruising grounds, places to formulate cultural theory, a chance to enact a new queer identity' (Gould 2002: 193). However, friendship norms such as exclusivity and conflict avoidance can undermine democratic projects (Polletta 2002: 222). In this chapter, I analyze the role of friendships and support networks in a bureaucratic feminist organization. In contrast to Polletta (2002) my study shows that those who felt marginalized left the organization rather than demanding the redistribution of power.

Feminist organizations can be defined very broadly as 'the places in which and the means through which the work of the women's movement is done' (Ferree and Martin 1995: 13). With respect to an organization's independence and its access to the available resources one can distinguish 'insider' and 'outsider' organizations (Katzenstein 1998; Spalter-Roth and Schreiber 1995). *Insider organizations* are part of and accountable to another organization – state agencies, social movements, political parties, or religious organizations. Accountability constrains the actions of an organization by defining with whom to form coalitions, what issues to address, and in what way to address them. Being part of an institution, however, also means having an 'official' status, credibility, and access to the resources of the institution. *Outsider organizations* are independent and thus less constrained, but they also lack official status and access to resources. Feminist organizations can be insider (femocratic) or outsider (autonomous) organizations. Autonomous feminist organizations are most accountable to feminist principles, while femocratic organizations are held accountable by the organization of which they are a part (Eisenstein 1995; Reinelt 1995). Feminist caucuses – feminist organizations that are not part of another organization but represent a certain constituency within a larger organization – have to negotiate whether they feel more accountable to the women's movement or to the organizational background (labor movement, peace movement, environmental movement, political party, voluntary association) from which they emerged.

The Coalition of Labor Union Women (CLUW) constitutes a feminist caucus in the labor movement and resembles the American Federation of Labor – Congress of Industrial Organizations (AFL-CIO). It is financially dependent on the AFL-CIO and the labor unions, although it also received funds from the feminist Ms. Foundation. CLUW seeks to empower women, improve their status, and address their needs. The organization was founded in 1974 during the height of the second wave of the women's movement and is one of the AFL-CIO's support or constituent groups. In contrast to autonomous organizations like Nine-to-Five, an organization of clerical workers, or Union WAGE (Balser 1987, 1993), CLUW set out to work within the unions rather than criticizing the labor movement from the position of an outsider. CLUW is restricted to union members and is shaped by the exclusionary solidarity (Ferree and Roth 1998) of the labor movement.[2] However, CLUW is not a union: it is an organization of union women. Membership in a union or collective bargaining organization is a precondition of regular membership in CLUW. This means that CLUW members are already members of (at least) one other organization, their union.

Membership in CLUW contributes to active membership and leadership in unions. Many CLUW members also have contact with women's movement organizations. Furthermore, a high proportion of members belong to civil rights organizations. CLUW has a high proportion of women of color which reflects the fact that, due to the racially and ethnically segregated labor market, a higher proportion of women of color than white women are union members. They joined CLUW because as women they felt isolated in male-dominated unions and as working class women felt alienated from feminist organizations that were dominated by white middle class women who did not address their needs (Roth 2003).

Network contacts play an important role in recruitment into the organization. A CLUW Membership Survey demonstrated that almost three-quarters of the membership learned about CLUW through a friend (13 percent), union member (27 percent), or through the union (union meeting 19 percent, union convention 4 percent, labor council 7 percent). Within CLUW, the incentives for participation are as much about solidarity and value realization as it is about power. CLUW is bureaucratic, but its informal structure also exhibits collectivist characteristics (Rothschild-Whitt 1979). For instance, social relations are often communal, holistic, personal, and expressive – typical of collectivist organizations – rather than impersonal, role based, segmented, and instrumental, which are more typical of bureaucratic organizations.

Feminist groups 'tend to cultivate a unique set of feeling rules and expression rules that both draw on and challenge the dominant ideal of women as nurturers' (Taylor 1995: 229). The emotion culture of the international women's movement promoted a loving community that transcended national rivalries (Taylor and Rupp 2002). Female bonding is an expression of a feminist 'ethic of care' which can be found in feminist organizations. Whether such bonding is best described as 'sisterhood' or as 'friendship' is subject to debate (Lugones and Rosezelle 1995). Lugones and Rosezelle (1995) argue that in contrast to sisterhood which implies the institution of a family, friendship is not an institutional relationship and does not have legal components. They suggest the term 'companera' for political relations among women. Weiss (1995) points out that women's relationships within traditional communities not only maintain the women but also help them to challenge their living conditions. Feminist communities are characterized by blurring the boundaries between friendships, families, the social, and the political (Weiss 1995: 12). In spite of the bureaucratic features typical of the labor movement, interaction at CLUW meetings and conventions is often shaped by the emotion culture of the women's movement.

CLUW provides friendships and support networks which play an important role for staying an active member in the organization. Members who felt that CLUW was neither effective with respect to pursuing its goals, nor with respect to providing a support network, left the organization. However, the friendships and networks that developed in the context of the organization continue even if members are no longer active in CLUW. The organization thus has long term effects by contributing to submerged networks for women in the labor movement and thus contributes to unobtrusive mobilization (Katzenstein 1998). The networks help to advance women's careers within their unions. Furthermore, through bringing CLUW members in union leadership positions as well as through conferences and other events, CLUW contributes to broadening the labor agenda by re-framing 'women's issues' as 'labor issues'and thus serves as a bridging organization between the women's and the labor movement and contributing to coalitions between women's, civil rights, and labor organizations (Roth 2003).

Data and methods

This chapter is based on a case-study of the Coalition of Labor Union Women (CLUW). For further information on the history of the organization and the methodology of the study see Roth (2003). Between 1991 and 1995, I conducted semi-structured interviews with 68 formerly and presently active CLUW members. Some interviews were as short as 15 minutes, while others lasted for several hours. On average, the interviews lasted one-and-a-half hours. Furthermore, 14 experts on the women's and the labor movement were interviewed. When I refer to these interviews, I use pseudonyms. During an internship in the CLUW Center for Education and Research in Washington, DC (summer 1994), I compiled a CLUW leadership directory which provided information about the 200 members of CLUW's national executive board, and in addition conducted a membership survey (N = 534, response rate 30 percent). On several occasions, I also engaged in participant observation at chapter meetings and national meetings.

Sisterhood and support networks

As already pointed out, CLUW members are also union members. Within CLUW, members can participate at the local level in chapters or at the national level in CLUW's national executive board. The friendships and support they find in CLUW are important for union women – regardless whether they are rank-and-file members just getting involved in their union, whether they have already achieved their first staff or officer position, or whether they have belonged to union leadership for a long time. Irrespectively of the position they hold within their union, they are often the only woman among the active members or leadership in their union. Especially for women in male dominated unions who have little or no day-to-day contact with other women in union leadership positions, CLUW offers an opportunity to come together with other union women. But even CLUW members who belong to unions that represent a predominately female work force and therefore have a higher proportion of women in union leadership positions sometimes feel isolated when they mediate among workers, union, and management. For example, Jody Hunter recalled that she thought 'it would be really good to know women who are involved in the unions.' She belonged to a male-dominated crafts union and was interested in networking with other union women. She emphasized that it is important for women to have 'their' network.

> Because traditionally I think the men's networks have been cut off from the women. And I think that . . . the informal network of CLUW is just as important as the formal things they do such as workshops. . . . I think the informal network of friendships is just being able to call somebody. . . . I just think that's worth a lot.

CLUW provided a space to find mentorship and to feel comfortable to ask for help. CLUW provides its members with a 'safe environment' or independent space (Needleman 1998) in which they can seek a piece of advice and share problems. Networking with women from their own and other unions, along with meeting union women from other countries, expands their knowledge about union and women's issues. In CLUW meetings they can exchange information, find allies, and build coalitions.

CLUW members appreciate the *sisterhood*, they found in the organization. The term *sisterhood* parallels the term *brotherhood*, which is common in the labor movement. The term implies a relationship that goes beyond a voluntary association; it suggests family bonds, personal and expressive relations among members and officers. As already noted, Rupp and Taylor (2002) identify an 'emotion culture' as typical for women's movement organizations. In their comparison of the male-dominated labor unions and the women's peace movement of the late nineteenth and early twentieth centuries, they argue that international solidarity was achieved by the women's movement but not by the labor movement through drawing on emotion templates like family relationships. However, Barker (2001) points out with respect to the burgeoning Solidarity movement in

Poland that labor organizing is also packed with 'human emotionality.'[3] He observed 'fear, courage, anger, laughter, nervous breakdown, pride and solidarity' (Barker 2001: 175). Similarly, Fantasia (1988) describes the development of 'cultures of solidarity' among female and male workers in labor disputes. Morris (1984) points to the generating of feelings of solidarity and emotions through hymns and spirituals in the civil rights movement. These examples show that emotion cultures are not restricted to the women's movement; however, the display of emotions is highly gendered and reflects emotion norms (Hochschild 1983). These gender differences are emphasized by Ella Turner who referred to CLUW as the 'women's AFL-CIO' and the CLUW leaders as 'sheroes.'

> Women have a different kind of what I call camaraderie than men do. And we tend to be much more understanding and much more caring about what happens to the person. And that's what CLUW has been for a lot of women. Whenever women run into problems within their respective unions or within their local unions or whatever, they can always call CLUW and ask, 'What is it that I should be doing?'

CLUW members, who joined unions – still predominantly male-dominated organizations – in order to fight for social change, appreciate the friendship, cooperation and mutual support in this women's organization.

Support and mentorship for new members

It is of crucial importance that women who feel otherwise alienated in the labor movement find a safe or 'independent space' (Needleman 1998) where they can turn to each other. It was evident from the women that I interviewed, especially those women who were not familiar with the labor movement, that they found CLUW allows them to become acquainted with the union culture. For example, My Chang had been a community activist before she became active in the labor movement, which she found very alienating. She stated:

> In my own personal career I give CLUW a lot of credit for keeping me more—, I mean for keeping my certain faith and [that I] stayed in the labor movement because I found the labor movement very alienating when I first got involved. And I think it was really from my joining CLUW and meeting people like [women labor leader] and others that made me feel like there is some hope for someone like me in the labor movement.

She found it inspiring to hear about the experiences of long time union members:

Well, one thing that inspired me is all the hardships that they had to go through in a very male chauvinistic AFL-CIO or their own union and how they were able to work their way through that. And then I was able to meet a lot of the strong women within the [garment workers union], like all around the country which was fascinating and then just get their tips on how they dealt with different situations in [garment workers union].

In addition to giving CLUW credit for keeping her in the labor movement, she also emphasized the mentorship that she experienced at the CLUW meetings. This included informal conversations over breakfast, lunch, or at the bar. Rather than receiving assistance from a single mentor, she found that CLUW provided its members with many mentors. Mentorship is crucial for the advancement of women in labor unions (Elkiss 1995). Several CLUW members reported that they had male mentors who encouraged them to take on leadership positions in the union. Furthermore, several interviewees found that women were not supportive enough of other women as I will discuss below Jackie Lanois who belongs to CLUW's national leadership recalled that her union mentor – a CLUW national officer:

insisted I did join [CLUW] and I think my life pretty much changed after that. And it's a good feeling, no matter where you go, where there is a CLUW chapter, and if you know somebody, to be able to network with that, that woman. And most of the women have so many skills which are different from mine. So if I ever had a problem in any area there is always somebody I can talk to for advice and it's a good feeling, it really is.

As these examples show, emotional support and sharing of skills are closely related. CLUW members feel comfortable to turn to another CLUW member if they need guidance or counseling, rather than being afraid of being belittled, turned away or not taken serious. Jacqueline Lanois emphasized:

What I really, really have been impressed with, is the fact that there's so many women who have joined together for a common cause. They're working together and working together in harmony and working together with the expertise and whatever is needed to really move forward, and the leadership, the genuine leadership they have there, and the willingness to be available to you.

Over and over, CLUW members emphasized that they felt 'comfortable' asking other members for advice. In this way, CLUW is experienced as a support group. Members emphasize the benefits of belonging to networks of CLUW. These networks offer access to resources and information, as well as assistance. Especially the conventions provide opportunities for getting together with friends and mentors. The younger national officers praised the older officers for being 'too willing to share their knowledge' and 'helping them up the ladder.'

Support for women in new leadership positions

Support networks are not only important for new union members but also for women who take on new leadership positions in the union to which they already belong. CLUW members in new leadership positions find the CLUW support crucial for carrying out their duties. Lydia Sellers remembered how she was elected to become the director of the newly established women's department of her male-dominated union. She recalled this as a very emotional situation which caused much hesitation and uncertainty:

> ... suddenly finding yourself in a new position that you're some national director for a newly established women's department that you know nothing about, and there has been nobody before you so you're like a pioneer trying out a new course in the wilderness, so to speak. I really just felt like, 'Hey, I don't need this. Not right now. I'm not ready to do this.' But I was just filled with emotion.

In this situation, she was very grateful for the support that she received in CLUW which she described as 'therapeutic.' As head of the newly created women's department she did not feel supported by her union board. She felt that CLUW helped her through the six years in which she was the director of the women's department. Sellers found that CLUW 'filled the void,' the lack of support that she faced in her union. She reported that when she 'was feeling down,' the participation in the National Executive Board meetings of CLUW 'revitalized her' because she could turn to her mentors who inspired her, she could call on them 'and ventilate [her] emotions or situations and ask for guidance.' The personal support, advice, and mentorship she received from CLUW members who had similar positions in their unions were crucial for Sellers. She therefore described CLUW as a:

> ... conduit for receiving and sharing resources. So it helped me grow as an individual, and it also helped me carry out my duties and responsibilities there in that new department. Because I had said many times that department I know, was set-up for failure. I think there were people assuming [as much] – I didn't have a budget, and I didn't have a secretary.

CLUW provided the resources that Sellers did not obtain from her own union. In turn, she invited CLUW members to participate in programs of the women's department or invited them to the national conventions of her union. CLUW's national officers emphasize that CLUW is less about individual careers, and more about issues and benefiting all women in the labor movement.

Support for long-time members

Emotional support is also very important for union staff and officers who are active in the labor movement for a long time, raising women's issues over and over again in their unions. Agnes Pardo, one of CLUW's national officers described the backing that she experienced in CLUW:

> The Coalition of Labor Union Women has been a cushion for me, while I have been out in the world dealing with the transient leadership or the political mountains that we had to climb, it has been great for me to run back to the Coalition of Labor Union Women and learn how to feel safer, to deal, to try out my speaking skills or my writing skills or my organizing skills in a safer environment, so I am more confident to go out and I have someone to talk to when I come back to the Coalition of Labor Union Women.

The long term members who had participated in CLUW since the beginning, experience CLUW as a support network. Respondents emphasized that mutual support was an important reason for them to participate in the national meeting:

> That's what the conferences are really about – to give you that extra energy. It's like a vitamin shot, you know. So that you can come back and feel that you are going to do this and you accomplish this for many women who need the help.

The encouragement they find in CLUW helped women union leaders to stay in their positions and continue their work in the unions. Cynthia Delgado, who was involved in CLUW from the beginning and is one of the founding members of the organization, explained how exhausting the participation in male-dominated unions was for women labor leaders:

> We come here so drained and so frustrated that we need that sort of a stimulation, listening to our sisters, or maybe just to hug, or a pat on the back. Or knowing that we all care about it, that we are working for the same thing. That it has given the greatest sisterhood to me that I have known. The church ... brings folks together from different walks of life, but the Coalition of Labor Union Women has brought women together for a common concern greater than anything in the history of the trade union movement.

Exchange and learning about women in other unions, networking with other union women, mutual support, and bonding: these aspects constitute a continuum from exchanging information to developing long-lasting friendships and are clearly intertwined. This echoes Aminzade and McAdam's (2001: 18) argument that rationality and emotionality are not mutually exclusive. While some see emotions as supporting rationality, others argue that emotion and reason must be seen as continuous.

CLUW constitutes a support group and is perceived as a valuable resource by its active members. The independent space it provides is important for creating a women-friendly organizational culture, and thus has feminist outcomes. In 1980, CLUW's national president Joyce Miller became the first woman on the AFL-CIO executive board. Until then, membership to the AFL-CIO executive board had been restricted to national presidents of unions. CLUW members head women's and civil rights departments of the largest US unions and participate as business agents, staff members and chapter presidents in a number of unions. Furthermore, the organization has contributed to bringing 'women's issues' like day care, pay equity, sexual harassment, and reproductive rights on the labor agenda (Roth 2003). However, CLUW offers less for non-unionized women or for union members who do not have the chance to participate in national meetings or who belong to chapters which include mostly retired or rank-and-file members.

Exclusionary solidarity

Solidarity is a key concept in the organizational repertoire of labor. As a labor organization, CLUW restricts the regular membership to union members – according to each union's definition of membership. For instance, if a union acknowledges workers who are currently laid off or between jobs as members, CLUW accepts them as regular members. The leadership of the organization emphasizes that restricting the membership to union members makes CLUW a unique women's organization with insider status in the labor movement. It makes CLUW an organization of and for unionized women workers. CLUW thus accepts the call of the labor movement for class solidarity as this concept was interpreted at the time of CLUW's formation. Such exclusionary solidarity (Ferree and Roth 1998) privileges one system of oppression – class – at the expense of gender since non-unionized women are excluded.

This restriction of membership to union members pre-empts the accusation of dual unionism that is, competing with existing unions and undermining union solidarity. The membership rule does mean, however, that retirees and men[4] who are union members could belong to CLUW as regular members, but working women who are not union members can become only associate members. The decision to restrict the membership furthermore reflects the political climate and the position of the AFL-CIO at the time CLUW was formed. The decision also excludes members of socialist groups, a legacy of McCarthyism (Schrecker 1998). Although some interviewees mentioned involvement in 'progressive movements,' membership in the Communist Party and other organizations of the Old and New Left was rarely discussed in the interviews. The category 'associate member' was created in 1979 and amended in 1984 in order to allow non-unionized members to join the organization, though not as full members. But few people are interested in paying dues without having the right to participate fully in the organization. Furthermore, associate members have difficulty finding a role in CLUW and feel marginalized. Some find it upsetting to be an auxiliary or associate member, but nevertheless stay active in their chapter and supported CLUW.

However, even within the organization, not everybody has the equal opportunity to participate. The participation at the national level, as a member of the national executive board or in the national officers council, is virtually restricted to union officers and staff. CLUW as an organization does not have enough funds to pay for the participation of the board members and so the unions pick up the travel costs for their members. There are only a few executive board members who pay for the participation in national meetings out of their own pocket. In contrast, participation at the chapter level is open to every CLUW member. Non-members or associate members can participate at the chapter level and at the national level as observers. Some members including those who are part of the networks and benefit from the support system of CLUW critically remarked that some members do not share these resources. Susan Carter was active both at the chapter level and at the national level; she belongs to the national executive board as a chapter delegate and stated:

> But I also feel that as women we sometimes forget to pull other women up along with us. You know what I mean? We get in a position where we can pull other women up along with us and we don't. We feel threatened. We feel challenged. You know? But it should not be that way.

While many members praise the support they receive through CLUW and being part of a network of union women, others who belong to the national executive board as chapter delegates, union delegates, or state vice-presidents dislike the idea of an 'old girls network' and found that women were not supporting each other enough.

Another long term CLUW activist who was active at the national level as a union delegate also critiqued the low leadership turnover within the organization. She suggested that terms should be limited in order to allow more women to develop leadership skills as well as open up the organization for new impulses. Otherwise, she was afraid that: 'if you have the same people, talk about the same stuff, with the same program, there is a tendency that the organization kind of dies.' She noticed: 'and we find ourselves criticizing the good old boys in the AFL-CIO, but we also find ourselves start emulating some of the ways of the good old boys and that would be bad, [laughs] particularly in a women's organization.'

Heather Stone, a state vice-president, also observed that 'women are their own worst enemies.' She stated that: 'our biggest challenge is to get women to be more supportive of women.' She found that women generally did not support women and women's issues. In her experience, many women labor leaders felt that they had achieved the success on their own and were not ready to support other women. She argued that men have more loyalty with men than women with women and, that while she could count on male support, she could not rely on female support. Stone also felt that women would criticize women, but would not criticize men for the same actions. With respect to backing women within CLUW she felt that members were of assistance to each other as long as their own positions and resources were not affected:

> I think they help other women to get in positions, as long they're not challenging their position. Yes, I think that they pretty much do that. I think CLUW as a whole definitely is supportive of women and women's issues. How supportive are they when it gets down to home turf and home network? I guess what you really need to try and discover is, if there is truly a different attitude between women and women in the labor movement and men and men in the labor movement.

While CLUW provides a support network for union women, not everybody feels assisted equally. As already mentioned, very few members can afford the financial burden of participating in the national meetings and thus only union members who are delegates and receive travel funds from their unions participate. This means that participation at the national level is virtually restricted to union staff members and officers as well as members of unions who also pay for the participation of their rank-and-file members. CLUW members thus compete for scarce resources for participation at the national level (Roth 2003). The fact that members hold onto positions of power points to the iron law of oligarchy (Michels 1962). Thus it seems that reciprocal emotions and affective solidarity (Aminzade and McAdam 2001) are restricted to a small number of activists who maintain control over resources and key positions. In that regard, CLUW is reminiscent of Rupp and Taylor's (1990) finding that during movement decline close ties among career activists maintain social movements in the doldrums.

Long term effects: submerged networks

All the current and former CLUW members I have interviewed emphasized the need for a 'free' or 'independent' space for union women, even if they had not necessarily found such a space in CLUW. Paradoxically, when women move up in their own union and can contribute to and benefit even more from the exchange with other women in union leadership which they meet through CLUW, they often no longer find the time (and motivation) to participate in CLUW. Those CLUW members who moved up in their union and who did not hold a position at the national level of CLUW often left the organization. In 1994, 8 percent of the CLUW's members were involved in the founding of the organization, 12 percent joined the organization between 1974 and 1979, 13 percent between 1980 and 1984, 18 percent between 1985 and 1989, and 37 percent between 1990 and 1994 (CLUW survey 1994). This shows, that the organization continued to attract new members. However, the leadership positions were often held by long term members. For example, Joyce Miller was CLUW's national president from 1977 until 1993. Gloria Johnson was National Treasurer from 1974 until 1993 when she became National President of CLUW (for an overview over CLUW's national leadership see Roth 2003: 104–5). Chapters differed with respect to the turnover of the leadership; some have the same president since the founding of the chapter, while others elect a new membership after several years.

Eleanor Junker, who participated in CLUW's founding convention and is working as a labor lawyer for a union with a high proportion of women workers is no longer active because she found that the chapter meetings she attended were restricted to socializing and were inefficient:

> I was a members years ago and then I dropped out, because I just did not see the point, I mean. I go to these meetings and there are three people there, and it was about some upcoming dinner or something. It just seemed like an incredible waste of time. I would never say that to [woman labor leader], because I think it is still important in terms of its potential. So, yeah, I am still a member.

Although formerly active members still see the organization as important, they do not find the support that they need at the chapter level, at least not in chapters which are dominated by rank-and-file members and retirees. After working long hours for their own union and often being active in other social and political organizations, their participation in CLUW feels more like a burden than a resource. But new members also find the informality of the meetings – at least initially – problematic. Jodie Hunter recalled that it took a while for her to get involved in CLUW since, at first, she felt excluded from the familiarity of other chapter members:

> When I first started I did not get involved immediately. I went to a couple of meetings and then I went to a workshop and then I didn't do anything for a while, because, I guess I didn't feel comfortable right away. Maybe it was just like I felt, like they weren't really organized or that maybe I felt like a lot of people that were first active in it all knew each other and I didn't really know them.

This account points to two aspects that prevented women getting involved. On the one hand, the organization does not seem to be clearly structured to the new member, it is not obvious how they can participate and what the organization accomplishes. On the other hand, the informality can give a new member the feeling that she does not belong. Later on, Hunter felt that she received a lot of support from the other chapter members and appreciated learning from other union women and receiving encouragement from them.

This shows that the informal atmosphere at chapter meetings can be evaluated quite differently depending on the relationship with other chapter members. CLUW members, who feel that other chapter members provide friendship and backing, appreciate the informality as an emotion culture typical of a women's organization. However, union women who do not have such relationships to other members, perceive the informality and contents of the meetings as a sign of inefficiency and irrelevance. But even then, members stay in the organization as dues paying members because they find the organization important 'due to its potential.' Some CLUW members are active in the organization because they want to support women in the labor movement, even though they do not feel that they personally benefit from the membership. For example, Samantha Torrel decided to stay active in CLUW because she felt she could support other members:

> I find that I'm now the support person for other people, but I still need support myself. So I have to go other places to find my support, that's all. No big deal. [laughs] But I still go to CLUW because I think people need the encouragement.

After Torrel moved up in her union and became president of her union local, she no longer found role models in her own CLUW chapter; she realized that she had become an exemplar herself. Her former role models had left the chapter and had become active in other organizations. Torrel felt that CLUW was no longer the place where she could let herself go and turn to for backing, but that now the chapter membership expected *her* to provide leadership:

> Well, when I first went it was more of a support group than it is now. I mean you could go in and say, 'Shit, I'm pissed off at these people!'

Now I can't do that because now I'm the big guy and they used to be the big guys, the other people that were there, and I was the little guy. Now I have to do it.

The CLUW members to which Torrell could 'bounce off' and ask for advice were no longer active in the organization:

A lot of people have dropped out of being active in CLUW who were my mentors, basically. Really. I still have contact with a lot of them, but it's just different.

If it is mostly rank-and-file members and retirees who are active in the chapter, then participation at the chapter level is no longer attractive for women who have moved up in union leadership. However, even those who are no longer active in CLUW emphasize how important the organization was for providing labor union women with support. Some formerly active members who felt that they can support working class women better through other organizations, point out that CLUW's leadership is successful – going to and speaking at conventions, achieving leadership positions in the labor movement, and getting media coverage. At the same time, a large group of working class women are neither connected to organizations of the women's movement like NOW, nor organized in unions and active in the Coalition of Labor Union Women. These former CLUW members miss working together and being supported by other women. Pat Garnet, who was not longer active in CLUW, explained:

It is interesting because any one of us, probably, who came out of the experience, misses CLUW or WREE and NOW is not involved in a specific women's focus kind of organization misses there is something very vibrant and dynamic of working with and supported of being part of the women, you know much more identified as women's movement and women's organization. It was a great time, I just enjoyed it.

Many formerly active CLUW members mentioned that they maintained friendships and networks with union women whom they had met through CLUW. Thus CLUW contributed to long lasting relationships and submerged networks within the labor movement.

Conclusions

In order to better understand social movement dynamics, more attention needs to be paid to the processes which contribute to staying in or leaving an organization. The case-study of the Coalition of Labor Union Women shows how the support networks and friendships in this feminist organization contributed to the participation in the still male-dominated labor movement. Reciprocal relationships (Jasper 1997) were crucial for maintaining the membership in CLUW. Through bringing more women into union membership and union leadership positions, CLUW changed the labor movement from within. However, the restriction of the regular membership to union members – due to the loyalty to the labor movement – excluded the majority of working women. Furthermore, participation at the national level of CLUW was virtually restricted to union officers and staff since other members could not afford to attend the national meetings. Thus, CLUW provided important resources for active members, but the membership and participation was severely restricted due to CLUW's character as an insider organization.

Networking, socializing and support are intertwined in this bureaucratic social movement organization. While personal contacts are important for joining CLUW, friendships are not a necessary condition. Instead friendships develop through active involvement in CLUW.[5] The organization is characterized by an ambiguous separation of business meetings and socializing. I have shown that members welcome the fact that socializing and business, exchange of information and emotional support are intertwined as long as they are part of those networks and find support from other members. Others, who are no longer active in the organization experienced the chapter meetings as inefficient. When participation no longer makes 'emotional common sense' (Gould 2002), members leave the organization.

The case-study shows very clearly that members do not differentiate between emotional support and technical expertise. The fact that they can turn to other CLUW members for advice alone is comforting. While they feel alienated and alone in male dominated structures, often being one of the few women in union leadership or the first to hold leadership position in their union, they are glad that they can turn to other women for advice and support and inspired by listening to the experiences of women in other unions.

Notes

1 I gratefully acknowledge the helpful comments of the editors, and Robin Leidner and Erika Summers-Effler.
2 A part of the membership was interested in organizing working women more broadly and therefore argued for opening the organization to all women, organized or not.
3 Thanks to Helena Flam for pointing out that there were many prominent women activists in the Solidarity movement. Barker (2001) describes the crucial role of several women in the strikes taking places in the summer of 1980.
4 Thirteen percent of the members are men (CLUW membership survey 1994). However, they did not tend to hold leadership positions but supported the organization with membership dues.
5 I cannot quantify how many friendships developed after joining CLUW.

References

Aminzade, R.R. and McAdam, D. (2001) 'Emotions and Contentious Politics,' in R.R. Aminzade *et al.* (eds) *Silence and Voice in the Study of Contentious Politics*, Cambridge: Cambridge University Press.

Balser, D. (1987) *Sisterhood and Solidarity: feminism and labor in modern times*, Boston: South End Press.

Barker, C. (2001) 'Fear, laughter, and collective power: the making of solidarity at the Lenin shipyard in Gdansk, Poland, August 1980,' in J. Goodwin, J.M. Jasper, and F. Polletta (eds) *Passionate Politics: emotions and social movements*, Chicago: University of Chicago Press.

Eisenstein, H. (1995) 'The Australian femocratic experiment: a feminist case for bureaucracy,' in M.M. Ferree and P.Y. Martin (eds) *Feminist Organizations: harvest of the new women's movement*, Philadelphia: Temple University Press.

Elkiss, H. (1995) 'Mentoring for union women: critical on-the-job leadership training,' *Workplace Topics*, 4: 45–57.

Fantasia, R. (1988) *Cultures of Solidarity*, Berkeley: University of California Press.

Ferree, M.M. (1992) 'The political context of rationality: rational choice theory and resource mobilization,' in A.D. Morris and C.M. Mueller (eds) *Frontiers in Social Movement Theory*, New Haven: Yale University Press.

Ferree, M.M. and Martin, P.Y. (1995) 'Doing the work of the movement: feminist organizations,' in M.M. Ferree and P.Y. Martin (eds) *Feminist Organizations: harvest of the New Women's Movement*, Philadelphia: Temple University Press.

Ferree, M.M. and Roth, S. (1998) 'Gender, class, and the interaction between social movements: a strike of West Berlin day care workers,' *Gender & Society*, 12: 626–48.

Flam, H. (1990) 'The "emotional man" and the problem of collective action,' *International Sociology*, 5: 39–56.

—— (1993) 'Die Erschaffung und der Verfall oppositioneller Identität,' *Forschungsjournal neue soziale Bewegungen*, 2: 83–97.

—— (1998) *Mosaic of Fear: Poland and East Germany before 1989*, New York: Columbia University Press.

Goodwin, J., Jasper, J.M., and Polletta, F. (2000) 'Return of the repressed: the fall and rise of emotions in social movement theory,' *Mobilization*, 5: 65–84.

—— (eds) (2001) *Passionate Politics: emotions and social movements*, Chicago: University of Chicago Press.

Gould, D. (2002) 'Life during wartime: emotions and the development of ACT UP,' *Mobilization*, 7: 177–200.

Hochschild, A.R. (1983) *The Managed Heart: commercialization of human feeling*, Berkeley: University of California Press.

Horowitz, D. (1998) *Betty Friedan and the Making of the Feminine Mystique: the American left, the cold war, and modern feminism*, Amherst: University of Massachusetts Press.

Jasper, J.M. (1997) *The Art of Moral Protest: culture, biography, and creativity in social movements*, Chicago: University of Chicago Press.

Katzenstein, M.F. (1998) *Faithful and Fearless. Moving Feminist Protest inside the Church and Military*, Princeton: Princeton University Press.

Lofland, J. (1996) *Social Movement Organizations: guide to research on insurgent realities*, New York: Aldine De Gryter.

Lugones, M.C. in collaboration with Rosezelle, P.A. (1995) 'Sisterhood and friendship as feminist models,' in P.A. Weiss and M. Friedman (eds) *Feminism and Community*, Philadelphia: Temple University Press.

Michels, R. (1962) *Political Parties: a sociological study of the oligarchical tendencies of modern democracy*, New York: Free Press.

Milkman, R. (1985) 'Women workers, feminism and the labor movement since the 1960s,' in R. Milkman (ed.) *Women, Work and Protest: a century of U.S. women's labor history*, Boston: Routledge and Kegan Paul.

Morris, A. (1984) *The Origins of the Civil Rights Movement: black communities organizing for change*, New York: The Free Press.

Needleman, R. (1998) 'Women workers: strategies for inclusion and rebuilding unionism,' in G. Mantsios (ed.) *A New Labor Movement for the New Century*, New York, NY: Garland.

Polletta, F. (2002) *Freedom is an Endless Meeting: democracy in American social movements*, Chicago: University of Chicago Press.

Reinelt, C. (1995) 'Moving onto the terrain of the state: the battered women's movement and the politics of engagement,' in M.M. Ferree and P.Y. Martin (eds) *Feminist Organizations: harvest of the new women's movement*, Philadelphia: Temple University Press.

Roth, S. (2003) *Building Movement Bridges: the coalition of labor union women*, Westport, CT: Praeger.

Rothschild-Whitt, J. (1979) 'The collectivist organization: an alternative to rational-bureaucratic models,' *American Sociological Review*, 44: 509–27.

Rupp, L.J. and Taylor, V. (1990) *Survival in the Doldrums: the American women's rights movement, 1945–1960s*, Columbus: Ohio State University Press.

Schrecker, E. (1998) *Many are the Crimes: McCarthyism in America*, Boston: Little, Brown.

Snow, D.A. and Davis, P.W. (1995) 'The Chicago approach to collective behavior,' in G.A. Fine (ed.) *The Second Chicago School? The development of a post-war American sociology*, Chicago: University of Chicago Press.

Snow, D.A. and Oliver, P.E. (1995) 'Social movements and collective behavior: social psychological dimensions and considerations,' in K.S. Cook, G.A. Fine, and J.S. House (eds) *Sociological Perspectives on Social Psychology*, Boston: Allyn & Bacon.

Spalter-Roth, R. and Schreiber, R. (1995) 'Outsider issues and insider tactics: strategic tensions in the Women's Policy Network during the 1980s,' in M.M. Ferree and P.Y. Martin (eds) *Feminist Organizations: harvest of the new women's movement*, Philadelphia: Temple University Press.

Taylor, V. (1995) 'Watching for vibes: bringing emotions into the study of feminist organizations,' in M.M. Ferree and P.Y. Martin (eds) *Feminist Organizations: harvest of the new women's movement*, Philadelphia: Temple University Press.

—— (1996) *Rock-a-by Baby: feminism, self-help, and postpartum depression*, New York: Routledge.

Taylor, V. and Rupp, L.J. (2002) 'Loving internationalism: the emotion culture of transnational women's organizations, 1888–1945,' *Mobilization*, 7: 141–58.

Taylor, V. and Whittier, N. (1998) 'Guest editors' introduction: special issue gender and social movements: Part I,' *Gender & Society*, 12: 622–25.

Weiss, P. (1995) 'Feminist reflections on community,' in P.A. Weiss and M. Friedman (eds) *Feminism and Community*, Philadelphia: Temple University Press.

Index

Abrams, P. 80, 94
activism-sustaining activities 7–8; co-counselling 150–65
activists: ACT UP 26, 190; left-wing 35
Adam, B. 124
Adbusters Media Foundation (AMF) 6, 12, 75, 99, 100–10, 112–15
agape 137–8, 139–41
AHL (HIV/AIDS-Organization) 173
AIDS 26, 173, 190
Alexander, J. 43, 45
America: Pacific Rim peace movement 16; social movements 36; women's caucus 8, 190; *see also* Coalition of Labor Women (CLUW)
AMF *see* Adbusters Media Foundation
Amin, S. 45
Aminzade, R. 2, 20, 41, 79, 189, 198, 200
Anderson, D.R. 138
anger 2, 4, 6, 12, 14, 21–30, 32, 34–7, 41–3, 44, 48, 58, 64, 65–9, 71–2, 81, 85–7, 102, 111–15, 141, 143, 156, 160–1, 166, 172, 180, 194; re-appropriation 26–8
anti-war demonstrators *see* Women in Black (WIB)
anxiety 5, 12, 16, 33, 43, 47, 48, 74, 107, 110, 112, 124, 145
April 27, 1989: Chinese student demonstration 86–9; *see also* Chinese student movement
Apter, D. 43
Aron, A. and E.N. 137, 147
Attac 14, 15
Australia: co-counselling 7–8, 150–65; refugee solidarity 17

Bakken, B. 92
Balser, D. 191
Barbalet, J.M. 66
Barker, C. 136, 193
Barnes, S.H. 31
Bartky, S.L. 123, 124
Bauman, Z. 127
Benetton spoof-ad 103–5, 113
Benford, R.D. 82, 137, 170
Ben-Ze'ev, A. 65
Berezin, M. 21, 25, 46, 110
Berger, P. 30, 34
Blumer, H. 41
Bourdieu, P. 91, 102
Bowden, P. 123, 124
breaching events 5, 58–60, 63–4, 74–5
Britt, L. 24, 26, 28, 112, 172, 185
burning: symbolism of 74
Bush, G.W. 16
Buy Nothing Day uncommercial 108, 113
bystanders 58, 59–60, 83, 88

Cadena-Roa, J. 58
Calhoun, C. 84, 91, 99, 111
Calvin Klein spoof-ad 106–8
care: emotional connotations 121–2; and feminism 7, 123–5; political construction of 119–20; *see also* personal assistants
carnivalesque protest forms 13–14, 29, 34
Carrithers, M. 141
Carter, S. 199
Castells, M. 100
Catholic worker community 138–47
Catholic workers social movement 137
cementing emotions 21